"*A Filtered Life* moves beyond simple denunciations of online sociality, exploring the promise and perils of our emerging digital age. This in-depth ethnographic analysis reveals how young adults craft selfhood and community through social media, with lessons for understanding an era in which digital technologies are part of everyday life from the outset."

Tom Boellstorff, *Author of* Coming of Age in Second Life *and* Ethnography and Virtual Worlds

"Taylor and Nichter show how complicated it can be to navigate the demands of authenticity in a competitive climate where everyone is editing themselves into a digital perfection. Read this book to learn the emotional costs of seeing and being seen as a 20-something under our contemporary online regime of self-branding."

Ilana Gershon, *Author of* The Breakup.20

"This lively study provides both compelling detail on a human level—the stories of young people who find themselves drawn into social media—and reflections on the broader implications for American culture. This book will interest all those who wonder about the impact of this enormously significant but little-understood aspect of contemporary life."

Peter Stromberg, *Author of* Caught in Play

"This engaging, timely, ground-breaking book provides important information about the smartphone-centered lives of today's emerging adults. It is a welcome and valuable contribution toward understanding the meanings that smartphones hold for emerging adults and will help them—and the rest of us—use them more wisely."

Jeffrey Jensen Arnett, *Author of* Emerging Adulthood: The Winding Road from the Late Teens Through the Twenties

A FILTERED LIFE

A Filtered Life is the first comprehensive ethnographic account to explore how college students create and manage multiple identities on social media.

Drawing on interviews and digital ethnographic data gleaned from popular social media platforms, the authors document and make visible routinized practices that are typically hidden and operating behind the scenes. They introduce the concept of "digital multiples," wherein students strategically present themselves differently across social media platforms. This requires both the copious production of content and the calculated development of an instantly recognizable aesthetic or brand. Taylor and Nichter examine key contradictions that emerged from student narratives, including presenting a self that is both authentic and highly edited, appearing upbeat even during emotionally difficult times, and exuding body positivity even when frustrated with how you look. Students struggled with this series of impossibilities; yet, they felt compelled to maintain a vibrant online presence.

With its close-up portrayal of the social and embodied experiences of college students, *A Filtered Life* is ideal for students and scholars interested in youth studies, digital ethnography, communication, and new forms of media.

Nicole Taylor is Associate Professor of anthropology at Texas State University and the author of *Schooled on Fat: What Teens Tell Us about Gender, Body Image, and Obesity*.

Mimi Nichter is Professor Emerita of anthropology at the University of Arizona. She is the author of *Lighting Up: The Rise of Social Smoking on College Campuses* and *Fat Talk: What Girls and their Parents Say about Dieting*.

A FILTERED LIFE

Social Media on a College Campus

Nicole Taylor and Mimi Nichter

Routledge
Taylor & Francis Group

NEW YORK AND LONDON

Cover image: © iStock / franckreporter

First published 2022
by Routledge
605 Third Avenue, New York, NY 10158

and by Routledge
2 Park Square, Milton Park, Abingdon, Oxon, OX14 4RN

Routledge is an imprint of the Taylor & Francis Group, an informa business

© 2022 Taylor & Francis

Library of Congress Cataloging-in-Publication Data
A catalog record for this title has been requested

ISBN: 9781032021362 (hbk)
ISBN: 9781032021348 (pbk)
ISBN: 9781003182047 (ebk)

DOI: 10.4324/9781003182047

Typeset in Bembo
by codeMantra

For our families
For all your love and support

CONTENTS

ACKNOWLEDGMENTS

We have both said many times over the course of this collaboration that we could not have written this book alone. Our history of working together was lengthy; Nicole had completed her dissertation with Mimi as her advisor, and her research topic aligned with much of Mimi's early work on body image. Over the years, we had published several articles together on college students, body image, and smoking, so we had confidence that we could conduct research and write together in a relatively seamless manner. When we first discussed starting a new project on social media use among college students, it seemed like a natural extension of our earlier work. And then, when we decided that the data we collected should be written up as a book, neither of us hesitated to sign on for the task. It has been an enjoyable collaboration as we brought different strengths to the project and learned from one another along the way. Nicole's taskmaster approach to meeting deadlines moved the project along in ways that were appreciated by Mimi, who values rumination, slow thought, and diving deep.

There are many people who assisted us in bringing this book to completion. First, we are grateful to all our participants who openly shared their experiences with social media and allowed us access to their accounts so we could more fully understand their performances on various platforms. Their thoughtful narratives, featured throughout this book, enriched our project and inspired us. We deeply appreciate their openness and honesty in walking us through their practices of editing and curating their online selves. Looking back, we acknowledge that at the onset of the project we understood relatively little about what online life was all about for 20-somethings.

There are many others to whom we are grateful. Research assistants Alejandro Allen and Angela Walton provided invaluable insights as interviewers and in discussions about emergent findings. We are also thankful for feedback we received on earlier chapters of this book from undergraduate students who read them as part of an anthropology seminar. Their positive feedback served as confirmation that our understanding of their online lives was on target.

On a personal level, there are many people without whose support this book would not have come to fruition. Nicole offers thanks to David Schachter for sharing insights from his experience working with youth and for picking up the slack at home so she could write. She is grateful to their son, Oliver, for his patience as she spent many hours locked in the study with noise canceling headphones while they were home together during the pandemic year. Mimi offers thanks to Mark Nichter who was always willing to discuss unfolding themes in the research, provide theoretical counsel, and follow ideas into their broader implications. She is always grateful to her two sons for enriching her life: Brandon, for ongoing discussions on issues of mental health on college campuses, and Simeon, for his loving support, enthusiasm, and ongoing interest in this research.

We also acknowledge that the universe threw us unexpected obstacles during data collection and the writing of this book. Deaths of family members and friends, sudden illnesses which derailed the writing process, and the multitude of challenges that came with Covid-19 were some of the difficulties we faced. Suddenly, we could no longer meet in person as had been our practice. Instead, we found ourselves relying on four- to five-hour Zoom meetings to review the interview data and discuss chapters. We adapted to our new normal, as did everyone around us.

At Routledge, we thank our editor, Tyler Bay, for his enthusiastic support of the project as it unfolded. Thanks also to Charlotte Taylor for providing answers to our many procedural questions. We are also thankful to peer reviewers who provided valuable comments on this book.

Many thanks also to Emily Repasky, Nicole's research assistant, for providing formatting help as we finalized the manuscript.

Finally, we are thankful to Jeffrey Mantz, Cultural Anthropology Program Director at the National Science Foundation, who believed in this project early on when it was only a rough sketch of an idea. Without this funding, we could not have seen the project to its completion.

INTRODUCTION

Sounds of Silence

Imagine a university hallway bustling with students rushing to and from class while others sit shoulder to shoulder on the floor, backs pressed against the wall, as they pass time during breaks in their day. Consider hallways so crowded they are difficult to move through, yet so quiet you can hear a pin drop. If we think back to just ten years ago, these halls were alive with a cacophony of conversation and laughter reverberating off the walls. Students talked and joked with each other as they congregated outside of classrooms, and they shouted greetings to friends and acquaintances who walked by. Today is a very different scene, one where students silently hunch over smartphones permanently affixed to their hands. If you were to stop and observe this scene for a few moments, you might notice the singular focus with which they stare into their handheld devices, seemingly unaware of what is going on around them. Those who walk down the hallway with eyes trained on their screens amble along slowly, weaving back and forth, occasionally stumbling as if they are drunk.

These observations were the genesis of our book. Beyond the intensity of the silent halls, we observed shifts in student behavior in other campus settings. Students checked their phones the minute classes ended, or even during lectures if the class size was large enough to ensure anonymity. Strolling across campus between classes, in-person sociality had transformed to near total immersion in one's phone. Although it was clear that college students were multitasking on their phones throughout the day—while studying, hanging out with friends, walking around campus, and even driving—we understood relatively little about the details of their everyday practices on social media.

DOI: 10.4324/9781003182047-1

As anthropologists who study the meaning of human behavior, we contemplated the shifts that we observed on campus and wondered what was happening in all of those smart phones. While we were certainly not exempt from the constant temptation of our own phones, we wanted to learn more about why digital worlds were so compelling to college students. What were they looking at? How did they interact and post differently across sites? Perhaps most importantly, what were the social and emotional implications of prioritizing a handheld digital environment over the physical social environment? As we began to envision a study, one of our initial goals was to gain a deeper understanding of how immersion in social media was affecting social relationships, creating shifts in communication styles, and the extent to which it affected one's sense of self. Toward this end, we designed an ethnographic study to understand the effects of intensive engagement in these digital worlds.

Social Media Use among Young Adults

The students we observed and interviewed on campus are part of a global phenomenon. Currently, 4.2 billion people (or 53 percent of the world's population) are social media users. That number has risen 13 percent in the last year.[1] The last two decades have seen an exponential rise in social media use among youth in the U.S. In 2005, only 12 percent of young adults used social media. Contrast this to today, where more than 90 percent of youth are social media users, and almost half (45 percent) report that they go online "almost constantly." This represents a 78-percent increase in use in 13 years.[2]

Important age-related differences exist in platform use among 20-somethings. Instagram, Snapchat, and Twitter, three of the most widely used sites by those in their early 20s, significantly decrease in use as youth approach their 30s. Instagram and Snapchat, used by three-quarters of those aged 18–24, reduce in use to 57 percent (Instagram) and 47 percent (Snapchat) among 25–29-year-olds. Forty four percent of 18–24-year-olds used Twitter as compared with 31 percent of those aged 25–29.[3] YouTube and Facebook become increasingly popular as youth move into their late twenties (93 and 84 percent, respectively). These findings suggest that interest in specific platforms changes over time, and that students may "age out" of the intense social media use that characterizes the college years. It is important to note that among all age groups in the U.S., researchers have not found notable differences in social media use by ethnic and racial group.

Smartphone ownership has been growing steadily among young adults aged 18–29. In 2021, 96 percent of young adults surveyed owned a smartphone.[4] Studies show that the number of times a person checks their phone has risen significantly over time as well: In 2017, young adults checked their phones 86 times per day.[5] By 2019, the number increased to almost 200 times per day.[6] We found that approximating how many times a day students check their phones was difficult to ascertain. In our initial survey with college students, their responses to questions about time spent online seemed greatly underreported. We did not think they were being dishonest, but from our observation of their use, it certainly seemed like they were checking their phones whenever possible. In interviews, they told us that checking their phones was the first thing they did when they got up in the morning, and the last thing they did at night. On campus and when hanging out with friends, they checked their phones continuously. The seamless nature of students' relationship with their phones made an accurate quantitative calculation difficult to provide.

College students—also known as members of Generation Z or the iGeneration (GenZ and iGen)—are often described as digital natives who have grown up with technology as a normal part of everyday life. Educator Marc Prensky coined the term "digital natives," which references a native speaker of a language, someone who knows a language from birth. Prensky observed that young people were native speakers of the digital language of computers, video games, and the internet.[7] Today, digital natives have extended their fluency in technology to embrace social media. They are the first generation to grow up in an "always on" technological environment.[8]

New technologies provide youth with powerful tools for self-presentation and opportunities for identity and gender performance. Identity exploration and the increasingly prominent role of social media in everyday life are key components of "emerging adulthood." This term, developed by psychologist Jeffrey Arnett, refers to the extended transitional years between adolescence and adulthood.[9] This life stage, comprised of those aged 18–25 and sometimes older, is defined by several key features, including an intense focus on the self; a feeling of being in-between, of not quite being an adult but not a teen anymore; continued identity exploration; and instability marked by multiple shifts in one's life and social environment.[10] We examine how some of these key features, particularly identity exploration and self-focus, affect media use. By documenting how media use unfolds in the daily lives of emerging adults, we highlight and make visible routinized practices of use, which are typically hidden and operating behind the scenes.

The college years, unlike earlier adolescent years, represent the first experience of living on one's own, away from the watchful eyes of parents. Social media provides an opportunity for emerging adults to plan everyday activities, meet up with friends at all times of day and night, and develop and maintain relationships. Youth today live in an age of increasing time compression resulting in greater opportunities for arousal (e.g., continuous connection to friends via digital social media) and diminishing tolerance for boredom.[11] Indeed, the very names of the two most popular platforms used by emerging adults—*Insta*gram and *Snap*chat—aptly capture the immediacy of communications. Social media, available 24/7, provides instant gratification for those in this life stage, characterized by exploring new freedoms and "living your best life."

Current Perspectives on Social Media Use

In recent years, popular news stories have focused on the emotional consequences of social media use among youth, including depression, anxiety, and social isolation.[12] Sensationalistic headlines such as "Have Smartphones Destroyed a Generation?" focus our attention on these negative impacts.[13] A popular documentary called *The Social Dilemma* reveals how social media companies have strategically engineered their sites to be addictive by tracking and manipulating users' perceptions and desires.[14] The focus of these journalistic and film accounts is engagement in debate about the extent to which smartphone use is harmful to youth. Popular books on the topic focus on this debate as well.[15]

For example, science, technology, and media scholar Sherry Turkle critiques the harmful effects of media, asserting that young people's excessive time online has resulted in reduced empathy and self-reflection, as well as less patience and imagination.[16] Despite constant online communication with others, Turkle finds that young people feel isolated and are fearful of face-to-face interaction. They know they should talk more in person than online, but it is difficult to do so. Texting or posting on social media is easier and a more comfortable way to communicate. Turkle's concerns about social media are particularly noteworthy as she was one of the first scholars to focus on the positive potential of the internet to enhance social relationships.[17] However, as time spent online has increased, Turkle has shifted her perspective and now expresses concern that our range of emotional expression is constrained by our phones and continuous use of social media.

Psychologist Jean Twenge, who has written several popular books on contemporary generational differences among American youth and their use of digital media, similarly concludes that frequent use lowers the psychological well-being of young people. In her purview, excessive time spent on smartphones promotes antisocial behavior and results in increasingly high levels of loneliness, anxiety, and depression. Her research among adolescents, tracking large-scale, nationally representative longitudinal surveys across the U.S., reveals trends away from in-person social interaction, such as hanging out with friends, partying, going to movies, and even going shopping.[18] These declines occurred at the same time digital media use (including internet, texting, and social media) among teens increased.[19] The amount of time high school seniors spent online doubled between 2006 and 2016; one survey found that the average teen spends 9 hours a day with digital media.[20] Twenge, similar to Turkle, expresses concern that reduced in-person interaction may affect the critical development of social skills during this life stage.

The field of psychology has dominated much of the academic research on youth and social media and has repeatedly highlighted the harmful emotional and cognitive impacts of new technologies.[21] In this book, we move beyond pathologizing depictions of youth and their social media use to examine some of the more fine-grained questions that remain unanswered. Our research methodology was designed to be bottom-up, meaning that we wanted to explore—by listening to the voices of students—how they were engaging with social media and how that impacted their sense of self.

Despite an abundance of survey research and experimental studies on social media and youth, we know little about the everyday online experiences of emerging adults in the U.S. While anthropologists have written on social media, to our knowledge, little ethnographic research has focused on emerging adults with few notable exceptions.[22] Anthropologist Tom Boellstorff was the first to conduct a long-term ethnographic study in an online setting. Based on two years of research in the virtual world *Second Life* where people interact with each other's avatars, Boellstorff explored identity play, sexuality, conflict, and other aspects of sociality.[23] In doing so, he introduced the concept of immersive ethnographic study of online worlds and provided important insights into methodological practices for engaging in this type of research.[24]

Anthropologist Ilana Gershon was the first to write an ethnography of college students and new media, which, at the time, included only Facebook, texting, email, and voicemail.[25] She explored how they negotiated social norms in these communicative channels through the lens of breakup narratives. Gershon found that college students did not have a shared understanding of social rules that guide breaking up online, which resulted in conflict and confusion.

In a follow-up study conducted eight years later, Gershon found that youth had become fluent in multiple social media platforms and moved easily between them to accomplish key social tasks during romantic breakups, including untangling their online connection, understanding the intentions of others, and managing the flow of information.[26] This work highlights the value in exploring processes of how people negotiate rules of etiquette and work toward developing shared social norms in a new medium. At a time when youth are constantly checking their phones and actively engaged in multiple social media sites, the need to negotiate rules of engagement both online and offline has become increasingly complex and labor intensive.

Anthropologist Daniel Miller and colleagues have made valuable contributions to the field in relation to how social media visually reproduces dominant gender norms through its feedback mechanism.[27] That is, self-presentation that aligns with normative gendered perceptions of how women and men should look and behave is rewarded with likes and positive comments.

> The point is that, as academics, we can now literally perceive cultural norms as the constant repetition of images—so also can the people whose images we are looking at. In particular, we can now "see" how the reproduction of gender identities works, often through a series of contrasting associations.[28]

The term "polymedia" refers to a dynamic model which incorporates the proliferation of new social media that "each acquires its own niche in people's communicative repertoires."[29] Importantly, this concept underscores that today's users rarely focus on a single platform but rather rely on an assemblage of media to accomplish their online goals. We build on these important anthropological concepts to explore how college students navigate the multiple options for sociality in terms of how they present different sides of themselves and manage social norms and audience expectations across sites.

More recently, Boellstorff has highlighted the interconnected nature of interactional contexts, arguing that digital worlds are as real as offline worlds.[30] He illustrates that what we do online affects life offline, challenging a pervasive assumption in contemporary research on technology and sociality that understands "digital" and "real" as binary opposites. We explore this notion by examining how online identity work and social interaction affected college students' sense of self and interpersonal relationships offline to illustrate the material implications of contextual intersections.

In practice, students engaged across all contexts, online and offline, as equally real spaces, and they understood that the consequences of online behavior extended to offline contexts. However, when discussing issues of identity and relationships during interviews, students often articulated conceptual distinctions between online and offline social norms and behaviors. For example, many of the women in our study cared more about looking good online than "in real life." Throughout this book, we attempt to honor students' articulated conceptual distinctions between "online" and "real life" while providing insights about the contiguous nature of these fully inhabited social spaces.

Background to Our Study

The aims of this study are threefold. First, we move beyond the crisis-oriented rhetoric that is pervasive in research and media presentations about social media use and youth. Just as linguists argue that language is dynamic and track how it evolves over time, we similarly explore social media engagement as a shift in communicative practices and sociality. Our focus is on how youth negotiate and adapt to new social norms and communicative expectations in these online worlds. Second, through an ethnographic approach, we unpack the lived experience of emerging adults on social media, paying attention to the process of editing the self, and the emotional vicissitudes of surveilled and self-regulated lives. Third, we explore the complexities of performances and presentations of self across multiple social media platforms.

A series of questions underpinned our research: What are the tacit rules and social norms that influence young people's online behavior? How do these rules and norms differ across sites? What are the ways in which youth garner social capital and maintain friendships in social media? How does continual observation of and comparison to others online affect how students feel about themselves? What are the mechanisms by which youth strategically highlight different aspects of their identities across online contexts? By carefully unpacking the production of multiple selves in social media, we share insights about the complexities of creating and maintaining an online life. We address these questions by offering a close-up look at the embodied experiences of college students with social media from their perspectives and in their voices.

To this end, we conducted two years of ethnographic research (2017–2019) with college students. Our methods included in-depth interviews, focus groups, and participant observation in the four most popular social media platforms for emerging adults at that time: Instagram, Snapchat, Twitter, and Facebook. The research setting, a large state university located in the southern U.S., serves an ethnically diverse student population. The university has been designated a Hispanic Serving Institution by the U.S. Department of Education since 2011. Currently, 57 percent of students enrolled identify as racial or ethnic minorities, which includes 39 percent Hispanic and 11 percent African American. Our sample closely reflects the university demographic. Fifty percent of our study participants identified as white; 32 percent identified as Hispanic, Latino, or Mexican; 13 percent identified as Black or African American; and 5 percent identified as other (Asian and Filipino). All of the students in our study were between the ages of 18 and 23 with a range of class standings.

Given the ethnically diverse nature of our research sample, we expected to find ethnic differences in online sociality. Our research team, which consisted of the authors and two research assistants, mirrored the ethnic composition of students in the study. However, we found that regardless of ethnic identity, students articulated similar experiences and social norms across sites. This may have been because our exploratory study was designed to mostly elicit student narratives across a wide range of social media-related topics. As such, we did not explicitly ask about ethnic differences. Strong distinctions emerged along gender lines and those are the focus of our analysis throughout the book. A study designed to explore ethnic differences in online sociality would likely uncover more nuanced data on the topic.

In total, 80 students participated in the study. We recruited 62 students for in-depth interviews (30 female and 32 male), and an additional 18 students participated in focus group discussions. Recruitment was done through class presentations and flyers posted across campus. Interviews, which lasted anywhere from 1 hour to 2.5 hours, explored online identity construction and self-presentation, social norms related to posting and giving feedback, body image, self-esteem, emotions and perceptions related to social media, ideas about friendship and connection, and gender differences in online behavior. At the end of each interview, we asked participants to "friend" our project social media accounts in Instagram, Snapchat, Twitter, and Facebook, which every student was willing to do.

After the majority of interviews were completed, we conducted participant observation in their social media sites over the course of a year. This involved developing various methods for systematic data collection, including capturing data across the sample and across platforms during certain times and days of the week as well as closely following a handful of participants to gather in-depth, concentrated data on their social media activity. We spent time observing and participating online, gathering screenshots of participants' social media images and comment threads in order to compare what students posted online with what they said in interviews and how they appeared in person.

We invited a handful of participants who were particularly insightful and forthcoming during individual interviews to gather a few friends for group discussions. We facilitated six group discussions, three of which were all women and three mixed gendered. Focus group discussions provided an opportunity for observing how friends talk with each other about social media and helped us understand the extent to which their perceptions, ideologies, practices, and experiences aligned. We were able to observe firsthand how friends negotiated communication norms. In our previous research on body image, we found that focus group participants who know and trust each other are more likely to talk openly and share personal experiences.[31]

In the midst of writing this book, Covid-19 happened, upending everyone's daily lives. Taking this as an opportunity, we gathered narrative data from college students about their experiences with social media and their observations of how online content and posting norms changed during this time. We provided 40 upper division anthropology students with a series of writing prompts that asked them to reflect on their shifting relationships with social media during quarantine and beyond, how posting during the pandemic changed, and how time spent on social media during the quarantine affected their social relationships and sense of self. These narrative essays provided invaluable insight into just how quickly and drastically online sociality changed because of Covid-19. We share themes that emerged from these data in Chapter 5, offering an initial glimpse into a topic that demands further ethnographic study.

Our approach to exploring identity creation among youth is unique in that we conducted long-term online participant observation of college students we interviewed across multiple social media sites. Comparing what youth said in interviews with our observations of their day-to-day online behavior across multiple platforms provided rich insight into online sociality. For example, we found that some students looked so different in their social media posts than they did in person that their online photos were unrecognizable. Some of these same students claimed they did not edit their photos and were even derisive of the concept. This observation led us to delve more deeply into the concept of editing, and we discovered that students might understand and define editing differently than we do. The ethnographic approach allowed us to study various online platforms as environments that each maintains their own editorial mandates.

We have included a handful of social media images from our research throughout the book to provide a visual complement to our narrative descriptions of what we observed online. We rendered these images as pencil sketches using an editing process in Adobe Photoshop in order to protect the confidentiality of participants. Through our research, we learned that a simple reverse image search on Google could readily identify participants in digital images captured from their social media sites, even if the most identifiable aspects of the photo were blurred or altered. The only way to ensure anonymity is to alter every pixel in the photo, which the pencil sketch rendering achieves. This method, used by other digital media researchers, provides the added benefit of retaining facial features and expressions, key elements for interpreting and illustrating image production on social media.[32]

We provide brief descriptions of participants throughout the book to help the reader assess their stories. Narrative renditions of students' affect, general appearance, and demeanor derive from our field notes, and descriptions of body size that appear in Chapter 3 derive from participants' own self-assessments during interviews. While we did not ask students to characterize their body size, they often did so in the context of discussions that focused on body image and social comparison. As anthropologists who value a holistic approach and contextualized narratives, our hope in adding these descriptive cues was to highlight participants as individuals as opposed to research subjects. All students mentioned in the book have been given pseudonyms to protect their confidentiality.

We identify and interrogate key contradictions that emerged from comparing interview data (i.e., what people said they did) and online observations (i.e., what they actually did). These contradictions, highlighted throughout the book, include the following: presenting a self that appears authentic but is actually highly crafted, curated, and edited; appearing happy and upbeat even during emotionally difficult times; and exuding body positivity even when you feel unhappy and frustrated with how you look. Most of the students we talked to wrestled with these contradictions and struggled to find ways to express themselves openly while simultaneously being mindful of cultural imperatives. They were reflexive in their interviews and welcomed the opportunity to share their perspectives with us.

Our title, *A Filtered Life*, is multi-layered in meaning. On the most obvious level, it refers to the use of filters available on many platforms to alter and enhance one's physical appearance and the background of an image. Beyond this interpretation, filters are a metaphor for strategically repackaging the self on different sites. Emerging adults filter their photos. They are also filtering their emotional selves and their life experiences to follow social convention, appear unique, and obtain the highest audience appeal. Notably, filtering the self is not just about how one looks; it is about every aspect of self-presentation, from the aesthetic of a person's feed and their physical appearance to the personality characteristics and lifestyle they want to convey. Yet, all of this is bounded by a generational desire to remain authentic, meaning that there are limits to strategic self-expression online. Ultimately, the audience decides whether a person has successfully walked that line between filtering the self and remaining authentic. As a creator, you must continually view your online self through the eyes of your friends and your imaginary audience to determine what they want and how they might interpret (consume) your posts.

Attention Economy, Convertible Capital, and Affordances

Before turning to key themes that emerged from our data, it is important to provide a brief background on the attention economy, convertible capital, and the concept of affordances, which we refer to throughout the book. The idea of an attention economy is attributed to economist Herbert Simon, who observed that in "information-rich" contexts, "What information consumes is rather obvious; it consumes the attention of its recipients. Hence, a wealth of information creates a poverty of attention."[33] While this term predates the multitude of online platforms that we have today, it has gained widespread usage in recent years, as has the term "attention capital," referring to the amount of attention that a specific communicator receives.[34] The attention economy underpins our discussion of social media as it positions attention as the most valuable commodity in achieving personal and professional goals.[35]

For emerging adults, garnering the attention of one's audience through artistic photos and self-branding on an image-based site like Instagram is paramount in the construction of the self. An important benefit of getting attention in the form of likes and comments from a wide audience is social capital, the actual or potential resources available through one's social network.[36] Having a large online following can be converted (in Bourdieu's terminology, *convertible capital*) into other forms of capital, such as economic capital (e.g., becoming an influencer) or cultural capital (e.g., in the form of enhanced social status).

Andrew Smith and Eileen Fischer, marketing researchers who focus on social media, discuss the concept of affordances as related to the attention economy.[37] They describe two components of affordances. First, affordances are features that enable use, such as likes, which allow one to know how much attention capital one's post has received, or hashtags, which allow for ease of categorization and searchability. Second, drawing on the work of social media scholar danah boyd, they outline four affordances that affect what we do in our online networks: persistence (how long your online content lasts), visibility (the potential audience who will see your content), spreadability (the extent to which content is sharable), and searchability (the ability to find someone's content). These affordances are important ways we garner attention and guide online interactions.[38]

Miller and colleagues point out that the four affordances boyd identified do not neatly align with some of the more recent social media sites, such as Snapchat and Instagram.[39] Most people now use multiple sites, so social media has become an ecology that offers many choices for sociality, ranging from small, private exchanges to public broadcasts. Miller and his colleagues refer to this as *scalable sociality*, a term they coin to describe the interconnected nature of social media, where individuals have a range of platform choices, degrees of privacy, and size of audience that they want to reach.

The Political Economics of Social Media

It is worth briefly considering how social media practices are situated within the broader context of capitalism in which these platforms have emerged and thrived. Media scholar van Dijck has described how the participatory terminology used in discussions of social media (e.g., *connectedness, sharing, social web*) serves to mask the capitalist ideology in which social media is rooted.[40] Even the term *platform* "conceals how all personal data is collected by private corporations through platforms' designs, features, and policies, curated, turned into commodities and sold to third-party advertising companies to make profit."[41] This is what has been referred to as *platform capitalism*, a process by which one's personal data—their likes, dislikes, and searches online—are commodified and later repackaged in offerings for new products.[42] As users become more entrenched in their favorite platforms, it becomes increasingly difficult for them to leave or opt-out, even for short periods.

Ads specifically targeted to viewer's interests appear frequently on social media. These targeted ads, wedged between users' content, are a result of demographic and lifestyle information made available to advertisers by social networking sites. These practices have proven to be extremely lucrative: in 2019, Facebook earned 70 billion dollars in advertising revenue—of this, 20 billion dollars came from ads posted on Instagram.[43] The key point to note here is that online advertising is more ubiquitous than ever, although it may not appear to be so, as it operates seamlessly in our everyday lives.

Social media is not just a convenient place to advertise—it is also changing how we think about what we need and want to consume. Advertising plays on our insecurities as well as our aspirations and provides us with visions of who we might become. Companies now have access to consumers throughout the day and night to display their brands; they also enlist and train influencers to present their products in ways that seem desirable, if not irresistible. Consider, for example, young women and clothing. In the contemporary world offline and online, many young women "feel an unspoken obligation not to repeat an #outfitof-theday."[44] A 2017 poll found that among women aged 18–25, over 40 percent reported feeling pressure to wear a different outfit every time they went out.[45] While purchasing new clothing frequently is certainly not available to all, it has become widely accessible to many by the growth of the fast fashion industry, which provides clothes at low cost. Fast fashion ads appear on popular apps, making new purchases cheap and easy to acquire. Considering the pressure emerging adults feel to continually post about their daily lives, it becomes clear that wearing the right clothes (and posing regularly in new outfits) is an important component of one's presentation of self and can help with quick shifts in identity.

Key Themes and Analytic Lenses

Social Norms and Tacit Rules Guiding Online Behavior

We have organized the book around several key themes. Importantly, we found that students could articulate a clear set of rules for posting and interacting in social media that differed by platform. In fact, these rules were so widespread and normative that they appeared to function as imperatives. "Everyone" seemed to know, at least in part, what was expected and desirable in the realm of editing the self—the do's and don'ts of self-presentation online, including what affect was acceptable to post in terms of mood and emotions. Throughout, we provide examples of how college students interpret and negotiate these rules in context and to what ends. There is a big difference between knowing the rules and choosing to follow them. We learned that sometimes, the rules are not quite so clear; a rapidly changing social media environment requires the constant interpretation and negotiation of emergent social norms. Thus, we unpack the fraught process of posting in platforms with ever-changing and emergent social rules that are subject to individual interpretation and the emotional whim of observers.

A useful concept for understanding online social norms and rules is *idioms of practice*, developed by anthropologist Ilana Gershon, to examine how young people utilize shared communicative practices within various media technologies. Idioms of practice emerge from talking to others and observing what they do online.[46] As Gershon explains, some of the rules are well known and explicit; others are implicit and known only when someone violates an expectation. For example, if a guy's girlfriend posts on Instagram, the expectation—the explicit rule—is that he should be among the first to like her post. Most college students were aware of that. However, it would probably be inappropriate if the same guy liked another woman's posts, particularly if she was considered attractive. No one really talks about that before the fact; instead, it emerges in context as breaking a rule.

Digital Multiples

Throughout the book, we reference *digital multiples*, a term we coined to explain how students strategically presented themselves differently across social media platforms. This process was guided by site-specific affordances, social norms, and perceived audience expectations. We unpack how students filtered their physical appearance, emotional expression, and social behavior across sites, and we examine the complexities and ramifications of creating and maintaining a site-appropriate self across multiple platforms. This is critical in an attention economy where the half-life of posts is limited and the burden of compulsory visibility is pronounced.[47] The desire for attention, commodified as the number of likes, views, and followers, has become such a valuable form of social capital that it is arguably reconfiguring human behavior.[48]

When we began research for this project, we conceptualized the online self as a digital double, thinking that students would have an online and offline presence that might or might not be consonant with each other. We recognized that online and offline selves are difficult to disentangle, given the pervasiveness of online participation. As Miller and colleagues have noted, "People now engage with a multiplicity of online and offline communications and identities with no clear boundary between them."[49]

Over the course of our research, we shifted our concept from the digital double to digital multiples once we recognized how much more complicated this issue was, considering how the platforms themselves required different presentation styles. For example, one young woman explained that if she had a difficult day, she would post about it on all of her sites, but not in the same way. Her Instagram post would feature an artsy photo of a glass of wine, using her signature colors as background. On Twitter, she would post a funny meme about getting drunk after a long day. On Snapchat, her post would include a video of her drinking the wine (since the post would disappear quickly). In contrast, her Facebook post would include a short narrative about why her day was hard without any mention of wine (since her parents might see it). The multiple online personas this student and many others described in their narratives paint a complex picture of how one creates digital multiples, an intricate and often time-consuming process.

Sociologist Erving Goffman described social life as a theater with interactions representing the interplay between actors and their audience.[50] Accordingly, as we move through our day, we foreground or background various aspects of ourselves depending on the social context and audience. For example, most people would dress and behave differently if they were going out to a party with friends than if they were going to a formal job interview; mixing those two worlds would be inappropriate or at least awkward for many American youth. This type of "audience segregation" allows us to keep the streams of our various social spheres separate.

Additionally, according to Goffman, we engage in "impression management" to control who sees what and when. To continue the example above, the impression young people want to make on a potential employer is probably different from how they want their friends to see them. Goffman contends that we are always performing to create an impression for an audience; we need an audience to see our performance and a backstage area where we can both relax and do much of the work necessary to keep up appearances.[51] Importantly, the self is not "a fixed, organic thing but a dramatic effect that emerges from a performance."[52] In our study, we observed that students portrayed themselves differently across social media platforms, depending on audience expectations and aspects of their identity they wanted to highlight.

If we consider the multiple contexts that college students traverse without factoring in social media, impression management is complicated enough. We can imagine that a typical day for college students might include interacting with peers, co-workers and supervisors, and professors in a variety of contexts such as home, campus, parties and bars, and workplaces. Once we layer in social media contexts that overlap and integrate with those face-to-face realms, the idea of managing one's impression, performing appropriately for the particular platform, and segregating audiences becomes infinitely more complex. Additionally, the digital multiples that one presents on various platforms reach diverse audiences, a factor youth must account for in the creation of a post.

This is what we refer to as digital multiples, which require a level of flexibility, wherein a person is willing to recraft their image repeatedly in accordance with site affordances and imagined audience desires. Once posted, viewers quickly rate and evaluate the performance through likes and comments. Beyond the number of likes, an important consideration is who has liked your post. All likes are not equal, with some valued more than others. Emerging adults are on shifting ground; they receive constant feedback on what is desirable and acceptable, and this information changes rapidly. The process of constructing and maintaining digital multiples not only requires strategic tailoring by site, but also needs to be sufficiently aligned with one's offline self and appearance to maintain an "authentic" identity.

Fluid Identities

The college years are a time of identity exploration and formation. Sociocultural linguists Mary Bucholtz and Kira Hall define identity as "the social positioning of self and other," a view that captures the dynamic nature of identity formation as emergent through discourse interaction and attention to context as well as relational to others, perceived identity categories, and ideological stances.[53] In other words, emerging adults negotiate or "try on" identities in specific social contexts and in relation to their perceptions of individuals with whom they are interacting. Thus, identities are collaboratively produced and managed both offline and online.[54] While identities are fluid and changeable, some aspects of identity can also be enduring and central to one's sense of self.

On social media, students aimed to create and maintain their identity on a platform like Instagram through the calculated development of an instantly recognizable aesthetic or personal brand that was consistent and uniquely associated with them. One's self-brand must be sufficiently recognizable in order to attract audience attention amidst noisy and crowded social media feeds. This was an iterative process; most students experimented with their look and created online selves that were responsive to their viewers by selectively deleting posts that failed to get sufficient likes. Some even rebranded themselves by deleting their entire posting archive and starting fresh at the junction of social milestones, such as beginning college or turning 21.

For some students, experimenting online was easier than trying on new identities in-person. Jayden, for example, who described himself as painfully shy, was different on Snapchat where he tried to be funny and outgoing. "Snapchat is allowing me to be the person I am becoming," he told us. Jayden observed that people responded so positively to his online humor that it gave him the confidence he needed to interact with people offline. Thus, positive feedback was validating in the development of his new identity. Snapchat was his preferred platform specifically because he could see how many people and who had viewed his posts, while not worrying about likes or comments. Another example of online identity experimentation was Mariana, a reserved and modestly dressed young woman, who told us she had limited self-confidence to talk with peers when she was around them. In contrast, her online personas were replete with photos of herself appearing sexy, glamorous, and full of confidence. For Jayden and Mariana, trying on new identities online offered less risk: Being humorous and not getting laughs offline might have proven overwhelming for Jayden, just as judgmental scrutiny and stares at Mariana's sexy attire at a party might have lowered her self-esteem. By comparison, online interactions carried less social risk; if students did not get enough likes, they could just delete the post.

Self-branding, Gender, and Authenticity

The half-life of the attention economy coupled with a strong desire for attention capital requires youth to devote time and energy to creating an easily recognizable branded self on social media. The desired outcome of this fashioning or self-branding is impression management, enhanced reputation, increased number of followers, and the potential to convert your online popularity to profit.[55] Considering the speed with which online images are consumed, self-branding projects need to be recognized as intense labor requiring continual refinements and upgrades. As anthropologist Alex Dent has observed, "The time between an initiation of communication and a response to that initiation is almost spontaneous."[56] We explore the compressed temporality of social media as well as the consequent demands and tensions inherent in such labor.[57]

Media scholars Brooke Erin Duffy and Emily Hund conducted research on female entrepreneurs who develop branded personas to promote their fashion blogs.[58] These "entrepreneurial aspirants" worked within the backdrop of neoliberal and post-feminist ideologies that emphasize the importance of self-governance, individual choice, and self-fashioning. The female bloggers in their study engaged in careful and fastidious online curation, articulating a vision of themselves as "destined to do passionate work" and "having it all." However, these gendered tropes obscured the difficult labor and level of self-discipline that were required to develop and maintain their brand.

While most of the college students in our study were not entrepreneurs, many of them—particularly the women—aspired to become influencers. About one-third had at least one friend who had an existing agreement with brands, and they saw their own self-brand and aesthetic as a potential pathway to material success. "Anyone who gets enough followers and posts the right way can get the attention of brands," one young woman told us. "Influencers are just everyday people who accumulate enough followers to become popular." Much like Duffy and Hund's description of female bloggers, some of our participants felt that becoming an influencer and earning a profit from their social media efforts was an attainable goal. Other students felt disturbed by their observations of how social media appeared increasingly packaged for the consumer. As one insightful woman explained:

> When I was in middle and high school, it seemed like social media was about connecting with friends and sharing life moments. Now it's like everyone is creating an image for others to consume. Online relationships are more transactional than they used to be.

Despite their recognition of and frustration with the shift in social media from peer-to-peer interaction toward a creator-consumer model, students continually felt compelled to perform visibility according to gendered scripts. For women, this required showing their bodies. Morgan, for example, who had close to a 1,000 followers, expressed frustration about needing to post images of herself scantily clad in a bikini to garner the maximum number of likes. "If I post a photo of myself that I like, hardly anyone else will like it," she quipped. Throughout, we examine the gendered scripts for appropriate presentation of self, paying credence to how women navigate popular expectations of heteronormative femininity online.

Media scholar Sarah Banet-Weiser has articulated how practices of self-disclosure, transparency, and authenticity underpin the creation of a digital self-brand for women.[59] By disclosure, she refers to ostensibly revealing one's everyday life for other's consumption; this practice is supposed to offer the audience a view of a person's "authentic" self. Banet-Weiser explains:

> Authenticity not only is viewed as residing inside the self but also is demonstrated by allowing the outside world access to one's inner self. . . . In the contemporary context, the creation of the "authentic self" continues to be understood as a kind of moral achievement . . . where to truly understand and experience the "authentic" self is to *brand* this self.[60]

Thus, self-branding is not externally imposed onto bodies, but is "rather the individual taking on the project herself as a way to access her true self."[61]

The concept of "authenticity"—revealing one's true self—emerged as an important theme in our interviews. Students emphasized the importance of "being real" online as a marker of honesty, trustworthiness, and integrity. They scrutinized social media posts for signs of over-editing, a faux pas that signaled inauthenticity and elicited derision. Among young women, authentic expression online often translates into beauty practices that highlight physical appearance. For the women we interviewed, the name of the game was to present both an authentic and an edited self that appeared effortlessly attractive. Successfully navigating this contradictory imperative required great skill, attention to detail, and vigilant monitoring of editing norms and feedback on posts. Men felt less pressure to post a flawlessly edited image, making it easier to achieve an appearance of authenticity. However, some still struggled with their online image and sense of self.

Both women and men were cognizant of the superficial nature of their editing practices: Students who did not edit risked critique for visible flaws and imperfections, and those who did edit risked critique for being inauthentic. Successfully striking a balance between real and fake in social media was a highly valued skill, and getting it right was important. This pressure underscores the imperative to impress an imagined audience, one that appears to value both perfection and authenticity, an impossible contradictory imperative.

Within a neoliberal and post-feminist environment, self-expression online has become a mechanism by which the female body and one's branded self is both produced and regulated. Post-feminist tropes of confidence, body positivity, and self-esteem are evident in popular culture and appeared in our study in young women's narratives.[62] Drawing on Foucault, cultural theorist Rosalind Gill details a gendered "technology of self" that "operates by inculcating a self-regulating spirit to locate both the source of the problems and their solutions within women's own psyches."[63]

In our interviews, we found that a consequence of frequently comparing oneself to others' bodies was an erosion of self-confidence and a hesitancy to post pictures of one's self. While this was true for women, we also found that men were not immune to feeling less than adequate online. Women—and some men—whose bodies did not conform to cultural standards for appropriate body size and shape, described how they developed strategies for hiding what they did not like about their bodies. Forms of self-governance and self-monitoring required to remake and maintain multiple selves was a frustrating venture.

The Works of Creating and Managing the Online Self

Throughout *A Filtered Life*, we highlight the *many works* involved in creating and maintaining a steady online brand. This is mostly invisible labor. In discussing *editing work*, for example, we unpack the intricate processes for perfecting social media content, involving taking multiple photos, attending to angles, lighting, posture, spacing, and background, as well as editing out perceived flaws and strategically posting during peak times to attract maximum attention.

Another important work is that of *identity and gender performance*, shedding light on cultural prescriptions for self-presentation, which remain equally robust online as they do offline. In an age where careful curating of the self is expected, we examine how the external body and the emotional self are presented. Under the constant surveillance of multiple imagined audiences, some young women and men were able to maintain the appearance of a seemingly "natural" aesthetic despite the tremendous effort required to produce content so that the "look" of their posts was eye-catching.

Beauty work describes the imperative to post your most attractive self and the production process required to achieve such perfection, including the work of micro targeting each body part to discover and then conceal one's flaws. In this process, social media practices are shaped by viewer expectations and site-specific conventions, as they converge with an online social milieu that values maximum visibility, adherence to cultural and gendered beauty ideals, and promotion of the self as a recognizable brand image.

Students engaged in the *emotional work* of anticipating audience desires and developing tailored content across sites designed to get as many likes and positive comments as possible, vigilantly monitoring feedback on posts, and the emotional vicissitudes of counting likes and reading comments. Emotional work also included the imperative to always portray a happy, upbeat self and package one's sad or angry emotions in socially acceptable ways, which differed by site. In this way, students needed to carefully produce and manage their emotional state. The work of remaining visible by posting regularly was also important. Posting infrequently suggested a lack of social life. Students worried that if they did not post regularly, friends would forget them. Being online constantly and seeing other people's posts of how they were living their best life often resulted in frustration and jealousy, especially when comparing your own life to that of people in your friend network who seemed to "have it all."

Finally, the *work of managing social relationships* involved scrolling through sites and liking others' posts. Students said it was especially important to like the posts of friends who regularly liked their posts. It was common for a student to call out their closest friends for failing to reciprocate in this way. The timing of a like was important as well. Being the first to like a post signaled a sense of desperation; conversely, students said it was strange to get a like on an old post, explaining that it could signal a sudden and intense focus on their feed. Through the lens of these various works, we can see how impression management becomes infinitely more complex and labor intensive when we take into consideration the multiple online worlds youth engage in daily.

Plan for the Book

Chapter 1: Media Landscape

This chapter sets the digital scene by broadly describing college students' experiences with and perceptions about social media, as well as the social norms that guide their behavior on Instagram, Snapchat, Twitter, and Facebook. These four were the most popular sites for college students in our study. We focus on how students used these platforms differently, including how social conventions, the imagined desires of their audiences, and site affordances guided their online behaviors. We also explore the reasons for posting, the meaning of likes, the many works involved in managing online popularity and social relationships, and the rules for phone use while hanging out with friends. This chapter provides context for subsequent chapters that explore in-depth students' social and emotional experiences with social media.

Chapter 2: The Editing Imperative

In anthropology, we understand identity as socially constructed through everyday practices and social interaction. This is true for social media as well, but we learned that the constructed nature of self is much more intensive and premeditated online. The confident, attractive, social media self was one that gave students a sense of pride, and importantly, garnered positive attention from others in the form of likes and comments. We describe how students cultivated and reproduced their public image using editing tools to create a personal brand that encompassed the internal and external self. Achieving a personal brand required that posts have consistent aesthetic elements including color scheme, composition, stance, mood, physical appearance, style, and personality traits. A successful post should appear natural, effectively masking the labor-intensive process of developing an instantly recognizable aesthetic. We explore the gendered aspects of editing and the social pressure (felt more acutely for women) to not only engage in these practices, but also master the impossible art of appearing both authentic and flawless. We pull back the curtain to reveal various works involved in the production process of a perfect post.

Chapter 3: The Body Imperative

While women have long been judged for their appearance, the social media age appears to have intensified body image dissatisfaction as it encourages frequent comparisons and a heightened awareness of others' evaluations. To a certain extent, these findings also apply to men, although most of the students in our study agreed that women worried more about their appearance and felt more sensitive to online feedback than men did. Accordingly, we explore a range of issues, including popular discourse about ideal body type, the ubiquity of social comparison, gender expression, and the impact of the body positivity movement on students' body acceptance. We highlight key themes that emerged from interview and focus group discussions on body image—authenticity, self-branding, surveillance, and the arduous work of image and identity among both women and men. We pay credence to gendered presentations of self on social media as compared to offline contexts. Most student narratives draw on references to Instagram, the most visual and curated site.

Chapter 4: The Positivity Imperative

What is the impact of engaging in a daily practice of packaging one's emotional self for viewers, of prioritizing the desires of an imagined audience over expressing your full self?

In this chapter, we explore the mandate expressed by college students to appear upbeat, happy, and excited online. The positivity imperative was particularly noteworthy considering results of studies that document the rise of anxiety and depression among young adults, especially those who spend a great deal of time online. Our in-depth interviews provided students an opportunity to describe the labor-intensive processes of curating a happy-go-lucky Instagram self—regardless of what they were feeling that day—and the socio-emotional impact of prioritizing this emotion over others. We describe how other sites, such as Finsta (fake Instagram), Twitter, and Snapchat, functioned as "emotional overflow" spaces where expression of sadness, anger, anxiety, and negativity were acceptable.

Chapter 5: Covid-19: Emerging Imperatives

In the midst of writing this book, Covid-19 emerged as a global pandemic that changed the way we work, socialize, and function in daily life. We suddenly found ourselves quarantined, unable to see friends and loved ones except online. In order to understand the effect on college students, we gathered data from student essays describing their experiences with social media amidst the Covid-19 pandemic. In particular, we wondered how the pandemic and quarantine had affected their relationship with social media in terms of frequency of use and sites where they spent the most time. This chapter explores the extent to which social media came to serve a different purpose for college students when it became their only, or at least, primary way of interacting with friends. We discuss what students said about the symbolic nature of posts with regard to masks and social gatherings, the heightened surveillance of friends and family on social media, the changing nature of social comparsion during quarantine, and how posting behaviors affected friendships during the pandemic. Through this discussion, we expand the understanding of risks associated with social media use and online sociality among youth, complicating the discourses that have emerged in popular culture.

Conclusion

We begin the concluding chapter by discussing social norms that guide on-line behavior and the complexity of students' experiences with social media. Students immersed themselves in their sites on a day-to-day basis; yet, they understood and articulated problematic as well as positive aspects of their social media use. We share students' reflections on their social media use, including the extent to which they saw themselves as dependent on popular platforms and how they imagine their relationship with social media might change after college. Finally, we discuss the broader implications of our findings and possible directions for future ethnographic research on this topic.

Notes

1 Kemp 2021.
2 Anderson and Jiang 2018.
3 Perrin and Anderson 2019.
4 Pew Research Center 2021.
5 Wolfe 2018.
6 Asurion 2019.
7 Prensky 2001.
8 Dimock 2019.
9 Arnett 2015.
10 Ibid.
11 Nichter 2015.
12 Ducharme 2019; Heid 2019; Julian 2018; Popper 2020; Twenge 2017.
13 Twenge 2017.
14 Orlowski 2020.
15 boyd 2015; Turkle 2015, 2017; Twenge 2018.
16 Turkle 2015, 2017.
17 Arnett 2015.
18 Twenge, Spitzberg, and Campbell 2019.
19 Twenge, Martin, and Spitzberg 2019.

20 Rideout and Robb 2019.
21 Stockdale and Coyne 2020; Twenge and Martin 2020.
22 Gershon 2010, 2020; Quintero, Bundy, and Grocke 2019; Ross 2019.
23 Boellstorff 2008.
24 Boellstorff et al. 2012.
25 Gershon 2010.
26 Ibid.
27 Miller et al. 2016.
28 Ibid., 119.
29 Madianou 2015, 1; see also Madianou and Miller 2013.
30 Boellstorff 2016.
31 Taylor and Nichter 2017.
32 Miller and Sinanan 2017; Tiidenberg 2018.
33 Simon 1971, 40.
34 Smith and Fischer 2021; van Krieken 2019a, 2019b.
35 Davenport and Beck 2001; Zulli 2018.
36 Bourdieu 1986.
37 Smith and Fischer 2021.
38 boyd 2010.
39 Miller et al. 2016.
40 van Dijck 2013.
41 Gangneux 2019, 1055; see also Fuchs 2014.
42 Srnicek 2016.
43 Carman 2020.
44 Monroe 2021, 78.
45 Ibid.
46 Gershon 2010.
47 Duffy and Pruchniewska 2017.
48 Zulli 2018.
49 Miller et al. 2016, 112.
50 Goffman 1959.
51 Hogan 2010.
52 Tolentino 2019, 14.
53 Bucholtz and Hall 2005, 586.
54 Edwards and Wang 2018; Giddens 1991.
55 Hearn 2010; Scolere, Pruchniewska, and Duffy 2018.
56 Dent 2018, 593.
57 Ross 2018.
58 Duffy and Hund 2015.
59 Banet-Weiser 2012.
60 Ibid., 61.
61 Ibid., 61.
62 Banet-Weiser 2015, 2018; Gill and Orgad 2017; Toffoletti and Thorpe 2018.
63 Gill 2017, 618; see also Foucault 1988.

References

Anderson, Monica, and Jingjing Jiang. 2018. "Teens, Social Media and Technology." *Pew Research*, May 31, 2018. https://www.pewresearch.org/internet/2018/05/31/teens-social-media-technology-2018/.

Arnett, Jeffrey. 2015. *Emerging Adulthood: The Winding Road from the Late Teens through the Twenties*. 2nd ed. Oxford: Oxford University Press.

Asurion. 2019. "Americans Check Their Phones 96 Times a Day." *Cision PR Newswire*, November 21, 2019. https://www.prnewswire.com/news-releases/americans-check-their-phones-96-times-a-day-300962643.html.

Banet-Weiser, Sarah. 2012. *Authentic: The Politics of Ambivalence in a Brand Culture.* New York: New York University Press.

Banet-Weiser, Sarah. 2015. "'Confidence You can Carry!': Girls in Crisis and the Market for Girls' Empowerment Organizations." *Continuum: Journal of Media and Cultural Studies* 29 (2): 182–193.

Banet-Weiser, Sarah. 2018. *Empowered: Popular Feminism and Popular Misogyny.* North Carolina: Duke University Press.

Boellstorff, Tom. 2008. *Coming of Age in Second Life: An Anthropologist Explores the Virtually Human.* Princeton, NJ: Princeton University Press.

Boellstorff, Tom. 2016. "For Whom the Ontology Turns: Theorizing the Digital Real." *Current Anthropology* 57 (4): 387–407.

Boellstorff, Tom, Bonnie Nardi, Celia Pearce, and T. L. Taylor. 2012. *Ethnography and Virtual Worlds: A Handbook of Methods.* Princeton, NJ: Princeton University Press.

Bourdieu, Pierre. 1986. "The Forms of Capital." In *Handbook of Theory and Research for the Sociology of Education*, edited by John Richardson, 15–29. Santa Barbara, CA: Greenwood Publishing.

boyd, danah. 2010. "Social Network Sites as Networked Publics: Affordances, Dynamics and Implications." In *A Networked Self: Identity, Community and Culture on Social Network Sites*, edited by Zizi Papacharissi, 39–58. New York: Routledge.

boyd, danah. 2015. *It's Complicated.* New Haven, CT: Yale University Press.

Bucholtz, Mary, and Kira Hall. 2005. "Identity and Interaction: A Sociocultural Linguistic Approach." *Discourse Studies* 7 (4–5): 585–614.

Carman, Ashley. 2020. "Instagram Brought in $20 Billion in Ad Revenue Last Year, More Than a Quarter of Facebook's Earnings." *The Verge*, February 4, 2020. https://www.theverge.com/2020/2/4/21122956/instagram-ad-revenue-earningsamount-facebook.

Davenport, Thomas H., and John C. Beck. 2001. *The Attention Economy: Understanding the New Currency of Business.* Cambridge, MA: Harvard Business School Press.

Dent, Alexander S. 2018. "What's a Cellular Public?" *Anthropological Quarterly* 91 (2): 581–601.

Dimock, Michael. 2019. "Defining Generations: Where Millennials End and Generation Z Begins." *Pew Research*, January 7, 2019. https://pewresearch.org/fact-tank/2019/01/17/where-milennials-end-and-generation-z-begins/.

Ducharme, Jamie. 2019. "Social Media Hurts Girls More than Boys." *Time*, August 13, 2019. https://time.com/5650266/social-media-girls-mental-health/.

Duffy, Brooke Erin, and Emily Hund. 2015. "'Having it all' on Social Media: Entrepreneurial Femininity and Self-Branding among Fashion Bloggers." *Social Media + Society* 1 (2): 1–11.

Duffy, Brooke Erin, and Urszula Pruchniewska. 2017. "Gender and Self-Enterprise in the Social Media Age: A Digital Double Bind." *Information, Communication and Society* 20 (6): 843–859.

Edwards, Simon, and Victoria Wang. 2018. "There are Two Sides to Every Story: Young People's Perspectives of Relationship Issues on Social Media and Adult Responses. *Journal of Youth Studies* 21 (6): 717–732.

Foucault, Michel. 1988. *Technologies of the Self: A Seminar with Michel Foucault.* London: Tavistock Publications.

Fuchs, Christian. 2014. "Theorising and Analysing Digital Labor: From Global Value Chains to Modes of Production." *The Political Economy of Production* 2 (1): 3–27.

Gangneux, Justine. 2019. "Logged in or Locked in? Young Adults' Negotiations of Social Media Platforms and their Features." *Journal of Youth Studies* 22 (8): 1053–1067.

Gershon, Ilana. 2010. *The Breakup 2.0: Disconnecting over New Media*. Ithaca, NY: Cornell University Press.

Gershon, Ilana. 2020. "The Breakup 2.1: The Ten Year Update." *The Information Society: An International Journal* 36 (5): 1–11.

Giddens, Anthony. 1991. *Modernity and Self-Identity: Self and Society in the Late Modern Age*. Stanford, CA: Stanford University Press.

Gill, Rosalind. 2017. "The Affective, Cultural, and Psychic Life of Postfeminism: A Postfeminist Sensibility 10 Years On." *European Journal of Cultural Studies* 20 (6): 606–626.

Gill, Rosalind, and Shani Orgad. 2017. "Confidence and the Remaking of Feminism." *New Formations* 91: 16–34.

Goffman, Erving. 1959. *The Presentation of Self in Everyday Life*. New York: Anchor Books.

Hearn, Alison. 2010. "Structuring Feeling: Web 2.0, Online Ranking and Rating, and the Digital 'Reputation' Economy." *Ephemera* 10: 421–438.

Heid, Markham. 2019. "Depression and Suicide Rates are Rising Sharply in Young Americans, New Report Says." *Time*, March 4, 2019. https://time.com/5550803/depression-suicide-rates-youth/.

Hogan, Bernie. 2010. "The Presentation of Self in the Age of Social Media: Distinguishing Performances and Exhibitions Online." *Bulletin of Science, Technology & Society* 30 (6): 377–386.

Julian, Kate. 2018. "Why Are Young People Having So Little Sex?" *The Atlantic*, December, 2018. https://www.theatlantic.com/magazine/archive/2018/12/the-sex-recession/573949/.

Kemp, Simon. 2021. *Digital 2021 Statbites: Quickfire Headlines and Highlights from the 2021 Global Digital Reports*, March, 2021. https://datareportal.com/reports/global-digital-statbites-001.

Madianou, Mirca. 2015. "Polymedia and Ethnography: Understanding the Social in Social Media." *Social Media + Society* (April–June): 1–3.

Madianou, Mirca, and Daniel Miller. 2013. "Polymedia: Towards a New Theory of Digital Media in Interpersonal Communication." *International Journal of Cultural Studies* 16 (2): 169–187.

Miller, Daniel, Elisabetta Costa, Nell Haynes, Tom McDonald, Razvan Nicolescu, Jolynna Sinanan, Juliano Spyer, Shriram Venkatraman, and Xinyuan Wang. 2016. *How the World Changed Social Media*. Vol. 1. London: UCL Press.

Miller, Daniel, and Jolynna Sinanan. 2017. *Visualising Facebook: A Comparative Perspective*. London: UCL Press.

Monroe, Rachel. 2021. "Ultra-Fast Fashion is Eating the World." *The Atlantic*, February 6, 2021. https://www.theatlantic.com/magazine/archive/2021/03/ultra-fast-fashion-is-eating-the-world/617794/.

Nichter, Mimi. 2015. *Lighting Up: The Rise of Social Smoking on College Campuses*. New York: New York University Press.

Orlowski, Jeff, dir. 2020. *The Social Dilemma*. Malibu, CA: Argent Pictures. Netflix.

Perrin, Andrew, and Monica Anderson. 2019. "Share of U.S. Adults Using Social Media, including Facebook, is Mostly Unchanged Since 2018. FactTank, Social Media

Usage in the US in 2019." *Pew Research Center,* April 10, 2019. https://www.pewre-search.org/fact-tank/2019/04/10/share-of-u-s-adults-using-social-media-including-facebook-is-mostly-unchanged-since-2018/.

Pew Research Center. 2021. "Mobile Fact Sheet." April 7, 2021. https://www.pewre-search.org/internet/fact-sheet/mobile/#who-owns-cellphones-and-smartphones.

Popper, Nathaniel. 2020. "Panicking about Your Kids' Phones? New Research Says Don't." *The New York Times,* January 17, 2020. https://www.nytimes.com/2020/01/17/technology/kids-smartphones-depression.html.

Prensky, Marc. 2001. "Digital Natives, Digital Immigrants." *On the Horizon* 9 (5): 1–6.

Quintero, Gilbert, Henry Bundy, and Michelle Grocke. 2019. "'I Want to See Those Memories': Social Affordances of Mobile Phone Cameras and Social Network Sites in College Drinking." *Contemporary Drug Problems* 6 (2): 180–197.

Rideout, Victoria, and Michael B. Robb. 2019. *The Common Sense Census: Media Use by Tweens and Teens, 2019.* San Francisco, CA: Common Sense Media.

Ross, Scott. 2019. "Being Real on Fake Instagram: Likes, Images, and Media Ideologies of Value." *Journal of Linguistic Anthropology* 29 (3): 359–374.

Scolere, Leah, Urszula Pruchniewska, and Brooke Erin Duffy. 2018. "Constructing the Platform-Specific Self-Brand: The Labor of Social Media Production." *Social Media + Society* 4 (3): 1–11.

Simon, Herbert A. 1971. "Designing Organizations for an Information Rich World." In *Computers, Communications, and the Public Interest,* edited by Martin Greenberger, 37–72. Baltimore, MD: Johns Hopkins University Press.

Smith, Andrew, and Eileen Fischer. 2021. "Pay Attention, Please! Person Brand Building in Organized Online Attention Economies." *Journal of the Academy of Marketing Science* 49: 258–279.

Srnicek, Nick. 2016. *Platform Capitalism.* Hoboken, NJ: Wiley Press.

Stockdale, Laura A., and Sarah M. Coyne. 2020. "Bored and Online: Reasons for Using Social Media, Problematic Social Networking Site Use, and Behavioral Outcomes across the Transition from Adolescence to Emerging Adulthood." *Journal of Adolescence* 79: 173–183.

Taylor, Nicole, and Mimi Nichter. 2017. "Studying Body Image and Food Consumption Practices." In *Research Methods in the Anthropology of Food and Nutrition,* edited by John A. Brett and Janet Chrzan, 58–69. Oxford, UK: Berghahn Books.

Tiidenberg, Katrin. 2018. "Ethics in Digital Research." In *The SAGE Handbook of Qualitative Data Collection,* edited by Uwe Flick, 466–479. Newberry Park, CA: Sage.

Toffoletti, Kim, and Holly Thorpe. 2018. "Female Athletes' Self-Representation on Social Media: A Feminist Analysis of Neoliberal Marketing Strategies in 'Economies of Visibility'." *Feminism and Psychology* 28 (1): 11–31.

Tolentino, Jia. 2019. *Trick Mirror: Reflections on Self-Delusion.* New York: Random House.

Turkle, Sherry. 2015. *Reclaiming Conversation: The Power of Talk in a Digital Age.* London: Penguin Books.

Turkle, Sherry. 2017. *Alone Together: Why We Expect More from Technology and Less from Each Other.* 3rd ed. New York: Basic Books.

Twenge, Jean. 2017. "Have Smartphones Destroyed a Generation?" *The Atlantic,* September, 2017. https://www.theatlantic.com/magazine/archive/2017/09/has-the-smartphone-destroyed-a-generation/534198/.

Twenge, Jean. 2018. *iGen: Why Today's Super-Connected Kids are Growing Up Less Rebellious, More Tolerant, Less Happy—And Completely Unprepared for Adulthood—And What that Means for the Rest of Us*. New York: Atria Books.

Twenge, Jean, Brian Spitzberg, and Keith Campbell. 2019. "Less In-person Social Interaction with Peers among U.S. Adolescents in the 21st Century and Links to Loneliness." *Journal of Social and Personal Relationships* 36 (6): 1892–1913.

Twenge, Jean, and Gabrielle N. Martin. 2020. "Gender Differences in Associations between Digital Media Use and Psychological Well-Being: Evidence from Three Large Data Sets." *Journal of Adolescence* 79: 91–102.

Twenge, Jean, Gabrielle N. Martin, and Brian Spitzberg. 2019. "Trends in U.S. Adolescents' Media Use, 1976–2016: The Rise of Digital Media, the Decline of TV, and the (Near) Demise of Print." *Psychology of Popular Media Culture* 8 (4): 329–345.

van Dijck, José. 2013. *The Culture of Connectivity: A Critical History of Social Media*. New York: Oxford University Press.

van Krieken, Robert. 2019a. *Celebrity Society: The Struggle for Attention*. 2nd ed. New York: Routledge.

van Krieken, Robert. 2019b. "Georg Franck's 'The Economy of Attention': Mental Capitalism and the Struggle for Attention." *Journal of Sociology* 55 (1): 3–7.

Wolfe, Anslee. 2018. "Guess How Often You Use Your Phone Every Day?" *Journal of Accountancy Newsletter*, April 2, 2018. https://www.journalofaccountancy.com/newsletters/2018/apr/how-often-use-phone-every-day.html.

Zulli, Diana. 2018. "Capitalizing on the Look: Insights into the Glance, Attention Economy, and Instagram." *Critical Studies in Media Communication* 35 (2): 137–150.

1
MEDIA LANDSCAPE

Chloe, a 21-year-old communications major, showed up to the interview wearing form-fitting jeans, a red tank top, and a trendy pair of horn-rimmed glasses. A petite Black woman, Chloe was outgoing, friendly, and eager to share her insights about social media. Chloe estimated that she is on her sites 6–8 hours a day, checking continuously, and posting daily. In addition, she maintains "streaks" with about 15 friends on Snapchat, which requires daily messages to each of them. Chloe had Instagram, Snapchat, Twitter, and Facebook accounts.

Chloe used her phone to avoid boredom and awkward social situations. For example, when her roommate was arguing with her boyfriend on the phone late one night, Chloe distracted herself by scrolling online. Being alone in a public space, whether walking or sitting still, felt uncomfortable to her unless she had something to do, so she used her phone as a tool to appear busy. Checking online regularly helped Chloe "to feel connected and like I'm part of something when I'm on there." At the same time, in order to limit her screen time, Chloe was currently posting only on Snapchat and Instagram, explaining, "I find constant online communication to be exhausting."

Despite her conflicted relationship with social media, Chloe said she feels "a deep anxiety at the thought of letting go of it, or even staying off of social media for a little bit because people will forget me if I don't have a presence online." Recently, when Chloe's phone stopped working for a couple of days, she constantly felt worried about what she was missing and wondered what people thought about her extended absence. She explained, "People don't necessarily exist, in a social sense, unless they are posting on social media and show other people what they're doing."

Chloe's narrative highlights how she, like so many other students, was immersed in these online worlds, and relied on them for a sense of escape,

DOI: 10.4324/9781003182047-2

connection, and self-worth. Even as these emerging adults recognized the downsides of social media, including the intensive labor required for maintaining online visibility, they felt compelled to stay connected for fear of being forgotten.

This chapter sets the digital scene by broadly describing college students' experiences with and perceptions about social media, as well as the social norms that guide their behavior on Instagram, Snapchat, Twitter, and Facebook. We focus on how students used these platforms differently, including how tacit rules, the imagined desires of their audiences, and site affordances guided their online behaviors. We also explore the reasons for posting, the meaning of likes, and the many works involved in managing online popularity and social relationships.

In 2020, after we had concluded data collection for this study, TikTok emerged as a favorite site among youth. According to the Pew Research Center, in 2021 emerging adults stand out for their use of Instagram, Snapchat, and TikTok.[1] Social media use among college students changed drastically in 2020 because of Covid-19, a trend that coincided with TikTok's increasing popularity among youth. We gathered follow-up data with college students during the pandemic to explore its impact on social media use. We share those findings in Chapter 5, including a discussion of why TikTok held such wide appeal among youth. Since we feature TikTok in only one chapter that appears much later in this book, we decided to describe it solely within the context of that chapter.

Social Media Use

Most of our participants began using social media in late elementary or middle school when their parents created a Facebook account for them so they could connect with family members. By the end of middle school, students had expanded to other sites they learned about from friends, such as Snapchat, Instagram, and Twitter. Once in college, they were already proficient online, and they had more freedom than ever to spend time on these sites.

Daily time spent on social media varied widely. Over one quarter (27 percent) of students reported spending more than 5 hours a day on social media; 31 percent spent 3–5 hours a day online; with the remaining 42 percent spending 1–3 hours a day on social media. Among those who spent more than 5 hours a day on various platforms, the majority were women. Several studies confirm that young women spend more time on social media than men do.[2]

We also asked participants to estimate how many times per day they checked their phones. Most found this question difficult to answer as the reflex was automatic and unconscious, making it nearly impossible for them to articulate an exact number. Checking their phones was as unconscious as swallowing or sighing—it was something they did automatically without thinking about it. Every time a notification pinged, students would look at their phones—it seemed Pavlovian. Chloe told us that she automatically reaches for her phone every time she hears a notification, and she "compulsively" unlocks her phone all day long. During interviews, students continually reached for their phones every time they heard a ping. More often than not, they resisted the urge to look at their phones while we talked, but it was clearly a struggle. Sometimes these moments evoked a nervous giggle from participants, especially when it happened during discussions about phone addiction.

Over the course of the interview, participants typically became comfortable sharing a more realistic assessment of their social media use. Even so, most had trouble approximating the total time spent because they checked their phones so frequently throughout the day. Encouraging students to walk us through their day and unpack the moments that prompted them to check their phone and distinguish between brief glances and periods of focused browsing helped us to understand in more detail how much time they were spending on social media. If we had taken their initial responses at face value instead of exploring questions further throughout the interview, we would have underestimated how much time these college students were spending on various sites.

Given these findings, it may not be surprising that studies suggest time spent on social media interferes with young people's studies and quality of sleep.[3] Social media use is also associated with anxiety for emerging adults, and compulsive use, in particular, contributes to increased anxiety and depression.[4] Findings on the socio-emotional effects of social media use are concerning when we consider just how often youth check their sites and how much time they spend on them every day.

Former technology executive Linda Stone has coined the phrase *continuous partial attention* to describe the effects of using social media while engaged in other tasks.[5] Social media requires a high level of vigilance that makes it difficult to focus on other activities at the same time. Specifically, multitasking between social media and schoolwork correlates with decreased ability to sustain attention and poor academic performance. Multitasking bottlenecks the cognitive processing and working memory aspects of the brain when students engage in social media while studying or listening to a lecture. As a result, they have trouble processing and remembering what they are learning.[6]

Boredom and Stimulation

Aside from notifications, students reported reaching for their phones any time they felt bored—during class, in between classes, while home alone, watching a show or movie, riding the campus bus, or during a pause in a conversation with friends. One of our articulate and introspective participants, Brian, explained:

> What compels me to go to Snapchat or Instagram or check Facebook is, like, if there's a lull in the conversation or if you're alone and you're not

being stimulated. There's always this constant barrage of stimuli. I feel like it would be very hard for someone to sit in a room and be bored and not check social media. . . . Our culture has kind of morphed us into a place where it's not okay to be bored. You always have to have some stimulation.

Here, Brian describes how any pause in interaction represents a gap that that must be filled; social media provides a quick, easy outlet to address this need.

Robert, a quiet and thoughtful participant with glasses and short brown hair, also described scrolling through social media "just 'cause I'm bored, and it gives me something to do. It's a constant source of entertainment." Reflecting more deeply on the connection between social media and boredom, he elaborated:

I often don't even know why I'm doing it 'cause, like, it doesn't necessarily make me less bored. I'm still bored. I guess it's just a habit I've gotten into. I'm sure reading a book would be significantly more entertaining for me. But, for whatever reason, like, that endless cycle is just hard to get out of.

In the absence of having something to do in any given moment, many students reached for their phones, a phenomenon Robert described as "instinctual."

A recent study found that the most common reason for using social media among adolescents and emerging adults was to alleviate boredom; this behavior increased from late adolescence to emerging adulthood.[7] In fact, a national study on smartphone use found that 93 percent of emerging adults used their phones to avoid boredom and 47 percent used their phones to avoid interacting with people around them.[8] Longitudinal studies indicate that over the past decade, boredom has been on the rise among middle and high school students, with increases being greater for girls.[9] Researchers have found that boredom and depressive symptoms are increasing among today's youth and have suggested a potential link to increased time spent on digital and social media and more time spent alone.[10]

After years of social enmeshment—even when physically alone—youth today may feel non-connectedness more acutely when compared to earlier generations of emerging adults. It seems plausible that growing up with constant technologically mediated stimulation could result in acute boredom when one is offline. Our culture provides easy access to hyper-stimulation at all times of day and night which, in turn, may intensify feelings of "lack" when there is nothing going on.[11] Students' comments about their social media use align with what college students told Mimi Nichter about smoking: "The sense of not having anything to do, of feeling somehow amiss without a connection to others, of needing to fill in time alone, comes to be recognized as a time for a cigarette."[12] For the students in our study, moments of boredom prompted an unconscious process of scrolling on their phones, which became a proxy for connection, filling an otherwise empty space.

Conversely, research also suggests that browsing through social media can result in feeling bored and disengaged. One study described a tipping point for teens who browsed social media for a long period; their experience shifted from feeling entertained to feeling bored and frustrated when content became repetitive and browsing got in the way of other activities, like studying or socializing.[13] Similar to students' comments noted earlier, even though scrolling through social media does not necessarily relieve boredom, it is a habit and, for some, an unconscious compulsion. The cellphone offers infinite opportunities for filling time, including scrolling through social media, watching videos, reading a book or the news, and searching for information, to name a few. However, the lure of social media appears to be especially irresistible for this age group.

Looking Busy

We learned that it was important for students to be, or at least appear to be, busy. When asked what prompts her to check social media when she is alone, one woman responded, "Mmm, if I'm not doing schoolwork, probably, like, that's what I do when I'm alone. Like, if I'm not busy, I'm checking social media." Checking social media to have something to do or "be busy" is similar to the themes of alleviating boredom and seeking stimuli discussed in the previous section. However, many students talked about using social media to look busy to others.

For example, Natalie, a communications major who described herself as anxious and socially awkward, said that when she is alone in public, she looks at her phone and refreshes the page repeatedly to look like she is busy, even if she is not interested in the content.

> I check social media when I'm with other people less often (than when I'm alone) 'cause I'm busy. I'm doing something. I'm entertained. So social media is my form of entertainment when I'm alone. If I have the entertainment already then I don't need the social media.

Here, Natalie illustrates Brian's earlier point that she seeks stimulus from her phone, suggesting the need for constant entertainment. However, Natalie also describes social media as a prop that she uses to look like she is doing something.

One student explained that he always scrolls through social media to look busy when he is alone in public: "Eating alone. That's a thing. So you're eating alone and you want to look busy. You don't want to be that lonely kid." Similarly, Aliyah said that when she is waiting for a friend to come pick her up, "I, like sit out front and I'll put my phone up to my ear pretending to talk. It makes me look like I have something to do." These examples illustrate that scrolling through social media can be as much about maintaining an image of being busy, being popular, and avoiding the discomfort of having nothing to do as it is about needing to feel constantly stimulated. In these examples, we see identity work and impression management at play; looking like one is alone can create an undesirable impression. Being busy on your phone, whether scrolling aimlessly or pretending to be in conversation with others, signaled that you were not alone, that you were visibly connected to your friends.

It is not only youth who face this desire for constant external stimulation and an expectation to be busy constantly (or at least appear so). Just being quiet and still is no longer sufficient. Nicole, one of the authors, experienced this pressure recently when she took her car to an auto shop for repair. She sat alone in the waiting room, enjoying the quiet solitude when an employee rushed in to encourage her to turn on the television and have some coffee. She said, "No thanks, I'm fine," which prompted him to ask incredulously if she had forgotten her phone. When she shook her head no, he nervously laughed as he asked, "What are you going to do? Just sit here and stare at the wall?" she nodded her head, and he seemed shocked, shrugging his shoulders with a perplexed and exasperated expression on his face as he turned to walk away. In this case, it was not an internal need to appear busy, but instead external pressure. The expectation to be constantly stimulated and always appear busy has become such a pervasive social norm that breaking this tacit rule resulted in confusion and irritation.

Avoiding Awkward Social Situations

Students said they looked through their social media to avoid awkward social situations as well. For example, Amber, a business major from a coastal town who posted a lot of beach and party selfies, talked about arriving at a party where she did not know anyone. She felt uncomfortable and started scrolling through her phone to have something to do. In effect, using her phone in this way, Amber created her own bubble—a space and time where she is alone but busy. Once her friends arrived and she had people to talk to, she put her phone away. In a similar vein, Nichter found that college students smoked at parties when there was no one to talk to in order to avoid seeming alone, bored, or, even worse, boring.[14] She observed that lighting up a cigarette at such times "can make it appear that you are self-engaged and occupied, rather than someone who is alone."[15] Having something to do when alone in a social space, such as scrolling through social media, provides a sense of purpose and engagement that can help youth feel more at ease and blend in with the crowd.

Students also used their phones to avoid interacting with people. As one woman explained, "Like if I come across someone that I don't want to talk to I'll just stay on my phone or pretend to be texting somebody that doesn't even exist (laughs)." Students said that riding the campus bus was both boring and awkward because no one talked to each other. The prospect of sitting silently in close proximity with strangers made them uncomfortable and looking out the window or staring down at their laps felt boring and awkward, so they scrolled through their phones instead. Shelby, a chatty student with a nose ring who rarely posted, explained:

> I was on the bus and I was just scrolling through my sites even though I had already looked at them, like, moments before. When I'm on the bus, if I look out the windows, there's not much to look at, so it's (looking at my phone) a way to fill time if I don't have a friend. And everyone's on their phone on the bus unless you have a friend. I don't know where to look, I don't know what to do. If I'm on my phone it avoids the weird eye contact.

In this case, the phone provided Shelby with a much-needed distraction from social discomfort and a way to fill time when she was alone. Social norms about whom you can talk to have shifted with social media. Now that everyone is looking at their phones in public, striking up a conversation with a stranger has become awkward and uncomfortable.

Procrastination

Procrastination was another reason students reached for their phones. As one woman said, "If I don't want to do my homework or laundry or something, I'll procrastinate by going through my (social media) sites. It's, like, 'Oh I'll just look through this one more time, or five more times' (laughs)." Another student said that he procrastinates on social media

> to the point where something that probably would have taken me 20–30 minutes to do had I just stayed off my phone, ended up taking me, like, 2–3 hours because I was on social media so much. I could have read an entire chapter of the book during that time.

For these students, social media provided an escape from work. What begins as a quick "brain break" can easily turn into hours of mindless scrolling. The expectation for constant stimulation competes, and often wins, over the need to study.

Some students had developed strategies for combating procrastination. For example, Shelby said that any time her phone lights up or buzzes she feels compelled to reach for it—she cannot help herself. Her phone was such a distraction that she had begun placing it out of reach when she needed to focus on schoolwork.

> You need to have it (your phone) turned on 'cause people contact you, so if I have things to do I keep it screen down ten feet away. That way if someone needs to contact me, I'll hear it but it's not in arm's reach.

Other students said they would put their phone away in a drawer while studying or silence it so they could focus. Youth are not the only ones who cave to the lure of social media when they should be working. This issue is so pervasive that there are at least ten apps available for download that allow you to block social media in order to focus on work.[16]

Rules of Phone Use While Hanging Out with Friends

Of late, researchers have studied the impact of being on one's phone while interacting with others, mostly in relation to one's romantic partner. Social media and marketing researchers James Roberts and Meredith David coined the term "phubbing," referring to "being snubbed by someone using their cell phone when in your company."[17] While multitasking and phubbing are clearly occurring when friends get together, we know relatively little about whether and how social norms are changing during these times.

Most students said they felt it was rude to scroll through their social media while socializing with friends. Yet, they admitted it was difficult to resist the urge, especially during a lull in the conversation. Brian explained:

> If there's kind of, like, a lull . . . like, if you're with friends, and there's not a lot going on. Maybe you're talking or when it gets to be a little slow and boring, people have the tendency, like me, to take out their phones and open Snapchat, go to Instagram, check Facebook. I would say we always want to be stimulated, and if the people we're with can't provide that then we want to get it from somewhere else.

As people have become used to constant stimulation, ordinary conversation can seem boring in comparison. When someone engages with their phone while hanging out and talking with friends, it is an implicit signal that they are no longer interested in the conversation.

Amber told us that she tries not to check her phone when she is with friends.

> I hate that. I feel like we should talk to each other. But, like, if the people I'm with, if they're all on their phones, then I'll get on my phone, 'cause I'm like, well, no one is talking to me anyways. Might as well look at Instagram or whatever.

When there is a lull in the conversation and her friends look at their phones, that often prompts conversations about videos and posts that they see on social media, which shifts the conversational focus from each other to someone's phone. Checking one's phone while socializing with others has become incredibly common. According to one national survey, 98 percent of emerging adults have used their phones during their most recent social activity with others.[18]

Students we interviewed explained that while hanging out, instead of or in addition to talking to each other, they would message each other through social media. Tania, an education major who described herself as a homebody who mostly posts about her dogs, explained, "My friends, when we hang out, we talk through Snapchat even though we're with each other. There's talking going on, too, but we're on our phones mostly." In this case, to an observer, it might look like a group of friends ignoring each other to look at their phones. In reality, they are engaging with each other online, as a complement to their offline face-to-face conversation.

Although Tania participated in communicating with her friends online while hanging out with them, she expressed increasing frustration with this dynamic because, "It feels rude. It looks bad. It looks like you're not actually enjoying each other's company." One of the benefits articulated by some students was that communicating with their phones while hanging out with friends allows them to connect over shared content. For some, it is also a way to be with friends without actively engaging in conversation. In this example, we see how social norms vary in relation to acceptable phone use when together with friends. Although one might assume that "phubbing" is a rude behavior, some college students recognized that using their smartphones when they were together with friends was integral to their interaction—giving them more to talk about—rather than a hindrance to time spent together.[19]

Nicholas, a media studies major who posted multiple times a day across his sites, told us that he and his friends have an "unspoken agreement" about when to put their phones away.

> If there's an active conversation going on, I'm not checking my phone at all because I don't want to be disrespectful. I feel like it's somewhat of an unspoken agreement. We don't necessarily tell each other, "Oh, we're gonna stay off our phones." But typically we're kind of just like, "Oh, well if you're saying words to me then I'm gonna put my phone down, and likewise, your phone is down, and we're communicating." But if we're all just hanging out and we're all just together, but not together, then we're all on our phones going through our social media.

Media scholar Sherry Turkle, who explores the role of technology in mediating interpersonal relationships, shares similar stories of youth who multitask with their phones while socializing.[20] We found that some friend groups explicitly set boundaries around phone use when hanging out in person. One young woman said that when her friends get together for a weekly dinner, they have agreed to put their phones face down in the middle of the table and focus on conversation for the evening. Because this was an explicit rule that everyone in the group had agreed to, she said they all comply. It helps that their phones are stacked slightly out of reach and therefore not readily accessible.

Quickly checking phones when notifications ping was also common practice while hanging out with friends. Students considered this practice less disruptive than scrolling through social media during a lull in the conversation. One student explained:

> We'll be hanging out, talking, and someone will look at their phone for a split second. It's all of us, and, I mean, it's not like constant, but it is, like, in the middle of a conversation. If you get a notification you'll check it. It's not as constant as when I'm alone, but it seems like someone is always picking up their phone.

The way students described this practice of quickly checking their phones made it seem like a natural part of the flow of conversation, no more distracting than when someone stops to take a drink of water or runs their fingers through their hair.

However, it is easy to imagine how even quickly checking one's phone can become a distraction from the conversation if the content is engaging or notifications are pinging frequently. Some students felt frustrated if their friends focused more on their phones than on the conversation at hand. Shelby said that she sometimes catches herself tuning the conversation out when she quickly checks her phone while with friends because she "sucks at multitasking." At the same time, when Shelby's friends tune her out while scrolling through their phones, she feels upset.

> I can tell when someone doesn't fully hear me. My roommate will be like, "Mm, yeah." And I'll say something completely off topic and she'll say, "Mm." And I'll stop talking until she looks up from her phone. Or I'll hit her phone. I do that a lot to try to get people to come back.

Jason, a fraternity member with a strong southern drawl, shared that he has one friend who gets on his phone while they are hanging out talking. "I'll start throwin' things at him (laughs) 'cause he'll be ignoring me (laughs). It's so weird, like, for someone in your friendship group to take out a phone while you guys are hanging out together!" As these examples illustrate, not everyone is on the same page when it comes to social norms about appropriate phone use while hanging out with others. Some expect focused attention during conversation, while for others, multitasking with a phone during conversation is acceptable. However, even among those who prefer to focus on the conversation at hand, it was often difficult to resist the lure of their phones.

Results of research confirm that smartphones have enabled both multitasking and multi-communicating.[21] That is, when friends spend time together, they expect to be attentive to one another but also available to other friends who may try to reach them. One study found that even though college students thought it unacceptable to text others while talking and hanging out with friends, they did it anyway.[22] This suggests that social norms of appropriate behavior with friends are fluid and are undergoing shifts.

How does multitasking in these ways affect friendships? Recent research has found that using a phone with friends can undermine the well-being that typically arises when friends spend time together. The researchers sent multiple short surveys to 120 college students over a five-day period. Each survey asked students to report how they had been feeling over the previous 15 minutes and to check all the activities they had been doing (e.g., socializing face-to-face, eating, studying). The researchers captured over 1,200 episodes in which participants reported face-to-face interaction, and they compared times when students used their phones and times they did not. Importantly, when students socialized with friends while also using their phones, they reported that they felt distracted, less socially connected, enjoyed themselves less, and were overall in a worse mood.[23]

Tacit rules about phone use differ by context and social hierarchy. For example, it would be considered rude for a student to check their phone while meeting with a professor during office hours; however, it would be acceptable for a professor to check her phone while meeting with a student. In the case of friends, a relatively horizontal relationship, the rules are more complex and often require negotiation. As we saw from the examples above, some students were offended when their friends looked at their phones during conversation. For others, it it was acceptable to quickly check one's phone while talking to a friend, but lingering on the phone was considered rude. Other students explicitly negotiated rules about phone use to facilitate smooth social interactions. Because social norms regarding phone use are so contextual, depending on the relationship of participants, their status in relation to each other, and the social setting, youth have to constantly shift their phone-related behaviors throughout the day. Understanding the boundaries of appropriate behavior in any given setting has become increasingly complex with smartphones and social media.

As we have seen, multi-communicating while hanging out with friends is a normative practice among today's college students. While some scholars have suggested that such practices can threaten the quality of interactions and diminish personal relationships, the voices of emerging adults reveal the complexity of these everyday behaviors.[24] Some students expressed frustration with friends engaging in moments of "absent presence," while many others accepted this as a new norm.[25]

The Purpose of Posting

One of the questions we asked students was why they post. Sofia, a congenial education major who mostly posted heavily edited selfies, responded, "I'm posting to get likes and posting so they can see how I look." We followed up by asking, "What if you post something and get no likes?" She explained, "I'll probably delete it honestly (laughs). I feel like nobody's seeing it, so I'll just delete it." We wondered, "So it's not important unless other people see it?" to which she replied, "I guess you can say that for social media, yeah." This quote captures the importance of online visibility and provides insight into why students deleted posts that did not receive enough attention. There was a widespread perception among students that if your life is not on display for others to see then it does not count. It appears that the point is not necessarily to live your best life but, instead, to perform living your best life for all to see.

We wondered about the purpose of likes—are they a public display of popularity, an internal boost to the individual's sense of self, or both? When we asked the question, "What does the number of likes mean to you?" mostly we heard from students that it made them feel seen, appreciated, and validated. Daniel, a self-described "social media expert" and frequent poster, explained:

> Like, that feeling I get when I'm done with a photo, and then, like, I post it, and then it gets all those likes. Not only does it make me feel validated, but it makes me feel like all the work I put into editing that photo paid off (laughs).

Most students talked about monitoring likes for their posts and feeling deflated or even anxious when they did not get as many as they had hoped for. It was a sign that they did something wrong, possibly miscalculating timing or audience expectations. Too few likes was a symbol of invisibility, an indicator that people were not interested enough in what you shared to spend a fraction of a second clicking on the emoji.

In contrast, accumulating likes felt rewarding—it meant that your audience approved, that your post was eye-catching enough that people stopped scrolling to provide feedback. It made students feel seen and valued. Students viewed their social media as an extension of self and likes represented external validation. Because the stakes for external validation were high, many students, particularly women, put a lot of thought, planning, and effort into creating the perfect post.

When our study began, Instagram had a built-in feedback mechanism that allowed friends and followers to publicly like or ignore posts. Partway through our research, in November 2019, Instagram rolled out a test program in the U.S. to hide the number of likes from followers. The C.E.O. of Instagram said, "The idea is to try and depressurize Instagram, to make it less of a competition, give people more space to focus on connecting with the people they love and the things that inspire them."[26] Individuals whose accounts Instagram selected to be in the test group could still see the number of likes each post received and who liked their posts, but their followers no longer had access to this information.

We wondered how hiding likes affected students' experiences with Instagram. Follow-up interviews revealed that most students had not been opted into the test program, so their likes continued to be publicly visible. For the handful of students whose likes were hidden from public view, they did not seem to care—they still counted likes as a measure of self-worth. Our findings suggest that likes represented a personal (as opposed to public) measure of self-worth. For this reason, hiding likes from public view may not have the impact Instagram intends. Although they learn how many likes to strive for and which types of posts get the most likes from studying other people's feeds, by the time Instagram had publicly hidden likes for some accounts, students had already internalized this knowledge and knew what they needed to post in order to get the external validation they craved.

The Science of Likes

Students shared their process for posting to get likes. Some, like Nicholas, had it down to a science.

> Typically, if I'm posting a picture on Instagram, I've already edited it. I've already made it look the way I want it to look. When it's time to post, it takes me forever to think of the right caption, who to tag, where to place those, if I should also post it on Facebook, what the location should be, and when to post it. I've actually been following a very strict timeline of when I post my pictures on Instagram even though that sounds bad. Because depending on the day and time you post, that's when you'll get the most activity, the most likes, the most comments (sigh). It's, like, a lot to think about.

Similarly, Jason said his strategy is to post when most people are on social media. He had found that posting between 8:00 and 9:00 p.m. resulted in the most likes. He imagined that was when most people had finished dinner and were sitting at home scrolling through their sites. After explaining this during the interview he jokingly said, "Not that I looked that up or anything (laughs). Well, actually I did."

Amber had a slightly different take on the importance of posting during peak hours.

> People want to get likes right away. Like, if I were to post a photo at 8:00 a.m. I might get a couple of likes right away, but I wouldn't get most of

the likes until later on. As stupid as that sounds, it's like, "Oh, I wanna get the likes now!" It's the truth (laughs).

The immediacy of the positive feedback was as important to Amber as getting numerous likes. In each of these examples, the amount of thought and planning that went into posting at just the right time is noteworthy. Posting strategy involved systematic research, including long-term observation of which posts get the most and least likes in relation to the day of the week and the time of day posted.

Monitoring likes was an important part of the process as well. Diego, an aspiring rapper who posted to draw attention to his music, described the process of tracking how people are engaging with his posts.

> So, I'll post something. Then I'll get a notification that somebody liked it. When you look at the notification, it just shows you one person, and then when you go into the app it shows you everybody who liked it. A heart will pop up and show how many likes you got. Yeah, it's just, I guess, you feel the need for recognition. You see the likes and you're like, "Looks nice!" So whenever I post I'll check on my newsfeed to see who liked it, who commented and stuff like that. I'll also check how many views I got if it's a video clip. And I'll check group messaging just to see what everybody's talking about, and if they're saying anything about my post.

Here, we see a glimpse of the work involved in monitoring feedback. Students repeated this process many times throughout the day, continually checking to see if their post had more likes than the last time they looked.

How did students respond when a post did not get as many likes as they wanted? Most told us they deleted it, sometimes reposting at a different time. Anthony explained, "It's likes. That's what drives Instagram. If you don't get the likes, you delete it and then you repost it. If you don't get the likes again, you repeat the cycle until you get the likes you want." What is missing from this description is a sense of how the person felt when they did not receive likes. Even if they can delete a post and repost it at a better time, they still may feel badly about themselves that they did not succeed in getting attention on their first attempt. Gabrielle described a different process she had observed from a friend:

> My friend Rachel, she's really obsessed with the way people see her. She just watches her own stories over and over again. And she, like, checks how many people have seen it and all that stuff. The other day she posted a picture. She was like, "I knew I should have waited. It wasn't the right time. Nobody's gonna see it. Nobody's liking it." And she was like, "I

can't delete it because then if I repost it, people are gonna be like, 'Oh my God! She's just looking for attention.'" And I was just like, "This is too much" (laughs).

We see how Gabrielle's friend behaves compulsively, worrying about getting sufficient likes for her post, and second guessing herself about the timing of her post. Her friend struggles with the knowledge that she cannot simply delete her unpopular post and repost it at a more suitable time (a common practice) because that will only serve to highlight her desperation.

While many students expressed frustrations about posting, there was also pleasure involved. Part of the excitement and fun of posting was anticipating how others would respond. Soon after posting, students awaited their audience response, forever hopeful for success. Brian told us about the sense of anticipation he experiences when he posts:

> I think about all of the details before I post a picture. Like, you know, should it be in color? Should it have a color tone to it? Should it be in black and white? What would look better? What will get likes? Then you post it, and your body, like, your brain just gets a shot of dopamine or whatever. Like, it really does! It's nerve-wracking and it's exhilarating to click "post" and put whatever you want out into the world. And then, you know, sometimes I think people, including myself, will take it down if they don't get enough likes, which factors into their concept of self-worth. They'll either change it or, a lot of times, people will delete it and start all over. It's a big cycle.

When we consider the expectation and hopes expressed by some students as they waited for likes, we can understand how checking for feedback could become almost compulsive. Some authors have compared social media's system of random rewards in the form of likes to slot machines.[27] *New York Times* columnist David Brooks wrote, "Tech companies understand what causes dopamine surges in the brain and they lace their products with 'hijacking techniques' that lure us in and create 'compulsion loops.'"[28] The dopamine surge keeps students continually clicking on their apps to check for content updates, likes, and comments.

Strategizing Likes

Social media feeds are crowded, and for most students, getting likes on any given post was a hit or miss process. It depended only partially on the time of day they posted and the post-worthy nature of their picture. Each post is in competition with all of the other posts in one's feed. That is, people judge posts against the other content that shows up in their feed at that particular time.

A post that may attract likes one day may not get any the next, depending on how many other people posted at a similar time and how eye-catching their posts are in relation to yours. Students had to continually plan and develop posts designed to attract likes in order to maintain their status. Likes, views, and followers represent a valuable form of social capital in the online attention economy where visibility is critical to success.[29] Students felt a lot of pressure to post regularly and maintain a strong presence on their sites.

The design side of social media apps also helps determine how much attention your post will receive. For example, a simple Google search displays numerous vlogs and blogs that unpack the Instagram algorithm. According to these sites, six factors influence which posts are most visible on your feed: interest, relationships, timeliness, frequency, following, and usage. Essentially, the Instagram algorithm analyzes your past behavior to predict which posts you are most likely to enjoy. It monitors your engagement with content and people in the form of searches, likes, comments, and direct messaging to determine which posts and stories should be most visible on your feed. What does this mean for our students who want likes? As one advertising blogger stated, "This is why showing up on Instagram is so important! It keeps you top of mind with your followers, helps your engagement, and helps your posts be seen by the algorithm."[30] This blogger goes on to provide numerous tips for getting the most attention, including posting regularly, replying to every comment on your post to build relationships with followers and encourage future likes, and enabling notifications so that your responses are timely.

Moreover, the Instagram algorithm constantly changes in response to the massive amount of data it gathers from users every second of the day. This destabilizes the science of posting and requires vigilance and continual research to maintain online visibility. In the next section, we shift focus to describe how usage norms differed for students across their favorite social media sites— Instagram, Snapchat, Twitter, and Facebook.

Instagram

Instagram is the most visual of the four platforms. Students explained that posting highly edited, aesthetically pleasing photos and videos was the expectation for this site. The name of the game was to attract as many followers and likes as possible. Instagram users have the option to make their account private; however, students we talked to thrived on attention and therefore chose public accounts. On Instagram, the people you follow and your followers may not match because users are not required to follow those who follow them. Instagram was a site for friends, acquaintances, and strangers to be able to follow students; they cared less about who their followers were than how many they had. A few had even purchased apps designed to increase their number of followers and/or likes.

Students told us that Instagram posts should highlight extraordinary, special moments in life rather than everyday moments. They saw Instagram as a space for sharing adventures, travel, milestones, such as birthdays, anniversaries, and graduations, and big social events. This meant that students posted only once or twice a week, much less frequently than they posted to Snapchat and Twitter. Yet, they spent more time developing content for Instagram than for any other site. Students felt a lot of pressure to live up to the exciting lives of those they followed on Instagram. This meant they had to either engage in exciting experiences at least once a week or make it appear as though they do.

One woman, for example, described herself as an introvert who only socialized a couple of times a month. Most weekends she enjoyed staying in and eating take-out while watching movies. During the interview, she sheepishly admitted to saving photos from social events and posting them throughout the month to make it appear that she has a more active social life than she does. Others created post-worthy moments by dressing up and taking photos with friends while hanging out at home. Photos of people laughing, smiling, and looking excited were a common theme across Instagram posts. The tone of these posts tended to be high energy and enthusiastic. In this way, students created a life that others can gaze at and admire.

Students also felt pressure to post beautiful, aesthetically pleasing photos— this pressure was a lot more intense for Instagram than for any other site. As a result, students put many hours into the development of one post. The "production process" involved multiple steps, including planning and dressing for a photo shoot, taking multiple pictures, reviewing the sometimes hundreds of photos to choose the best one, carefully editing the image using filters, developing a clever caption, posting it at the best time for optimal attention, and monitoring likes in subsequent days.

The level of stress and anxiety generated by the comparative, competitive nature of Instagram was unparalleled. Many of the students we talked to cared deeply about getting likes for their posts. They worried if certain people did not like a post, if not enough people liked a post, or if the ratio of likes to followers was low. A few had even developed a formula for evaluating the ratio of likes to followers—if a post did not meet a certain ratio threshold, then it was promptly deleted. Students described apps for tracking how often followers liked posts so they could delete followers who never liked their posts, thereby increasing their ratio of likes to followers. In contrast, no one worried about likes, followers, and developing a perfect post to this extent on any of the other sites.

Snapchat

In many ways, Snapchat is the opposite of Instagram. While Instagram represents exciting milestones and adventures, Snapchat represents the everyday, mundane moments of life. While Instagram consists of carefully posed and edited photos designed to impress, Snapchat consists of hastily snapped pictures and videos meant to reveal raw, candid aspects of oneself. While Instagram represents an archive or digital photo album of milestones designed to last, Snapchat represents a fleeting snapshot of everyday life that disappears after 24 hours. In contrast to Instagram, where the goal is to have as many followers as possible, most students we interviewed limited their Snapchat audience to a relatively small group of carefully selected friends. Whereas a person's Instagram followers may not be the same as those they follow, in Snapchat, someone has to accept your friend request before you are connected.

Perhaps one of the most notable differences between the two platforms is that Snapchat has no feedback mechanism for posts—it is not possible to like or comment. The only way to provide feedback is through the chat function. There are two ways to communicate with friends in Snapchat—post to one's story and chat with individual friends or groups of friends. Students reported posting to their Snapchat stories daily, often multiple times a day, as this was quick and easy to do. In short, students saw this platform as a way to share ordinary, unfiltered moments, with friends.

Students frequently described Snapchat as "funny," "everyday," and "random." One woman said, "I just use Snapchat for fun and to, like, play around." Similarly, Amber explained, "I post random, everyday things on Snapchat, like videos of my friends doing something stupid, or a picture of the coffee cart in the quad." Comparing it to Instagram, she added, "It's not, like, as important to get the perfect shot, you know." This is a noteworthy comment from Amber because in that same interview, she described a painstaking photoshoot process with friends that involved taking hundreds of pictures to get just the right one for Instagram. Snapchat provided Amber and others the freedom to have a more carefree posting attitude. Overall, students felt less concerned with their image on Snapchat because posts disappear and their audiences were smaller and more intimate.

Many students offered examples of how they used Snapchat to share what they considered humorous moments from their day. For example, one woman laughed as she told us she was taking a video of campus while she was walking when she tripped and fell down the stairs. She posted it to her Snapchat story because she thought it was funny. Similarly, Aliyah posted a video of her roommate playing the ukulele loudly and off key to share a laughable moment with her friends. Jayden, a self-effacing business major, posted on Snapchat multiple times a day, and it was the freedom to be funny that drew him to this platform. He explained that offline, he is shy and quiet, but on Snapchat, he is funny and outgoing. Jayden sees his Snapchat friends as his audience, and he enjoys entertaining them. His friends often send him chats letting him know they liked his posts; this feedback has given Jayden the confidence to be more outgoing in person.

In addition to posting funny and silly photos and videos, students also shared the more mundane aspects of their days. For example, Sofia said:

> On Snapchat, I post, like, whatever I'm doing. So, if I'm sitting and reading, I'll post a picture of the book. If I'm studying, I'll post a picture of my computer screen. There is no need to filter because it's just my friends who see it, and I know it's not gonna be there for long.

Similarly, Anthony described his process for capturing everyday life: "I'm just walking around and I see, like, a squirrel eating and I think, 'Okay that interests me.' So I'll let other people see what I'm interested in at this moment, at this time, at this place."

Some students also described Snapchat as a safe space to vent emotionally. For example, Jayden said he had been experiencing a lot of conflict with his roommate lately, and Snapchat provided an outlet for him to complain.

> It's (the conflict) upsetting and I don't like to have it all bundled up inside me, so I will just express that on Snapchat. Like, I don't really say his name, but I'll say, "I'm ready for a new roommate" or something like that.

While Snapchat does not have a feature that allows people to comment on posts, Jayden said friends often send supportive messages via chat when he vents. Whether to elicit social support or simply rant about a frustration, Snapchat provided students the space to express unhappy emotions to a select group of friends without worrying about their image.

In some cases, the uninhibited space Snapchat provided invited racy posts of partying and sexual behavior. Students told us they and their friends posted videos of risqué behaviors you might not expect to see on social media. These types of posts were most common late at night during the weekend when students had been drinking. From our own observations of Snapchat, we saw videos of students giving drunken, nonsensical monologues, drunkenly singing and dancing along with music at a party or bar, slamming shots or guzzling beer, and smoking cigarettes, e-cigs, or joints. Most students who alluded to sexual behavior that appeared on Snapchat were unwilling to provide details. However, Anthony described a woman friend's post that made him very uncomfortable—it was a video of her having sex with a guy.

Robert said that people feel safe posting illicit behavior on Snapchat in part because Snapchat alerts users if someone takes a screenshot of their post. He learned about this feature when he took a screenshot of someone's post in order to get the address for a party. Apparently, someone in the post was talking about marijuana and they panicked upon receiving the screenshot notification, and worried that Robert might show it to the police. As several students pointed out in interviews, once someone has taken a screenshot, you have no control over what they might do with that image. The carefully selected audience, temporary nature of posts, and screenshot alert feature, all contribute to a carefree posting environment where students let go of their image concerns and show uninhibited behaviors that ranged from mundane, lighthearted, and grumpy to wild, illicit, and racy.

Anthropologist Gilbert Quintero and colleagues have studied how college students post pictures of themselves engaged in extreme drinking and drinking competitions as an expression of "edgework"—voluntary risk-taking, wherein a person tries to skillfully negotiate the boundaries of risk.[31] Posting their risky behavior online enables a person to chronicle and communicate their activities to their peer network, which may help them to garner prestige or social status. In this way, photos and videos of drinking serve as trophies and enable college students to "perform the work of memory making that constructs this aspect of their collegiate social experience."[32]

Another notable feature of Snapchat is "streaks," which is a running count of how many consecutive days two people have sent chats to each other. Ten of our participants, an equal number of women and men, told us that they maintain streaks with friends on Snapchat. Some managed streaks by sending out a mass chat, while others felt strongly that it is important to send individual, personal messages to each friend for whom they are maintaining a streak. One woman, who had 12 or 13 streaks going at the time of the interview, told us that she sends each of her streaks three pictures every day. She feels like it is important to give personal attention to each of them.

Nicholas, on the other hand, had about 30 streaks going at the time of the interview, which he said felt a little overwhelming to maintain at times. He explained, "I try to personalize it, just because I know that when people do that for me I feel special. But sometimes I do send mass Snapchats, like, early in the morning just to get it out of the way. I guess it kind of feels like a chore." We asked Nicholas what he gets out of doing this every day, and he replied, "I guess it's just fun to see the number of streaks between us rise and to know that I have such a connection with this person."

On the one hand, streaks felt like meaningful connections for students because of the commitment required on both sides to sustain them over time. On the other hand, the connection itself, in the form of a message or photo, is brief and lacks depth. A streak on its own would not contribute to deepening a relationship; instead, it serves as a daily reminder of friends who share an affinity for one another and take the time to say a quick "hello" virtually. It is important to note, however, that not all streak participants were enamored with the process. Diego had maintained some of his streaks since high school and described them as "the worst thing ever!" Though a part of him wished he could stop, he felt overcome with a sense of anxiety at the mere thought of breaking them.

Twitter

Students described Twitter as the "wild west" of social media, where "anything goes." Content can be funny, sad, angry, political, informational, personal, or vague, and many students said that most Twitter feeds they follow represent the full range of content, with no discernable pattern. A number of students mentioned that President Trump's tweeting behavior contributed to the random, volatile nature of content on Twitter. Trump's well-publicized pension for constantly tweeting his unfiltered thoughts normalized that behavior on the site.

There are two types of posts on Twitter—tweeting an original post and re-tweeting someone else's post. Most students reported re-tweeting multiple times a day and tweeting only occasionally, which ranged from several times a week to several times a month. Twitter posts are limited to 280 characters, which encourages brevity over depth and likely shapes the content and frequency of tweeting. Twitter allows users to make their accounts private; however, all of our students chose to keep their accounts public. Like with Instagram, the people you follow will not necessarily be the same as those who follow you.

Mariana, whose favorite site was Twitter, told us that she re-tweets 30–40 times a day. What she loved about Twitter was the constant activity and new content. She said, "You can just post back-to-back all day long and people are always on it tweeting and re-tweeting." She re-tweeted anything that caught her attention, including news headlines, funny memes, and song lyrics that described how she felt at that moment. Diego told us that he enjoys creating polls on Twitter. For example, during final exams, he tweeted, "When you're not doing schoolwork are you: (A) watching *Stranger Things* or (B) crying yourself to sleep. He felt entertained by the fact that everyone chose option B. Another student said he mostly re-tweets but sometimes tweets a running commentary of things that happen during the day, like, "I just tripped in front of everyone," or "I dropped my phone."

When talking about Twitter, students used descriptors such as "political," "funny," "angry," "opinionated," and "random." Nicholas' description of Twitter captures what many had to say about this site:

> Twitter is absolutely crazy. It's anything from politics, pop culture, music, film, funny memes. Like, literally anything can go on Twitter. Sometimes I'm posting about how I had tickets to see an artist, then I couldn't go and I'm sad. I'm posting about what my philosophy professor said in class. I'm re-tweeting how much money Rihanna made this year. I'm re-tweeting something Barack Obama said. I'm re-tweeting something about weather, something about current news, events, or something funny. Literally, anything goes on Twitter. It's basically this huge free for all of social media.

One student described Twitter as having a culture all its own. Content that "goes viral" or becomes most popular through re-tweets on Twitter would probably not gain widespread attention on any other platform. He explained:

> So, something funny that would go viral would be, like, someone falling over a plant. Then someone would re-tweet it and say something like, "Yo, that's me!" And then it would get lots of re-tweets and everyone would be talking about it.

He also described someone who became Twitter famous for posting "tiny food" he had created, which illustrates the truly random nature of what becomes popular on this site.

The random and rapid-fire nature of Twitter posting created a sense of freedom from caring about image and popularity. Whereas students kept track of how many likes and/or views their posts garnered on Instagram, most did not pay attention or care about getting feedback on Twitter posts. For example, Daniel was so concerned with how many likes his Instagram posts received that he had developed a formula for calculating his ratio of likes to followers, and if a post did not meet his minimum threshold for number of likes, he would delete it. In contrast, Twitter provided a space for Daniel to post whatever he wanted without worrying about what people thought.

> For Twitter, things randomly pop into my head, and I just wanna express it on social media, even though, like, I know nobody cares and no one will like it, and no one will see it. I have Instagram to like, validate me, essentially. So, I don't need Twitter to validate me, too.

Students also referred to drama and emotional content on Twitter during interviews. One student laughingly referred to Twitter as "vent-book." This site served as an outlet for venting about relationship drama, generally through sub-tweets, which are intentionally vague posts meant to call someone out without naming them. Sub-tweets serve a dual purpose: They indirectly criticize someone you are upset with, and they signal to followers that you are struggling emotionally. For example, one student told us about a sub-tweet his friend posted recently after her boyfriend broke up with her: "She posted, like, 'I've never seen somebody change gold for copper. Like, she was gold and the other girl was copper, you know.'"

Shelby said that after she broke up with her ex-boyfriend, he posted three significant dates from their relationship in separate tweets. In a fourth tweet, he wrote, "I thought these were going to be important forever." She felt embarrassed by the dramatic nature of his posting, even though he did not name her. Only someone who was close enough with those directly involved might understand the meaning of such vague tweets. To everyone else, these kinds of tweets simply signaled relationship drama of some kind.

Twitter represented a space where people could explicitly express difficult emotions as well. One woman explained, "On Twitter, like, you're just so angry or passionate about something and you just type it and post it. Whatever you're feeling. Rather than the other sites where you have to censor things a little bit more." The culture of Twitter, where anything goes, likely contributes to people freely posting about their feelings. However, the rapid flow of tweets also helps to lower the stakes for showing vulnerability, as posts become quickly buried in one's feed. The likelihood that very many people will see any given post is low.

Facebook

Facebook was the site students had been using the longest. On this platform, someone must accept your friend request before you are connected. Posts allow feedback in the form of emojis that represent a range of emotions including love, caring, sadness, anger, shock, and the traditional thumbs up. Friends can also leave comments on posts. For most, Facebook was their least favorite site because their "friends" included parents and other family members. Facebook was fraught for many students because they felt like they needed to edit themselves to be "family friendly." For example, one young woman said she would post about having a bad day very differently across the four social media sites. On Instagram, Snapchat, and Twitter, her posts would involve some mention of or allusion to wine consumption.

However, on Facebook, she said she would just post about having a bad day without any reference to drinking wine.

> Like, I have my dad and my grandma on there (Facebook), so, like, I'm not going to post, "Oh I want to go home and have a whole bottle of wine." I would definitely get a call about that. My family would be like, "Oh, you have a problem." I don't have a problem. I just had a bad day!

Another student similarly explained that whatever he posts on Facebook is the "PG version" of what he posts elsewhere. He said, "I only post content that I'm totally okay with my 95-year-old grandma seeing. You know, it's like updates on accomplishments, cute pictures of me in class, that sort of thing." Students did not want to have to explain posts to their family members or receive phone calls from concerned parents. Consequently, Facebook was a challenge for them.

Because students felt like they had to edit their posts so carefully on Facebook, they checked this site infrequently, and hardly ever posted here. Most posted only two to three times a month, sometimes less. The purpose of posting here was primarily to update family members. Nicholas considered posting occasional photos to Facebook his duty, like calling home to check in. When students were on Facebook to post photos for their family, they would occasionally share on their timeline a meme or funny video that caught their attention. Some said family members tagged them in posts, which would show up in their feed, a further disincentive from using Facebook to connect with friends. Overall, students tended to view Facebook as a site for older people, probably because for many, their parents introduced them to the site, and it is where their older relatives were most active on social media.

Summary

In this chapter, we explored social norms of phone use and posting. We found that smartphones have intensified and complicated the work of negotiating social rules, in part because students must navigate multiple online contexts continually and simultaneously as they interact across their sites all day long. At the same time, they are operating across multiple contexts offline, continually attending to those social norms, which have become more complex because of phones. Of course, the work of constantly dipping in and out of multiple contexts and attending to the social norms of each environment all day long requires a completely new level of multitasking and multi-communicating, especially when we consider how much time youth spend on their phones. The online personas (i.e., digital multiples) that one presents on different platforms reach diverse audiences who may have divergent expectations about what is like-worthy. Online social norms require that emerging adults pay attention to these nuances and site affordances while creating an image and posting.

Our discussion of phone use while hanging out with friends highlighted the struggle to navigate increasingly complex norms of interaction. Some friend groups had agreed to explicit rules about phone use while they were together; however, most operated under a false assumption of shared norms. This resulted in miscommunication and frustration at times, requiring constant negotiation of rules and social etiquette. For example, some felt like it was fine to check their phones while hanging out with friends, and others felt offended by it. Some felt like a quick peek at their phones was fine, but anything beyond that was rude; others unapologetically turned to their phones when they felt bored by the conversation. Phones also served as a social lubricant for friends hanging out together, providing content to share and discuss. One thing is clear—phones loomed large in these offline settings as objects to be negotiated, resisted, and shared among friends.

We also explored the purpose of posting and the meaning of likes. Students described the many works associated with worrying about their online popularity, measured in likes, as "a lot to think about" and "a big cycle." It was time-consuming and emotionally exhausting. However, the potential reward outweighed the downsides. Students had come to rely heavily on external validation of likes as a measure of self-worth. The labor involved in attending to likes was continual and invisible; it involved figuring out what to post and when, liking your followers' posts so they will like yours, monitoring how many likes your posts get, and managing the embarrassment and disappointment of too few likes. This process was an emotional rollercoaster, from the adrenaline rush associated with posting to the letdown and worry students felt when their posts did not get enough attention.

During interview discussions, students clearly described their labor in terms of time spent on their posting endeavors and the emotional work associated with monitoring and interpreting feedback. Many also expressed frustration with the intensive and consuming nature of maintaining visibility and popularity online. At the same time, most were willing participants in the process and viewed it as a normal and acceptable part of social media use. For these digital natives, the invisible and continual labor associated with social media felt seamlessly integrated into their daily lives to the extent that it largely operated at the level of the subconscious.

Notes

1 Auxier and Anderson 2021.
2 Leyrer-Jackson and Wilson 2018; Scott et al. 2017; Twenge and Martin 2020.
3 Garett, Liu, and Young 2018; Leyrer-Jackson and Wilson 2018; Woods and Scott 2016.
4 Dhir et al. 2018; Vannucci, Flannery, and Ohannessian 2017.
5 Stone 2009.
6 Junco and Cotten 2012.
7 Stockdale and Coyne 2020.
8 Smith 2015.
9 Weybright, Schulenberg, and Caldwell 2020.
10 Martz et al. 2018; Spaeth, Weichold, and Silbereisen 2015; Weybright, Schulenberg, and Caldwell 2020.
11 Nichter 2015.
12 Nichter 2015, 160–161; see also Stromberg, Nichter, and Nichter 2007.
13 Weinstein 2018.
14 Nichter 2015.
15 Ibid., 55.
16 Campbell 2019.
17 Roberts and David 2016, 134.
18 Rainie and Zickuhr 2015.
19 Yang and Christoffereson 2020.
20 Ibid.
21 Smith 2015, Turner, and Reinsch 2011.
22 Harrison, Bealing, and Salley 2015.
23 Dwyer, Kushlev, and Dunn 2018.
24 Reinsch, Turner, and Tinsley 2008; Turkle 2008.
25 Gergen 2002.

26 Brakkton 2019.
27 Griffiths 2018; Parkin 2018.
28 Brooks 2017.
29 Duffy and Pruchniewska 2017; Zulli 2018.
30 Warren 2020.
31 Quintero, Bundy, and Grocke 2019; see also Lyng 2004.
32 Ibid., 14.

References

Auxier, Brooke, and Monica Anderson. 2021. "Social Media Use in 2021." *Pew Research Center*, April 7, 2021. https://www.pewresearch.org/internet/2021/04/07/social-media-use-in-2021/.

Brakkton, Booker. 2019. "Instagram Will Test Hiding 'Likes' on Some U.S. Accounts Starting Next Week." *National Public Radio*, November 9, 2019. https://www.npr.org/2019/11/09/777906177/instagram-will-test-hiding-likes-on-some-u-s-accounts-starting-next-week.

Brooks, David. 2017. "How Evil is Tech?" *New York Times*, November 20, 2017. https://www.nytimes.com/2017/11/20/opinion/how-evil-is-tech.html.

Campbell, Courtney. 2019. "10 Apps that Block Social Media So You Can Stay Focused and be More Productive: Shut Down and Get to Work." *Reviewed.com*.

Dhir, Amandeep, Yossiri Yossatorn, Puneet Kaur, and Sufen Chen. 2018. "Online Social Media Fatigue and Psychological Wellbeing—A Study of Compulsive Use, Fear of Missing Out, Fatigue, Anxiety and Depression." *International Journal of Information Management* 40: 141–152.

Duffy, Brooke Erin, and Urszula Pruchniewska. 2017. "Gender and Self-Enterprise in the Social Media Age: A Digital Double Bind." *Information, Communication and Society* 20 (6): 843–859.

Dwyer, Ryan J., Kostadin Kushlev, and Elizabeth W. Dunn. 2018. "Smartphone Use Undermines Enjoyment of Face-to-Face Social Interactions." *Journal of Experimental Social Psychology* 78: 233–239.

Gergen, Kenneth J. (2002). "The Challenge of Absent Presence." In *Perpetual Contact: Mobile Communication, Private Talk, Public Communication*, edited by James E. Katz and Mark Aakhus, 227–241. New York: Cambridge University Press.

Garett, Renee, Sam Liu, and Sean Young. 2018. "The Relationship between Social Media Use and Sleep Quality among Undergraduate Students." *Information, Communication & Society* 21 (2): 163–173.

Griffiths, Mark D. 2018. "Adolescent Social Networking: How Do Social Media Operators Facilitate Habitual Use?" *Education and Health* 36 (3): 66–69.

Harrison, Marissa A., Christine E. Bealing, and Jessica M. Salley. 2015. "2 TXT or not 2 TXT: College Students' Reports of When Text Messaging is Social Breach." *The Social Science Journal* 52 (2): 188–194.

Junco, Reynol, and Shelia R. Cotten. 2012. "No A 4 U: The Relationship between Multitasking and Academic Performance." *Computers & Education* 59 (2): 505–514.

Leyrer-Jackson, Jonna M., and Ashley K. Wilson. 2018. "The Associations between Social-Media Use and Academic Performance among Undergraduate Students in Biology." *Journal of Biological Education* 52 (2): 221–230.

Lyng, Stephen. 2004. "Crime, Edgework, and Corporeal Transaction." *Theoretical Criminology* 8 (3): 359–375.

Martz, Meghan E., John E. Schulenberg, Megan E. Patrick, and Deborah D. Kloska. 2018. "'I Am So Bored!': Prevalence Rates and Sociodemographic and Contextual Correlates of High Boredom Among American Adolescents." *Youth & Society* (50): 688–710.

Nesi, Jacqueline, and Mitchell J. Prinstein. 2015. "Using Social Media for Social Comparison and Feedback-Seeking: Gender and Popularity Moderate Associations with Depressive Symptoms." *Journal of Abnormal Child Psychology* 43 (8): 1427–1438.

Nichter, Mimi. 2015. *Lighting Up: The Rise of Social Smoking on College Campuses.* New York: New York University Press.

Parkin, Simon. 2018. "Has Dopamine Got Us Hooked on Tech?" *The Guardian*, March 4, 2018. https://www.theguardian.com/technology/2018/mar/04/hasdopamine-got-us-hooked-on-tech-facebook-apps-addiction#img-1.

Quintero, Gilbert, Henry Bundy, and Michelle Grocke. 2019. "'I Want to See Those Memories': Social Affordances of Mobile Phone Cameras and Social Network Sites in Collegiate Drinking." *Contemporary Drug Problems* (46): 180–197.

Rainie, Lee, and Kathryn Zickuhr. 2015. "Americans' Views on Mobile Etiquette." *Pew Research Center: Internet and Technology*, August 26, 2015. https://www.pewresearch.org/internet/2015/08/26/americans-views-on-mobile-etiquette/.

Reinsch Jr., N. Lamar, Jeanine Warisse Turner, and Catherine H. Tinsley. 2008. "Multicommunicating: A Practice Whose Time Has Come?" *Academy of Management Review* 33 (2): 391–403.

Roberts, James A., and Meredith E. David. 2016. "My Life Has Become a Major Distraction from My Cell Phone: Partner Phubbing and Relationship Satisfaction among Romantic Partners." *Computers in Human Behavior* 54: 134–141.

Scott, Carol, Laina Bay-Cheng, Mark Prince, Thomas Nochajski, and Lorraine Collins. 2017. "Time Spent Online: Latent Profile Analyses of Emerging Adults' Social Media Use." *Computers in Human Behavior* 75: 311–319.

Smith, Aaron. 2015. "U.S. Smartphone Use in 2015." *Pew Research Center: Internet and Technology*, April 1, 2015. https://www.pewresearch.org/internet/2015/04/01/us-smartphone-use-in-2015/.

Spaeth, Michael, Karina Weichold, and Rainer K. Silbereisen. 2015. "The Development of Leisure Boredom in Early Adolescence: Predictors and Longitudinal Associations with Delinquency and Depression." *Developmental Psychology* 51: 1380–1394.

Stockdale, Laura A., and Sarah M. Coyne. 2020. "Bored and Online: Reasons for Using Social Media, Problematic Social Networking Site Use, and Behavioral Outcomes across the Transition from Adolescence to Emerging Adulthood." *Journal of Adolescence* 79: 173–183.

Stone, Linda. 2009. "Beyond Simple Multi-Tasking: Continuous Partial Attention." *Lindastone.net*, November 30, 2009. https://lindastone.net/2009/11/30/beyond-simple-multi-tasking-continuous-partial-attention/.

Stromberg, Peter, Mark Nichter, and Mimi Nichter. 2007. "Taking Play Seriously: Low Level Smoking among College Students." *Culture, Medicine, and Psychiatry* 31 (1): 1–24.

Turkle, Sherry. 2008. "Always-On/Always-On-You: The Tethered Self." In *Handbook of Mobile Communication Studies*, edited by James E. Katz, 121–137. Cambridge: The MIT Press.

Turkle, Sherry. 2017. *Alone Together: Why We Expect More from Technology and Less from Each Other.* 3rd ed. New York: Basic Books.

Turner, Jeanine Warisse, and N. Lamar Reinsch Jr. 2011. "Multicommunicating and Episodic Presence: Developing New Constructs for Studying New Phenomena." In

Computer-Mediated Communication in Personal Relationships, edited by Kevin B. Wright and Lynne M. Webb, 181–193. New York: Peter Lang.

Twenge, Jean M., and Gabrielle N. Martin. 2020. "Gender Differences in Associations between Digital Media Use and Psychological Well-Being: Evidence from Three Large Datasets." *Journal of Adolescence* 79: 91–102.

Vannucci, Anna, Kaitlin Flannery, and Christine McCauley Ohannessian. 2017. "Social Media Use and Anxiety in Emerging Adults." *Journal of Affective Disorders* 207: 163–166.

Warren, Jillian. 2020. "This is How the Instagram Algorithm Works in 2020." *Seotomize,* February 3, 2020. https://seotomize.com/this-is-how-the-instagram-algorithm-works-in-2020/.

Weinstein, Emily. 2018. "The Social Media See-Saw: Positive and Negative Influences on Adolescents' Affective Well-Being." *New Media & Society* 20 (10): 3597–3623.

Weybright, Elizabeth H., John Schulenberg, and Linda L. Caldwell. 2020. "More Bored Today than Yesterday? National Trends in Adolescent Boredom from 2008 to 2017." *Journal of Adolescent Health* 66: 360–365.

Woods, Heather Cleland, and Holly Scott. 2016. "#Sleepyteens: Social Media Use in Adolescence is Associated with Poor Sleep Quality, Anxiety, Depression and Low Self-Esteem." *Journal of Adolescence* 51: 41–49.

Yang, Chia-chen, and Kaia Christofferson. 2020. On the Phone When We're Hanging Out: Digital Social Multitasking (DSMT) and Its Socioemotional Implications. *Journal of Youth and Adolescence* 49: 1209–1224.

Zulli, Diana. 2018. "Capitalizing on the Look: Insights into the Glance, Attention Economy, and Instagram." *Critical Studies in Media Communication* 35 (2): 137–150.

2

THE EDITING IMPERATIVE

Daniel flashed a friendly smile as he arrived at the Student Union for his interview. He was casually dressed in a long-sleeved tee shirt, ripped jeans, and blue converse sneakers. A 20-year-old marketing major with fair skin and blondish hair, Daniel exuded a nervous energy. Early on in our meeting, he self-identified as a gay man and a "social media expert." Daniel started using social media at age 13 with Facebook, but he now considered that site outdated for his generation and rarely checked it. Instead, his go-to sites were Instagram, Snapchat, and Twitter. He posted on these sites regularly and checked each of them throughout the day. Most of his time was devoted to Instagram, which he described as his passion.

For Daniel, cultivating his brand on Instagram was both an art and a science. He used a professional camera to take photos, carefully constructing his expression, posture, stance, and outfit against strategically selected backdrops to achieve just the right look. He explained, "There's a high standard in Instagram and meeting that standard requires hard work." He went on to describe it as a "highly controlled space where people only post the best things about themselves." Daniel recognized that Instagram has an algorithm that is "designed to keep popular people popular and unpopular people unpopular," explaining that the platform highlights posts from individuals who get the most likes at the top of their friends' feeds where they are seen first.

When we asked Daniel what he finds so compelling about social media, he responded by focusing on Instagram, explaining that he appreciated the permanent nature of posts. He took pride in creating "perfect posts" that represented a catalogue of his life's best, most glamorous moments. Daniel enjoyed scrolling through his own feed to admire his work and reminisce about memories captured there. He especially appreciated that, with careful editing, he was able

DOI: 10.4324/9781003182047-3

to make even ordinary memories seem exciting. Daniel described his time- and work-intensive process for editing photos, explaining that he often spends hours perfecting each post. He had purchased several professional editing apps to manipulate contrast and lighting, add filters, and change his appearance. Daniel always whitened his teeth, hid his acne with skin smoothing filters, and brightened his eyes. He even used an app that simulates what the photo will look like on Instagram compared with other photos in his feed to make sure it aligns with his overall aesthetic.

Daniel's Instagram posts received an average of 280 likes (he had done the math to calculate that average). He carefully monitored his followers to determine who likes his posts regularly, and he deleted followers who rarely or never like his posts. Daniel referred to this as "the likes-to-followers ratio" and explained that it is important to manage that ratio to maximize the number of likes. He had business cards printed with a professional looking headshot and his Instagram handle so that people could easily find him online.

As proud as he was of his scientific method for maintaining a certain level of visibility and popularity online, Daniel was also aware that his approach resulted in constant comparison of himself with others, which affected his sense of self. He understood that the other side of validation was insecurity, and that if he halted his calculated efforts to maintain popularity, his self-esteem would suffer. Daniel reflected on this contradiction:

> Honestly, everyone is like that, but a lot of people won't be as blunt about it as I am. I think it comes from the culture we live in, like celebrity culture, that makes people feel bad about the way they look and seek validation.

Daniel's narrative provides insight into a young man who has fully embraced the challenges of social media with a calculated eye focused on the perceived prize of obtaining maximum likes. As with most students, Daniel engaged, on a near daily basis, in labor-intensive work to develop and maintain a recognizable brand that highlights his personal aesthetic. He felt motivated by a strong desire for attention capital, which would attract the focused gaze of others and help him remain at the top of his friends' feed. His formula for maximizing likes resulted from careful study of the platform's affordances, a term social media scholar danah boyd uses to describe design features of a site that guide how people post and interact online.[1]

Technology affordances, including how long content lasts, who sees it, how shareable it is, and the ability to find someone's content, are dynamic, fluid, and contextual as participants co-construct online social norms and contexts.[2] In Daniel's narrative, we see how he strategically uses his knowledge of Instagram's algorithm for visibility along with the site's accepted practices, which value a cohesive aesthetic, highly edited images, and a highlight reel of the most glamorous moments, to maximize positive attention and feedback.

Social media provided an outlet for college students to cultivate online personas (i.e., digital multiples) and manage their impressions with various audiences. A confident, attractive, social media self was one that gave students a sense of pride, and importantly, garnered positive attention from others. Students we interviewed created their best online selves through use of editing tools, angles, filters, poses, and captions that enhanced their physical appearance, but also extended beyond beauty and attractiveness to create a personal aesthetic. As one student explained:

> You can see someone's feed and you'll know from just looking at the picture, you don't even need to look at their username. You'll know that the picture came from that person because of how they follow, I guess, an Instagram aesthetic. It's really fun to see people's different personalities come to life in their pictures.

Communication and media scholar Brooke Erin Duffy writes about the importance of editing in creating a personal brand. She explores the Instagram filter as a metaphor that references "the culture of vigilant self-monitoring on social media, particularly as individuals internalize directives to brand the self with resolve."[3] Duffy writes, "We un-tag unflattering photos, we build credibility through 'friend' and 'follower' counts, and we harness our online personae to pithy self-descriptors that function as digital sound bites."[4] Though Duffy's focus is on youth who aspire to make a living in the social media economy, our research highlights the effects of online aspirational culture on youth seeking external validation and popularity in their personal lives.

Among our participants, the imperative to edit was too strong to resist. If everyone else edits and you opt out, then your blemishes, freckles, shiny complexion, and uneven skin tone appear magnified in comparison. As one man said:

> You really do get more likes if you look better. That's just the brutal truth (laugh), and so if you post something unedited on Instagram, like, it's not gonna get that many likes. Even though that would be an ideal culture of people just posting your natural looks. But that's not the society we live in, and that's not what's gonna get likes.

This comment highlights a cynical acceptance of "the society we live in," where "your natural looks" are not enough. Underpinning the editing imperative is a deeply internalized knowledge, honed by trial and error, of the need for self-enhancement by using filters and other modification tools.

Goffman's metaphor of social life as a theater that we discussed in the introduction is particularly useful for understanding how students presented themselves online.[5] In this case, Instagram represents a Broadway theater version of the stage, with the goal of achieving a flawless performance in front of a sold-out audience that elicits a standing ovation or as many likes as possible. Though one's Instagram aesthetic must be memorable, it cannot appear overly dramatic or edited lest it reveal the labor involved. Each post must strike a perfect balance between natural and glamorous, flawless and effortless.

In anthropology, we understand identity as socially constructed through everyday practices and social interaction. This is true for social media as well, but we learned that the constructed nature of self is much more intensive and premeditated online. Though it was difficult for participants to estimate how long the entire process of creating an Insta-worthy post took, the process of choosing the best pictures, editing them, and writing the perfect caption for one post took an average of 2–3 hours. One woman said she could easily spend 2 hours just creating a caption. That, of course, does not include time spent planning the photo shoot and strategizing the best photo opportunities at the event. It also does not include the hours spent monitoring how many likes a post accumulates. For many, the effort that went into creating a perfect post was worth the confidence boost they experienced.

This chapter explores how students cultivated and reproduced their public image using editing tools to create a personal brand. We unpack the invisible labor behind this process and discuss the pressure students felt to edit themselves in an online culture that promotes competition, social comparison, and external validation through public feedback channels. Instagram is our focus in this chapter, as students felt the most pressure to cultivate an ideal self on this site.

Instagram as a Personal Memory Bank

Students saw Instagram as a site of "permanent" identity work with some describing it as a digital photo album that represents who they are at a given moment and catalogs their personal development and major life events. One woman underscored the importance of carefully cultivating your online self: "Because that is gonna be on your page for a long time. So you wanna post things that are probably more true to yourself on Instagram than you would on Snapchat. On Instagram, you're building a profile." In this case, a profile is like a personal brand—it represents your image with the goal of making a favorable and memorable impression. Similarly, one man analogized Instagram to a written journal where he could record important memories.

> It's not a journal in the sense of, like, writing about emotions. It's more of a journal in the sense of having a memory that I'm hoping will last forever 'cause my memory will only let me hold so much information. Sometimes I have a hard time recalling certain things. Having a picture with a phrase reminds me of that time and, like, the feeling I had when I was there. It helps me pull that memory back out.

He went on to say that when he is going through a difficult time emotionally, looking back through happy memories on Instagram gives him perspective and improves his mood. Of course, this online journal is a filtered memory bank, only showing a stylized highlight reel of joyful, exciting moments.

Instagram served as a personal memory keeper as well as a public representation of self. Whereas a traditional paper photo album is generally created for the consumption of the individual and, perhaps, family members or a few close friends, the Instagram album has a much wider audience that includes the self, close friends, acquaintances, and sometimes, even strangers. Instagram users have the option to make their profile private; however, students we talked with preferred to keep theirs public in hopes of accumulating as many followers as possible.

The concept of Instagram as a permanent memory bank, echoed by many of our participants, can be further unpacked. In truth, this was a highly selective set of memories because students continually deleted posts that failed to obtain sufficient likes. Some students updated their feeds by deleting old pictures from middle and high school to make a fresh start in college. One student deleted everything he had ever posted in anticipation of his 21st birthday because he wanted to create a new, more "mature aesthetic." His pre-21 aesthetic consisted of bright colors and playful graphics overlaid onto his photos (Figure 2.1).

FIGURE 2.1 In his pre-21 Instagram image, this college student has overlaid playful graphics, including a ferris wheel and a bright purple sky with stars to create a whimsical and carefree feel.

He described his post-21 aesthetic of black- and white-themed photos as "edgy and urban" (Figure 2.2).

Thus, the concept of permanence is relative, reflecting students' desire to see their identities as enduring and immutable, even as they selectively retain and delete memories to preserve only certain images.

In the introduction, we described how identity is relational, contextual, and socially negotiated.[6] This theory of identity provides a useful framework for understanding the Instagram "aesthetic." Social media is a space where youth can "try on" identities and experiment with different forms of expression across platforms, a process that is negotiated within the constraints of each site's affordances and social norms. Identity is particularly relational when it comes to Instagram, where feedback in the form of likes is the desired outcome. Maintaining visibility and popularity on Instagram requires constant attention to audience expectations and a willingness to refine the self to please followers.

These negotiated identities are flexible and fluid in the sense that a person can experiment with various presentations of self; aspects of one's identity may also be enduring and essential to how one sees themselves over time.[7]

FIGURE 2.2 In his post-21 Instagram image, the same college student has repurposed his look into a more mature, serious aesthetic to create an edgy and urban feel.

Students act in accord with what Bourdieu terms as *habitus*, a set of dispositions, internal to the individual and shaped by gender, class, ethnicity, and the historical moment. While habitus shapes and produces practice (what one does in everyday life), it does not determine it. Habitus is dynamic and fluid and follows a practical logic.[8] A flexibility of practice, informed by habitus, has been compared to a jazz musician who improvises within the constraints of their instrument and jazz traditions.[9] In students' editing on Instagram, we see both habitus and improvisation at play; while there are limits to the versions of themselves they can create, the options for self-improvement are plentiful. Improvisation keeps one's personal brand lively; while the aesthetic needs to be recognizable and familiar, each post must show something new. Otherwise, there is a risk that your followers will get bored.

A Branded Self

During interviews, students talked about creating themed posts that represented not only their best look but also aspects of personality they wanted to highlight. Some students created an aspirational Instagram self that represented who they hoped to be in the future rather than who they actually were in their day-to-day lives. Instagram provided a space for exuding confidence, energy, and passion in a cultivated, stylized way that is not possible offline. Here, we present two in-depth case studies of students who strategically created and maintained branded selves.

Chelsea—Sexy, Confident, Artistic Hula Hooper

Chelsea, a petite white woman with long golden hair, big blue eyes, and a fair complexion, enjoyed hula hooping and creating art; she used Instagram to highlight her hobbies. Chelsea's posts often featured videos of her hula hooping to music or photos of her posing provocatively with her artwork or hula hoop. In one photo, she stood facing the camera at a slight angle, illuminated in golden sunlight, with the hoop resting on her head. She wore tight red pants and a loose, dense tangle of thin copper wire that was all that appeared to cover her torso. Her back arched slightly, accentuating her chest and hips, and her shadow appeared on the wall behind her. The caption read, "Made dis wire corset for my soft sculpture class" (Figure 2.3).

Chelsea used editing tools to develop a personal brand, which included brightening the color and intensifying contrast to achieve a vintage Technicolor look in her posts. This creates an effect of "visual harmony" across Chelsea's posts, which is what she aimed for—her Instagram page was a collage of color-themed, artistic selfies intended to highlight her creativity, beauty, and confidence. Chelsea, like many other students whose posts we observed, was talented at creating a professional, polished collection of Instagram images.

FIGURE 2.3 Chelsea, an aspring artist, poses with her hula hoop in a dreamlike state. The visual she creates represents her overall Instagram aesthetic.

Chelsea's posts were provocative, often focused on showing off her body. In many of the photos, she used angles and poses to highlight her butt, hips, or breasts. For example, in one photo, she and a friend were both standing to the side with their backs arched wearing skimpy swimsuits that showed off their bare legs and revealed the sides of their breasts. Chelsea's friend stood behind her with her hand resting on Chelsea's waist, suggesting a close or physical relationship. Both women wore red lipstick and looked suggestively at the camera. The caption read, "Ready for them summer nights." The reproduction of similar images throughout her Instagram account projected an image of Chelsea as sexy, confident, and artistic. None of these qualities came through in the interview where Chelsea seemed shy, unsure of herself, and highly self-conscious about her acne, which was visible in person, but not in any of her social media posts. Instagram provided a space for her to express a different side of herself, to experiment with being bold and self-assured. The numerous likes her Instagram posts received bolstered her confidence and provided a sense of external validation about her physical appearance and her artistic abilities.

Comparing Chelsea in person with her curated Instagram posts, we see how her self-presentation and identity is not fixed but rather is fluid, emergent in relation to context and performance. In her posts, Chelsea highlights her sexuality and her artistic side to her audience, obfuscating her everyday shy and self-conscious behavior, which is evident in offline interactions. Although Chelsea's self-confidence appears strengthened by her audience response, we can question the extent to which the attention that her online aspirational self receives influences her offline sense of self, beyond the high of momentary likes. Is the experience of her digital multiple—the woman she has created online—empowering in her everyday life? If so, for how long? Self-confidence may be a double-edged sword; while it feels good in the short term, it requires that Chelsea live up to the image that she has created. While we do not have answers to these questions, they are important to consider, not just for this case study but for the many other students who shared fluid identities online that may not match their offline selves.

Diego—Tough, Sensitive, Fun-Loving Rapper

Diego, a tall, slender Latino student, was a self-described rapper with a unique style. He showed up to the interview wearing tight maroon pants, a fitted black t-shirt, and a bandana tied around his head. He wore his dark loose curls long only on top, with the sides and back cut short. Diego posted his homemade rap videos on Instagram, and he devoted a great deal of time and effort creating an Instagram feed that would draw attention to his music. During the interview, Diego described strategies he used to make his feed aesthetically pleasing and readily recognizable.

> I try to make the page look appealing. So, like, I'll have two videos and then a picture in between, and then another two videos and a picture in between. I try to keep it consistent. I feel like if somebody visits your page, it's more attractive to see, like, a clean kind of interface, I guess. So I try to keep the colors the same, too. I'm into pinks, purples and blues. I try to keep it the same so that when people open my page it's an eye-catcher, it's attractive.

Diego's color scheme and patterned posts represented his brand. He aimed to create an aesthetically pleasing Instagram "look" that his followers would immediately associate with him when one of his posts showed up in their feeds.

When asked about why he chose those colors specifically, Diego explained that purple was his grandmother's favorite color and he chose it in honor of her. His use of blue was a strategic choice; a YouTube video on how to get more likes on social media recommended adding a blue tint to photos. He described the blue tint he adds to all of his Instagram posts as a "placebo effect" because it makes him feel more confident that people will like his posts. Similarly, displaying pink as one of his themed colors on Instagram helped him feel more confident wearing pink offline. Diego used to be afraid to wear the color because it is associated with femininity. However, getting positive feedback while wearing pink on Instagram empowered him to feel bolder in his style choices.

His posts reveal a complex person who is alternately funny and playful, somber, emotionally vulnerable, tough, and flirtatious. For example, one post included two pictures; in the first, he looks directly at the camera with a serious expression. The portrait style photo is taken from the waist up, which draws attention to his t-shirt featuring a picture of rapper Ice Cube leaning against a classic car with a blue sky in the background. The second photo, taken from more of a distance, includes Diego's face and torso down to his knees. He is wearing the same serious expression and the same t-shirt. This time we can see his multi-colored green, pink, and blue shorts. He stands in front of what appears to be a hot tub and pool with green and purple light reflecting off the tile. We can see the face of a beige, floppy eared dog standing at his side. The caption reads, "Ice cube face + nice guy just got a mean flow=pooch." Here, as in many of his posts, Diego shows us his multifaceted identity work as both a tough, serious rapper and a man who loves to hang out with his dog. Regardless of which side of himself Diego reveals, his color scheme and posting pattern remain consistent. As a result, at a glance, Diego's feed has a recognizable look.

Diego said that because he is shy, social media feels "safer" for initial encounters with strangers and interactions with acquaintances. Getting positive feedback in the form of likes increases his confidence to not only continue to post, but to also experiment with his identity in terms of style, music, and revealing his sensitive side. During the interview, he showed us examples of posts where he shared his emotional self. For example, in one selfie that features him staring off into the distance, the caption reads, "Self-love is the best kind of love." Similarly, in a video post, Diego sings a rap song about love with a caption that reads, "How far will you go for that special someone <3." For Diego, social media allowed him to experiment safely with expressing vulnerability. His online social capital derives from people liking his music, clever captions, and overall design aesthetic.

Diego's case study reveals a multi-vocality; unlike Chelsea, he presented different sides of himself to his audiences, attempting to balance private and public aspects of his self. For example, Diego's use of the color purple in his posts was sentimental and coded as a tribute to his grandmother. Others would not be able to interpret the real meaning of this color choice. For both Chelsea and Diego, meaning derived from the work of production (hula hoop, art, and music videos). In both cases, they are packaging their brand, resulting in a product for others to consume sensorily. This packaging of an authentic self into a product that will appeal to others while masking perceived imperfections was a goal for many students.

In these two examples, we see that once a person has developed a branded self, they have to engage the social life of their posts within the framework of the brand. In other words, they must create a context, or a series of contexts, in which to insert their branded self. Chelsea and Diego have developed their digital identities as a social product, which requires an ongoing investment of time, thoughtfulness, energy, and placement. They have to invest resources to maintain their brand and to ensure that their digital multiples have full social lives in appropriate settings.

Much of the work involved in creating and maintaining a branded self on Instagram is invisible labor seamlessly woven into everyday social media use. Students were aware of the time and effort required for creating a consistent look and developing the social life of their brand; they readily described and reflected on it during interview discussions. Many expressed frustration about the imperative to edit, but felt unable to opt out because the pressure to live up to normative image expectations on Instagram was too great. As digital natives who began editing and posting selfies in middle school, they had accepted, if grudgingly, the necessary labor involved in editing photos.

The Photo Op

Some participants planned photo ops in advance of an event, carefully thinking through the various "candid" photos they wanted to capture. In one extreme case, Nicholas, a self-described gay man with an intense, but friendly demeanor, planned his birthday photo shoot months in advance. During the interview, he contrasted the ease and effortlessness of posting on platforms like Twitter, Snapchat, and Facebook with the time-consuming nature of preparing a post for Instagram.

> Instagram is a whole 'nother thing. I've already planned my twentieth birthday pictures for Instagram, and I turn twenty in three months. That's how far ahead I'm planning the posting of those pictures and how they're gonna look and how the caption's gonna look. And it's honestly crazy that I even do that.

Though Nicholas acknowledged that his approach is extreme, he was nonetheless committed to it. Of those who planned Instagram photo shoots ahead of time, most did so several days in advance. Others divided their time at social events between hanging out with friends and looking for optimal photo opportunities. All agreed that it is very important to document their lives and events on social media. There was a pervasive sentiment that unless it appears on social media it did not really happen.

Interestingly, we are seeing this phenomenon nationally, as large crowds of people flood to #Instafamous tourist sites to take selfies for social media. According to a *BBC News* article, 259 tourists died globally between 2011 and 2017 while taking "extreme selfies."[10] At Yellowstone National Park, after a woman was gored by a bison while attempting to take a selfie with the animal in 2015, park officials instituted a safety pledge for visitors that includes the warning, "No picture is worth hurting yourself, others, or the park."[11] Though students in our study did not necessarily travel to faraway places for their post-worthy photos, they did dress up specifically for the purpose of Instagram photo shoots, plan photo ops in advance of upcoming events, feel pressure to cultivate a fun, exciting self, and document their experiences on Instagram for public consumption.

Students, especially women, reported taking multiple photos for one post, depending on the social media platform. In a few extreme cases, photo shoots could produce 100 or more pictures for one social media post. Amber, a fitness enthusiast from a coastal town who had long blonde hair and a perpetual golden tan, explained that when she goes back home, she and her friends will do hours long photo shoots on the beach.

> We take, like, 100 (photos) per person, just 'cause you're, like, moving around and you're doing different angles and stuff. You're in the water, you're out of the water, you're lying on the sand, you're doing all sorts of poses. So we take a lot of photos. Then I'll choose one to edit and post.

For Amber and her friends, the photoshoot itself is an event; it is how they enjoy socializing and spending time together, but it is also an opportunity for identity work.

Editing the Self

We wondered how self-improvement and editing practices have changed in the age of social media, when the opportunity to perfect one's appearance is readily available to everyone with a smartphone. Online, alterations in how one looks are attainable through various photographic techniques as well as through editing tools that allow you to change your facial features and body proportions. These techniques require a certain level of knowledge and skill, but an abundance of YouTube video tutorials and a little bit of practice are all these digital natives needed to become proficient. Morgan, a self-described social media cynic who nonetheless engaged in the editing imperative, explained, "It used to be Playboy and Maxim models were just in magazines. And now any ordinary girl can be that." To illustrate her point, Morgan opened Facetune (a free editing app with enhanced features available for a monthly fee of $5.99) on her phone and exclaimed, "I'm going to blow your mind with how crazy this rabbit hole of fake happiness is." She proceeded to manipulate a photo of herself with the app, changing the size of her nose, lips, and eyes, all of which only took a couple of minutes.

Nicholas, a keen observer of social media practices, described friends who are:

> . . . a bit crazy with editing apps . . . making their boobs look bigger, or, like, shrinking their stomach or making their butt big, erasing pimples, contouring their nose, making their teeth whiter, or making their eyes pop more.

He explained, "On Facetune, you can pretty much do anything." His quote underscores the endless possibilities for changing your appearance through this widely used app. To provide a sense of just how popular Facetune is, the app has been downloaded 50 million times since it was launched in 2013. Half a million people currently subscribe to the app, and 70 percent of those are women.[12] Recent research found that 80 percent of girls have used an app to change their appearance before the age of 13.[13]

Offline beauty practices range from the more mundane end of the spectrum, such as exercise routines, use of makeup, and body shaping underwear to the extreme end of the spectrum, which includes cosmetic surgical procedures, such as breast augmentation, liposuction, nose reshaping, and tummy tucks. Botox is particularly popular among young adults who are adopting a proactive approach to aging. According to *Forbes* Magazine, "Within just five years, Botulinum Toxin (Botox) use among people aged 19 to 34 increased by 87 percent."[14] A recent *Vice* article explores why Botox is so popular among young people. One 22-year-old woman explained:

> I think that the younger generation—like around my age and younger— has a huge understanding that what you see online is not real. But they're more willing to look not real because that's what they've grown up with. Yeah, so you can show them a picture and be like, "Look how photo-shopped that is," and they'll say, "I know, and I also know that this look is attainable to me in some way."[15]

Though none of the students we interviewed talked about getting Botox or other procedures, this example underscores the blurry boundary between online and offline appearance norms as youth spend increasing amounts of time staring at edited images on a screen. It also speaks to the normalization and acceptance of photoshopped selves.

Certainly, an expansive array of beauty tools has been around for years. What digital technology adds is widespread access to seemingly limitless possibility in changing your appearance. Digital technologies make the full range of beauty tools accessible to anyone who is willing to learn the skillset. With only a few clicks and swipes, you can completely alter your facial features and body proportions in a photo. However, as discussed above, online editing is creating interest among some young adults to seek out non-invasive procedures, such as Botox, to achieve that flawless look offline as well. Sociologist Dana Berkowitz conducted research on Botox and found that "some practitioners expressed concern that young women were being sold the idea that Botox was preventive."[16] Botox was "often cast as an appearance intervention that could yield psychological, social and economic benefits."[17] It has become such a ubiquitous, normalized beauty tool that the question is no longer if young women need it but at what age they should begin getting these injections. Widely available appearance modification tools available online and offline highlight the neoliberal emphasis on personal choice when it comes to beauty practices. Within this framework, social media users may interpret the editing imperative as a form of empowerment as it encourages them to take control of their look.

In 2019, 72 percent of American Academy of Facial Plastic and Reconstructive Surgery members reported seeing patients who were seeking cosmetic procedures to look better in selfies.[18] After using editing apps and "improving" themselves online, many people seek to create that look permanently offline. Known as *snapchat dysmorphia* or *selfie dysmorphia*, this phenomenon refers to a disorder where one is preoccupied with a slight defect in their physical appearance.[19] The ability to enhance how one looks online has resulted in greater acceptance of plastic surgery, even among college students.

"It's Like Steroids for Athletes"

Because the use of editing tools and filters was so normalized, most of the women we interviewed felt pressured to use these beauty tools. Morgan explained:

> It's hard to not do it (using filters and editing tools). It's almost like steroids with athletes, where if one person does it, then it ruins the game for everyone, and everyone has to do it. That's almost what Facetune is like. It's like, everybody knows about it. Every girl who is on social media feels like she has to do it.

The normative nature of editing meant that choosing not to edit makes it appear as if you are the only one with flaws, essentially amplifying your imperfections. The "natural" body is seen as increasingly flawed. Good editing techniques allow the skillful "practitioner" to move beyond these perceived deficits to create a better self. The culture of editing is so widespread that it has become an imperative.

Morgan further develops the steroids metaphor from the example above, explaining that both steroids and editing create an unfair advantage: "It's cheating, but, like, I get why you do it. You're competing with others. . . . You should see the girls on there. It's crazy! No one looks like that, you know?" Just like in a sports context where none of the players can compete with a fellow athlete who is taking steroids, in social media a woman cannot compete with her peers who are editing away their flaws. The only way to keep up is to engage in the practice yourself, whether it is taking steroids in athletics or editing in social media. Much like the dependency that can develop for an athlete on steroids, emerging adults may develop dependency on editing tools so they can compete successfully.

Tacit silence about the labor involved in achieving flawlessness obscures the effort, highlighting instead the result. Under the constant surveillance of multiple imagined audiences, which include friends, acquaintances, and strangers, some young women, like Morgan, were able to mask the tremendous effort these practices required. Here, students measured online beauty work by both its invisibility and its proximity to dominant gendered appearance ideals. This behind-the-scenes work mirrors what women have long been doing offline. In fact, the imperative to manage appearance both online and offline has multiplied beauty labor.

"I Don't Care How I Look in Person"

For most women, getting likes on their social media posts was more important than getting positive feedback for how they looked offline. For photos, women spent a lot of time doing their hair and makeup and choosing a cute outfit, even if they were just taking the photo at home. In contrast, many said they felt less concerned with how they looked offline. During interviews, women would point out that they were wearing sweats and no makeup, with their hair thrown up in a messy ponytail. Sofia, a friendly woman with a big smile and long, wavy dark hair, contrasted her online and offline looks during an interview discussion about beauty norms. She explained, "I won't post anything if I don't have makeup on or if I'm not dressed up. Like, for Instagram, I won't sit here and take a picture and post it right now." She explained that she currently looked "ratchet," which "is how I normally look in real life." Sofia described "rachet" as atrocious or ugly, exemplified by sloppy hair and mismatched or rumpled clothing.

Sofia felt pressure to live up to her online presentation of self, and she felt unattractive compared to her highly constructed image. Here we see how the imperative to maintain one's digital multiples extends to offline beauty work, in the sense that one may feel inadequate in everyday life because the presentation of self on social media is so curated. For many college women, perfecting an online look was their primary focus, to the neglect of their everyday offline appearance. Thus, social media not only invites comparison of the self with others, but of one's online self with the offline self. It is like a social media version of a house of mirrors where the distorted reflections are ubiquitous and overwhelming; instead of seeing yourself distorted, you see a perfected self.

Like Sofia, Amber, the blond fitness enthusiast, readily admitted to looking quite different online than she does in person. Offline, she did not style her hair or wear makeup, and she dressed very casually. However, her social media self was heavily cultivated; in her posts, Amber always wore makeup and had her hair styled. Either she appeared dressed up to go out in form fitting dresses or jeans and low-cut tops, or she was sporting a string bikini on the beach. Amber explained:

> I feel like I look better in pictures (laughs). Just based on how I present myself in photos and how I edit and stuff. I don't really care about what

people think of me in person, but I want people to think I have good pictures (laughs). As weird as that sounds.

When we consider the number of hours students spent online, it is easy to imagine how their close examination of their curated digital multiples could result in a growing dissatisfaction with their offline self.

Women talked at length about scrutinizing every detail of the photo, including all of their individual facial features, the way their bodies looked, and background images in making decisions about which photos to include in their posts. Morgan's description of her photo scrutiny process reveals how her microanalysis of her appearance online affects her self-esteem offline.

> I feel like when you take pictures of yourself, you just notice, like, your flaws more often. I can take a picture with my friends and I'll just look bigger than them. And sometimes the lighting will hit you wrong. It's just unfair. I don't mind my nose, but sometimes how a shadow hits my nose, or, like, my lip comes under my gums when I smile. If I can tweak those things, I will.

Despite her self-criticism, Morgan mostly posted sexually provocative pictures of herself wearing bikinis on Instagram. Online, she came across as confident and bold; her posts received hundreds of likes and affirming comments about how attractive she looked. Despite all of the external validation she received, Morgan's micro-critical evaluation of her appearance online led to heightened self-criticism offline. The normative culture of filtering and editing photos to appear flawless invited scrutiny that amplified "flaws." With every post deemed a success, Morgan felt pressure to ensure subsequent posts lived up to her online hype.

Gabrielle also had a fraught relationship with the production process—she put time into creating perfect posts, but she felt frustrated sometimes at the effort involved.

> I do it because I want to post nice pictures of myself. So I can't say anything negative about it, but it's really a hassle sometimes. Like, sometimes, it's just not worth it 'cause there's a lot of work that goes into it. And I just don't have time for that.

Despite their mixed feelings about the process, women felt compelled to devote time and effort into cultivating their online image, accepting that the work was a necessary part of posting.

Even if men and women both cared about how they look online, the pressure was greater for women to attend to the details of their appearance. Gabrielle described how the normalization of editing creates a distorted perception of how people actually look. She believed that seeing positive feedback for people who heavily edit their images on social media doubly reinforced the editing imperative. Not only does abstaining from editing practices amplify your flaws in comparison to all of the perfected images of others, but also the tangible rewards of creating a flawless image are difficult to resist. In a context where people measure success in likes and flawless images garner the most likes, what is the point of posting an unedited image? The examples above highlight competing beauty labors of maintaining online and offline looks that approximate your most attractive self and resemble each other, a task that proved difficult and labor intensive. Most women found it too time-consuming to maintain a perfect, seamless look across contexts, which resulted in an exclusive focus on the social media self.

Angles and Poses

Many of the students we talked to, both male and female, said they use angles to highlight their best features and downplay their least favorite features. Andre, a theater major who sought a large Instagram following to boost his chances for becoming a professional actor, had his pose "down to a science." He explained, "It's, like, head tilted to the left, the bright smile, the jaw line." True to his word, Andre's social media selfies did reflect his signature pose. Andre described in detail how he uses angles to accentuate and downplay certain features.

> I have very white, straight teeth. I always have a bright smile just 'cause it's a trait that I find, you know, very share worthy about my face. Yeah, and it's always been, like, a tilt of my head. 'Cause for the longest time, I didn't have a neck. I was a very fat kid. Um, and so having a neck is very important to me. And usually I like distance because, um, it's not that I don't like my nose, it's just a little large. It's a very traditional Filipino nose. So it's nice and it's cute, but it, like, spreads when I smile because I smile so big. I look really good behind a person in a selfie. If I take a selfie, I'll be like on the edge so you only see half of my face. I'm always off to the side and tilting my head to get a jaw line.

Here, Andre reveals how he analyzes his individual facial features for their share worthiness. The detailed description of his nose is particularly striking. It is clear that he has scrutinized his nose in photos, evaluating how it looks close up and at a distance, and how it changes during certain facial expressions. Andre describes several techniques for obscuring his nose, including taking a photo at a distance, standing behind someone when posing for a picture, and positioning himself so only half of his nose appears in the photo. He seemed to have internalized the idea that a Filipino nose is not attractive, and therefore puts quite a bit of effort into hiding it.

A recent ethnographic account of young women in the Philippines who purchase makeup to minimize the appearance of their nose also highlights cultural notions of beauty in relation to specific facial features.[20] Andre's narrative reveals an intense level of micro-targeting body parts online (by himself and others) as anyone can zoom in on your photos and scrutinize every feature up close, looking for flaws. The practices of editing, zooming in to evaluate one's features and flaws, and frequently revisiting posts to check likes and comments encourages constant self-critique and comparisons with others.

Andre unabashedly explained how shooting from specific angles to hide parts of himself and using filters to maximize his attractiveness was something he regularly did. Reminding us that posting skills in his generation have been honed over many years, Andre explained that he had grown up in a culture where everybody edited their photos, and "that was kind of the norm so I've never thought anything about it." From his perspective, fixing your photos was a good thing to do to boost self-confidence. He explained:

> It's not necessarily that you're trying to fool anyone to think that you don't look the way you look, because your face is your face. There's nothing you can do about that. It's one of those things where you obviously shouldn't go to extremes and, like, do physical harm to yourself or anything like that. But if you need to take a couple steps back so you can get that perfect lighting, do it. I think it's just one of those things where if this is what you need to feel confident about yourself, I am 100 percent here for it.

Andre acknowledged that it is not easy for everyone to post, and yet people his age needed to have an online presence. His positive view of editing was striking—if it helped, why not do it?

An especially popular angle was the "bird's eye view" or having someone take a photo of you from above. Most of the selfies we saw on college students' social media posts featured this angle with the person looking up at the camera. One man told us that many of his friends like to have their photos taken this way for aesthetic reasons, explaining, "They'll take the picture from high lookin' down 'cause you have to look up and you get good natural light in your photos."

Women talked about using this top-down photo angle as a way to look thinner. Though most of the selfies we observed in people's social media were from a top-down perspective, some women were derisive of the way other women used this angle, describing it as an obvious plea for attention. Amber, for example, said that she has a friend who takes photos top down, while cropping out her bottom half to make sure her protruding stomach and large thighs are out of the picture. When asked how people respond to these posts, Amber said that while people do give her positive feedback online, they secretly criticize her.

> A lot of people will talk about her behind her back because they notice that she's doing it to get attention. Like, they'll comment, "Oh you look

so good" on her post. Then they'll be like, "She's just doing this for people to give her compliments" behind her back.

Tania agreed that using the "bird's eye view" was a desperate attempt to get attention on social media. She explained:

> I think a lot of people will post pictures . . . like taking the picture from the top down, so people can be like, "Oh you're so pretty." I don't do that. I think that's just really desperate, asking for likes. It's kind of like you're buying your friends.

Despite their critiques of the "bird's eye view" angle, both Tania and Amber posted photos angled this way in their own social media accounts. Their comments speak to both the normalization of editing techniques and the importance of subtlety in editing. Everyone edits and everyone knows that social media posts are not real; however, if one's use of angles, poses, or filters was too obvious, viewers interpreted it as an indicator of insecurity and an attention-grabbing ploy, revealing a level of vulnerability frowned upon in social media.

A Filtered Self

Filters were the most commonly used and socially acceptable editing tool for men and women. Instagram and Snapchat have multiple options for filters that can change the lighting and color contrast; smooth out skin tone; overlay animated images, such as blooming hearts or flowers, twinkling stars, and glitter sunglasses; morph your face into a dog, cat, or rabbit; and distort your features in similar ways as funhouse mirrors. Using filters is even easier than using editing tools, such as Facetune. When you take a picture with the Instagram or Snapchat camera feature, the filter options automatically appear on the screen with the photo, inviting you to scroll through and try out each option. In fact, filters were such a seamless part of these apps that many students did not think of them as editing tools. Choosing a filter was simply part of preparing a post, similar to coming up with a caption to go along with one's photo. In fact, students considered filters that created subtle effects, like smoothing out skin tone to even out the complexion and erase blemishes, creating a warmer or cooler color tone, or adjusting contrast, a normal part of everyday posting.

Natalie, a communications major who described herself as socially awkward and fidgeted with her hands throughout the interview, said that she likes to use filters because they make her pictures look more like professional photos. She pulled up a recent Instagram picture of herself smiling into the camera with her hands on her hips. She had used lighting to hide aspects of herself in the photo. Her face was illuminated and stood out as the focal point; in contrast, shadows and dim lighting obscured her body, revealing only the form of her confident stance but none of the details. Many of her social media posts followed this theme in terms of stance and lighting. Natalie revealed during the interview that she struggles with anxiety and that social media allows her to express herself more freely than she feels comfortable doing offline. In person, her anxiety is observable in the way she nervously fidgets, shifts uncomfortably in her seat, and furrows her brow when she talks. Social media provides a space for Natalie to "hide behind" the bold image she creates, and filters help her achieve that effect.

If you were to follow Natalie's Instagram account without having ever met her, you would likely think of her as confident, provocative, and a little edgy. In the photo Natalie pulled up on her phone during the interview, she explained that she had used a filter to illuminate her face and make her eyes appear larger because she thinks they are her best feature. Manipulating her photos to highlight certain aspects of herself enabled Natalie to project a better self, even if it is a filtered self (Figure 2.4).

FIGURE 2.4 Natalie, an otherwise shy woman, poses in a confident stance wearing a lacy maroon bra and matching satin jacket. As in all of her Instagram photos, she has brightened her face and enlarged her eyes.

In a sense, Natalie is filtering not only her physical features, but also her personality. Her story reveals how social media can provide a space to express or cultivate your digital multiples and how filters and lighting can serve as tools in masking insecurities and body parts deemed unacceptable. Identity work involved in maintaining digital multiples is complex as it goes well beyond the superficial layer of appearance; it encourages and facilitates a remaking of the whole self, including one's affect.

Cody, a self-effacing gaming enthusiast, viewed filters as important and useful props in helping to mask insecurities. He noted:

> I don't really see a problem with them. I know a lot of people will hide behind those filters to hide insecurities. I've noticed that people . . . if they have low self-esteem, they'll purposefully look bad in a photo . . . they'll take a stupid angle, they'll give themselves the exaggerated fat neck, or they'll do that zoomed in, out of focus thing, or whatever. They do it because they're like, "Oh well, if the photo looks bad on purpose, then no one can make fun of me for looking like garbage." I feel like a lot of people do the same thing with those filters. They'll hide behind the bunny ears, because they're like, "Oh well, I don't like this about my face, and this bunny filter makes it go away."

By using filters to hide parts of themselves or to morph body parts so they appeared out of focus, participants were adopting a strategy that Cody observed pre-empts negative comments from others. By saying that you already know that the photo is bad (or, in reality, that you are not attractive or photo-worthy), you preclude others from saying so.

Gender Expression in Editing Practices

Most participants, male and female, voiced the opinion that women care about their online image and men, for the most part, do not. Gabrielle, a soft-spoken woman with chin length blonde hair and cat-eye glasses whose online images were so heavily edited that she was hardly recognizable, talked about gendered differences in appearance.

> Guys don't really care (about how they look). But, like, there's a standard for girls. Like, you try to make it (your photo) flawless, because if you don't people are gonna talk shit and pick it apart and stuff. But guys don't take good pictures anyway. So it's kind of expected for it to not be a great picture of a guy. Whereas for girls, if the picture isn't good, it's like, you don't know how to take a selfie.

Most men confirmed this gendered stereotype. One man explained: "I'll take maybe two or three. If I don't get the right picture, sometimes, like, I don't care and that's it. I don't want my friends to think, like, I have too much flash." Similarly, another man who said he takes only one picture described feeling pressured to take multiple photos for an Instagram post at the insistence of his sister.

> That was 'cause my sister made me. After the first one, I said, "It's fine. Post it." She's like, "No, the lighting is horrible. We've got to fix this. It won't look good." And I said, "Okay." If my sister is not involved, I take one picture and post it. That's it.

This gendered exchange reflects the heteronormative expectation that concern with image is associated with femininity, a norm that heightens the pressure women feel to enhance their photos.

Women described photo shoots with friends that involved taking multiple pictures to get the right one and carefully attending to their online image. For example, when asked how many photos she typically takes, one woman replied, "I'm not going to lie. I'll probably take, like, a 30-minute session (laughs). Sometimes me and my roommate will be like, let's go take pictures, and we'll go outside, and we'll just start taking pictures of each other." When asked how many photos a typical session produces, she replied:

> It's a lot. Like, this weekend I went to a pumpkin patch with my boyfriend and a friend. Our friend was snapping pictures the whole time. You know, on the iPhones they just snap fast if you hold your finger on the button. That's what she did, and when I got back to the car, oh my God! My album was over 1,000 pictures just from that day. I had to go through them all to find one to post.

Part of the reason for taking so many photos was that women felt pressure to display mastery of photography technique as well as their editing abilities in each Instagram post. For women, these skills are an implicit extension of self—likes are a reward for both being attractive and having the skills to enhance one's appearance. Here, in these contiguous worlds (i.e., offline and online), skills developed and honed in one space are shared and appreciated in the adjoining space.

The stereotype that men do not worry about their image is nothing new.[21] Just like the college men in this study told us they quickly snapped a picture or two and posted without care, teen boys from Nicole Taylor's earlier research talked about picking up clothes off the floor and throwing them on before school, without worrying about how they looked.[22] Teens from both of our earlier studies even spoke to the pressure guys feel to "play it cool" and pretend not to care even when they do.

Even so, several men we interviewed challenged this gendered trope in relation to social media. Andre, for example, explained:

> Guys care about their image just like girls do. But caring about how you look and wanting pictures of yourself that look good is almost, like, tied in with being effeminate. It's a trait that is associated with women, so guys are ashamed to say it. It's one of those things where, like, even if a guy doesn't feel confident with his picture, he's not gonna ask to have it taken again because he's afraid that this will, like, make him not a man anymore, which is fucking stupid!

It is noteworthy that only three of the men we interviewed told us they edited their photos in order to look more attractive online (including Andre), and they all self-identified as gay. In the examples below, we highlight two men who told us they edited as a way of drawing attention to their skills, and both of them self-identified as straight.

Diego, the aspiring rapper highlighted in an earlier section, admitted to taking many pictures to get the right one. He focused on getting the right angles, poses, and color schemes for each post to create a recognizable brand that would draw attention to his music. Yet, Diego felt awkward asking his male friends to take multiple posed pictures of him because he worried about what they would think. To avoid the social discomfort, Diego bought himself a tripod so that he could do photoshoots of himself without anyone's help.

Javier, who sported a beard and rectangular glasses, unabashedly discussed his extensive editing of photos for social media.

> I'll make sure to, like, get a good angle, and depending on the natural lighting around me, I might have to edit to get it to look how I want. My friends do the same thing. I got really into editing once I figured out that my friend was really into photography. Now our whole friend group is into that. Like, if you look at our social media, you can tell when we started paying more attention to editing our photos. Usually, I'll mess with the color temperatures, exposure levels and all of that. I can soften or sharpen the image, too.

Javier said he liked editing because "it could be helpful at some point." He talked about how professionals get paid to edit television, movies, and social media, explaining that "editing is just a big part of the culture right now." At some point, he hoped his skills might help him succeed in the job market. Both Diego and Javier gave somewhat practical reasons for editing—in Diego's case, he aimed to create a brand to promote his music, and in Javier's case, he was perfecting a craft that could translate into a job someday. In contrast to Andre, who edited to accentuate his best features, Diego and

Javier edited as part of a strategic effort to attract attention to their respective entrepreneurial skills.

Steven, an alpha male with a serious demeanor who sported a crew cut and aspired to join the Marines after college, did not view caring about one's image as a gendered issue. Initially he said, "I feel like girls care more about how they look because of their nature. They're typically more insecure." Upon further consideration, he added, "Um, but there are a lot of insecure guys, too. I feel like the people who are more into their, like, image, care more about how they look on social media." As an example, he contrasted himself with his younger brother:

> I don't mean to sound prideful or anything, but I just don't care what people think about me. So for me, I don't find a need to take more than one picture or edit or use filters or anything. But, like, my little brother has always been scrawny and so he's insecure. Growing up, I was always into working out, but he was never interested. Now he's a total gym rat and so when we take a picture together, I feel like he's always trying to make himself look bigger. It's like an ego thing because he was always viewed as, like, inferior to me. I've noticed that he also edits his pictures to, like, whiten his teeth and get rid of acne and stuff.

To our surprise, when we scrolled through Steven's social media posts, they appeared highly edited and body focused. Most featured his large, muscular shoulders and arms as he flexed for the camera. One shirtless photo, taken from the back, highlighted his well-defined back muscles. Offline, Steven had acne and a ruddy complexion, but online his face was smooth and without pimples. We found that editing was such a seamless part of the posting process that students did not consciously think about it. Outside the context of an interview where we asked students to reflect on image refinement, the labor of editing was as invisible to our participants as it was to their Instagram followers.

Though most of the men in our study did not edit or filter their photos, it was common for them to scrutinize pictures before posting. In response to a question about how they decide if a picture is post-worthy, Nicholas, one of the few men we interviewed who readily admitted to caring a lot about his online image, explained:

> It could be anything, like, how I'm standing. If the way I'm standing makes my body look slimmer, if it's bringing out features I don't necessarily want people to see. How my smile looks, if it's crooked, if my teeth are a certain way, if I'm smiling too much and my eyes are, like, really small, and one is smaller than the other. If, like, one eyebrow is higher than the other. Like, it's honestly a lot because you are your worst critic. So, everything I see on me, if I don't like it, it's not going to be posted.

While none of the self-identified straight men admitted to such an intense level of scrutiny, many told us they check certain aspects of their appearance before posting, like making sure their teeth look white, their smile is symmetrical, their hair looks nice, there is equal spacing between people in the picture, and no one's face is obscured by shadows. For example, Jason, a golf enthusiast and fraternity member with a strong southern drawl, said, "If someone takes a picture of me, I have to make sure it looks good. I want to make sure someone wouldn't have a negative, like, impression of that picture." He explained, "I would want to retake the picture if, like, I'm not looking at the camera, my hair is messed up, or I have a half smile." Many of the men we interviewed said they examine the background imagery in the photo before posting, checking to make sure it was framed well and symmetrical in the picture. Thus, while men were interested in their online presentation of self, they concentrated on different aspects of their posts when compared to women.

In our earlier work, when teen boys claimed not to care about their appearance, we had no way of knowing if that was true because we could not observe them getting ready in the morning.[23] However, for this project, we observed social media posts, and it was often obvious when students used filters or edited their photos. Once we became attuned to the techniques students used to cultivate their looks, such as angles, poses, framing, filters, and editing, we were able to identify them pretty easily in social media images. Even light editing, such as the use of built-in Instagram skin-softening filters, became evident to us over time. When comparing our offline and online observations, we noticed that a majority of our participants, including men, filtered or edited their photos to enhance their appearance.

The Importance of Authenticity

The concept of *authenticity* emerged as an important theme in our interviews. Students emphasized the importance of "being real" online as a marker of honesty, trustworthiness, and integrity. They scrutinized social media posts for signs of over-editing, a faux pas that signaled inauthenticity and elicited derision. Social media researcher Duffy points out that ads in the U.S. have highlighted authenticity as a central value for decades, citing Coca-Cola's earliest marketing slogan ("the real thing") and, more recently, Dove's "real women" ads.[24] She explores how authenticity came to be a proxy for empowerment among millennials who value individual expression. For young women, authentic expression online often translates into beauty practices that highlight physical appearance. For women we interviewed, the name of the game was to present both an authentic self and an edited self that appeared attractive yet natural. Successfully navigating this contradictory imperative required great skill, attention to detail, and vigilant monitoring of editing norms and feedback on posts.

Mariana, a reserved woman with big brown eyes and a shy smile, described degrees of fakeness and underscored the importance of being only a little fake.

> It's like if somebody wears makeup and they also filter and soften their skin (in posted photos), and then, like, when you see them in real life, they're in their sweats, no makeup, and they look totally different. It's like, "You're in your sweats! What are you doing?" So, when I post pictures, I try not to wear anything too extravagant 'cause then if they see me in a t-shirt in real life they'll be like, "Oh that's Mariana. Like, I know who she is." Or whenever I'm already wearing makeup, I won't soften my skin with a filter 'cause I'm already wearing makeup. So, it's like I'm not going to be two times fake. I'm just gonna be one time fake.

Mariana emphasized the importance of "keeping it real . . . well, as real as you can be online." Her quote above illustrates the work that goes into walking the fine line between real and fake—Mariana carefully considered her editing practices in the context of how she appeared offline as compared to her online look. In order to strategize for her post, Mariana must imagine how her audience will react—will the image represent too drastic a departure from her everyday look "in real life," or does it represent a fairly realistic version of her best self? She must consider how her friends will react to her post and edit to elicit emotional responses that will result in likes.

Chloe, a forthcoming woman who expressed strong opinions about social media, claimed that she did not use any filters or editing tools, but she had a lot to say about her friends who did.

> Oh my God, I have friends who will use these editing apps where they whiten their teeth and airbrush their faces, or they take a little chunk of fat off their arm and, like, try to slim down. And it's just like super, super edited. I don't like to do that because that's a little too unrealistic. Like, I don't look like that. It's almost like they'll airbrush you until you look like you're literally glowing and it's not real. I sent my friend a picture that we took and I posted the original one, and she posted the edited one. It was so very different. Like, she had edited our faces, whitened our teeth, I think she even cropped out a piece of my arm to make me look slimmer. Like, anybody had to know that's not real.

Many participants, like Chloe, were derisive of the heavy-handed editing apps that could drastically change one's appearance in a photo. At the same time, we felt surprised by some of the women in our study who looked quite a bit different online, specifically on Instagram, than they did during our interviews.

It appeared that the line between real and fake was subjective and varied among students. Everyone agreed that it was important to be the same person online and offline and that light editing of images was acceptable as long as you still looked like yourself and the edits were not obvious; yet, when we observed their social media posts, we found that many students had edited their photos in an obvious, sometime heavy-handed way. For Natasha, extreme editing was a sign of dishonesty.

> I feel like online you should be the same person you are in real life. I've seen pictures of people that are super edited and, like, when you meet the person you don't even recognize them. I think that's wrong.

Most students we interviewed felt similarly, even those who edited their photos before posting.

Men felt less pressure to post an edited self, making it easier to achieve an appearance of authenticity. However, some still struggled with creating an online image. Robert, a soft-spoken man who carefully considered our questions before responding, shared his journey of coming to terms with the effects of editing on his sense of self. Robert used to apply skin-softening filters to erase his acne, but he no longer worried about that. Instead, he had begun selecting the right filters to enhance the quality of his photos rather than his own appearance. For Robert, who had struggled with body image issues his whole life, shifting from editing his own appearance to the overall quality of the photo represents progress toward accepting his body.

Robert's realization that hiding his perceived flaws in photos does not improve his sense of self highlights the superficial nature of these editing practices. It also underscores the imperative to impress an imagined audience, one that appears to value both perfection and authenticity, an impossible contradictory imperative: Students who did not edit risked critique for visible flaws and imperfections; those who did edit risked critique for being inauthentic. Successfully walking the line between real and fake online was a highly valued skill, and getting it right was critical.

The Price of Inauthenticity

When we asked students the question, "How important is it for you to look similar online to how you look in person?" the answer was consistent and emphatic— very important! One woman's response exemplifies what most had to say:

> Huge! I feel like it's dumb if you don't look the same (online as offline). People will make comments, like, "That's not what she looked like online." Why have people talk about you like that if you know it's gonna happen? Like, do you think they don't know that you edited?

Students often followed up on comments like this by taking out their phone to show us an over edited photo of a friend in their social media, which prompted further commentary about how ridiculous the photo looks.

Shelby, a talkative young woman who was eager to share her thoughts on social media, explained:

> I have this friend I wanna show you. She's a beautiful girl. So pretty! But, like, see how her face is blurred and her teeth are extremely white? Look at how big her eyes are. That's just not what she looks like! Even the setting is a completely different color. Like, everything in this picture is not real.

Amber also talked about a friend who over edits to the point that it looks obvious. When asked how others respond to such pictures, she replied, "They'll tell her she looks great to her face or in comments. But a lot of people will talk about her behind her back because they notice that she's doing it to, like, get attention."

We asked Shelby if she knows why people edit their photos so heavily. Has she ever asked her friends? Is this something people talked about openly? She replied:

> I asked one of the sorority girls I live with and she was, like, "Well, you have to look good." Like, I get that. And she was like, "If you want a guy you have to look good. They want that." But for me, I wouldn't want a guy I like to see a super edited post. If he's your boyfriend, I assume he's gonna see you in real life, like, without makeup. I just don't see the reasoning behind it.

Her response led us to ask if guys really do prefer the heavily edited photos. She said, "They know! Like, they know the difference because I'll be sitting with people and they'll be like, 'That's not what she looks like. I saw her earlier today and she has a pimple.'"

Guys had a lot to say about crossing the editing line as well; they told us they felt tricked when a woman looked different online than offline. Steven explained:

> I guess if it (editing) makes you feel better then I don't see any harm in it. But when it comes to people who, like, make themselves look way different that's a problem for me (laughs). Everyone makes themselves look better on social media. Everyone makes their lives look better. But if you're making yourself look different, and I'm not talking about a filter. I'm talking about, like, editing, and, like, making yourself look how you think someone wants you to look. If you're doing that then you're not

acting the way you act in person, and you don't look the way you look in person, so any person who finds you attractive online is not gonna feel that way when they meet you. That's messed up in my opinion (laughs). Like, that's not okay."

Steven said that the phenomenon of over editing to the point that a woman looks different online than she does offline is so common that guys joke about it.

Yeah, like there's a joke among guys, like, take her swimming on the first date in case she's wearing, like, four pounds of makeup on her face. So that it comes off in the water. Like, it's a thing guys say if it seems like their picture is very doctored.

Jason said he finds a woman who looks different offline than she does online unattractive. By way of example, he told an elaborate story about a woman his friend had dated recently.

Online she seemed fun, but she was a dud in person. Like, she was just boring to talk to, and she wasn't as attractive as she portrayed online. I mean, once that happens, like, you're on edge about whether that person is trustworthy or not, whether they'll lie to you in the future.

When we asked Jason to describe how she looked different, he offered to show us pictures. Though Jason was never able to find them on his phone, he continued the story while he searched and frantically texted friends to see if they could send the pictures to him. He said, "Oh, I wish I had those pictures because it's like night and day. She looked like a whole different person." He had captured the pictures from her Snapchat account and sent them around to his guy friends, all of whom scrutinized the pictures and made fun of the woman and their friend who was dating her. Months after they had captured the woman's photos, Jason and his friends were still talking about her. When Jason texted several friends to see if they still had the photos it prompted a fresh round of jokes and laughter among them during the interview, all of which played out over texting.

Such gossip and teasing only served to heighten the anxiety of women who knew others were scrutinizing their social media images. One woman explained, "Whenever a guy sees a selfie of a girl, um, they can always criticize that girl. Like, 'Oh, her eyes are too far apart or, like, her nose is too big, or her smile is kinda weird.'" On the one hand, it is no wonder women feel such immense pressure to edit. On the other hand, they are damned if they do edit and damned if they do not edit because, unless they somehow strike the "perfect" balance, they open themselves up to scrutiny and critique. Worse, they may never know if they cross the editing line since no one is likely to tell them that they have over edited. Instead, people whisper and laugh behind their backs. Some students negotiated this impossible imperative to be both real and fake by maintaining two different Instagram accounts—a main account where they highlighted their most attractive, edited self and a Finsta (fake Instagram) account that featured their authentic, unfiltered self.

Anthropologist Scott Ross found that maintaining fake and real Instagram accounts allowed college women to enact these competing identities.[25] He wrote, "As the media ideologies my interlocutors had about Instagram became too strict, they did not attempt to break taboos on their accounts, nor did they abandon the app altogether—instead they turned to Finstas."[26] Though his focus was on identity and affect, we can extend the analysis to appearance norms. Some students maintained real and fake Instagram accounts in order to present the edited and unedited versions of themselves to different audiences. Women felt so much pressure to strike a perfect balance between authentic and flawless on Instagram that some found solace in Finsta, a safe space for sharing unfiltered (in all aspects of the meaning) photos of themselves. Appearing both authentic and perfectly edited in their main Instagram accounts was a key component in attracting likes and an important form of social capital in Instagram. It was like walking a gauntlet—you either succeeded or failed with no in-between.

Researchers Duffy and Chan introduce the concept of *imagined surveillance* to explore how young people navigate potential scrutiny on social media.[27] Though they focus on how college students mitigate social media risks related to surveillance by potential employers, the concept aptly describes how students we interviewed felt surveilled by their peers online. Those who struck the right balance between an authentic and perfect look got the most likes and, importantly, avoided being the object of gossip. All of the students we interviewed readily admitted to engaging in surveillance and scrutiny of others' images; consequently, they knew their own images were under constant evaluation as well. Further, they knew that no one would tell them if they went too far with their edits. In this case, the number of likes is not an accurate measure of success. Never knowing when you have crossed the editing line adds to the stress of posting.

Summary

This chapter highlights the invisible labor involved in the creation of an online self within the larger digital multiples project. The Instagram self requires a great deal of time, skill, strategy, and maintenance—it represents one's perfect self and personal brand. Most participants articulated a gendered trope that women care a lot about their online look and men do not care at all. Those who challenged this stereotype agreed that men who care about how they look in their online photos feel pressured to hide behind a "whatever" attitude or cloak their image concerns in entrepreneurial efforts. The exception was men who self-identified as gay; they felt freer to discuss their appearance-focused editing practices at length.

For women, online social capital mostly depended on physical appearance—how closely a woman aligns with dominant beauty ideals and her ability to edit in a way that enhances her best features. Women who struck the perfect balance between perfection and authenticity were able to attract the most likes. This contradictory imperative was impossible to achieve. They described a process that involved taking many photos to get the right one and zooming in to examine every pixel of the image for potential "flaws" that could be fixed with editing.

The editing imperative led women to engage in micro-scrutiny of their appearance online, which affected their sense of offline self. The complexity of social media resulted in a multitude of comparisons: Women continued to compare themselves to other women (friends, roommates, classmates) in their everyday offline lives; they compared their own posts online to those of other women; and they were mindful that their posts matched how they looked offline. Many women struggled with the dissonance of their edited, flawless Instagram image and their everyday offline look, leaving them dissatisfied with their appearance. Individual whims of online followers determined the extent to which one's posted images achieved a perfect balance between natural and glamorous, flawless and effortless.

Moreover, when women got it wrong, the social consequences were dire; they became the topic of gossip and jokes among their peers. The blurry boundary between "one time fake and two time fake" only served to heighten women's anxiety about posting. This chapter reveals how the online world affects the offline world in unexpected ways. A constant focus on micro-targeting body parts to identify and fix possible "flaws" online with the knowledge that their followers also had the ability to zoom in and examine the details of their photos affected how women felt about themselves offline.

Notes

1 boyd 2010.
2 Marwick and boyd 2014.
3 Duffy 2017, 187.
4 Ibid., 187.
5 Goffman 1959.
6 Bucholtz and Hall 2005.
7 Ibid.
8 Bourdieu 1990.
9 Ibid.; Wacquant 1992.
10 *BBC News* 2018.
11 Hegyi 2019.
12 GMA Team 2018.
13 Haines 2021.
14 Rabimov 2018.

15 Lemiski 2019.
16 Berkowitz 2017, 55.
17 Ibid., 55.
18 American Academy of Facial Plastic and Reconstructive Surgery 2019.
19 Haines 2021.
20 Taqueban 2018.
21 Nichter 2000; Taylor 2016.
22 Ibid.
23 Nichter 2000; Taylor 2016.
24 Duffy 2017.
25 Ross 2019.
26 Ibid., 3.
27 Duffy and Chan 2019.

References

American Academy of Facial Plastic and Reconstructive Surgery. 2019. *Annual Survey Statistics, 2020.* https://www.aafprs.org/Media/Press_Releases/News%20Stats%20AAFPRS%20Annual%20Survey.

BBC News. 2018. "Selfie Deaths: 259 People Reported Dead Seeking the Perfect Picture." *BBC News,* October 4, 2018. https://www.bbc.com/news/newsbeat-45745982#:~:text=Selfie%20deaths%3A%20259%20people%20reported,the%20perfect%20picture%20%2D%20BBC%20News.

Berkowitz, Dana. 2017. *Botox Nation: Changing the Face of America.* New York: New York University Press.

Bourdieu, Pierre. 1990. *The Logic of Practice.* Stanford: Stanford University Press.

boyd, danah. 2010. "Social Network Sites as Networked Publics: Affordances, Dynamics and Implications." In *A Networked Self: Identity, Community and Culture on Social Network Sites,* edited by Zizi Papacharissi, 39–58. New York: Routledge.

Bucholtz, Mary, and Kira Hall. 2005. "Identity and Interaction: A Sociocultural Linguistic Approach." *Discourse Studies* 7 (4–5): 585–614.

Duffy, Brooke Erin. 2017. *(Not) Getting Paid to do What You Love: Gender, Social Media and Aspirational Work.* New Haven, CT: Yale University Press.

Duffy, Brooke Erin, and Ngai Keung Chan. 2019. "'You Never Really Know Who's Looking': Imagined Surveillance across Social Media Platforms." *New Media & Society* 21 (1): 119–138.

Goffman, Erving. 1959. *The Presentation of Self in Everyday Life.* New York: Doubleday.

GMA Team. 2018. "How Do Photo Retouching Apps Affect Impressionable Teens on Social Media." *ABC News.* https://abcnews.go.com/GMA/Living/photo-retouching-apps-affect-impressionable-teens-social-media/story?id=56928554.

Haines, Anna. 2021. "From 'Instagram Face' to 'Snapchat Dysmorphia': How Beauty Filters are Changing the Way We See Ourselves." *Forbes,* April 27, 2021. https://www.forbes.com/sites/annahaines/2021/04/27/from-instagram-face-to-snapchat-dysmorphia-how-beauty-filters-are-changing-the-way-we-see-ourselves/?sh=375bfaf74eff.

Hegyi, Nate. 2019. "Instagramming Crowds Pack National Parks." *National Public Radio,* May 28, 2019. https://www.npr.org/2019/05/28/726658317/instagramming-crowds-pack-national-parks.

Lemiski, Mica. 2019. "We Asked Young People Why They're into Botox." *Vice*, March 7, 2019. https://www.vice.com/en/article/mbzkkv/we-asked-young-people-why-theyre-into-botox.

Marwick, Alice, and danah boyd. 2014. "Networked Privacy: How Teenagers Negotiate Context in Social Media." *New Media & Society* 16 (7): 1051–1067.

Nichter, Mimi. 2000. *Fat Talk: What Girls and Their Parents Say about Dieting*. Cambridge, MA: Harvard University Press.

Rabimov, Stephen. 2018. "The Millennial Approach to Remaining Young and Beautiful." *Forbes*, February 27, 2018. https://www.forbes.com/sites/stephanrabimov/2018/02/27/the-millennial-approach-to-remaining-young-beautiful/?sh=5bca6fcd12c6.

Ross, Scott. 2019. "Being Real on Fake Instagram: Likes, Image, and Media Ideologies of Value." *Journal of Linguistic Anthropology* 29 (3): 359–374.

Taqueban, Efenita, M. 2018. "Lipstick Tales: Beauty and Precarity in a Southern Philippine Boomtown." PhD diss. Amsterdam Institute for Social Science Research.

Taylor, Nicole. 2016. *Schooled on Fat: What Teens Tell Us about Gender, Body Image, and Obesity*. New York: Routledge.

Wacquant, Loic. 1992. "Toward a Social Praxeology: The Structure and Logic of Bourdieu's Sociology." In *An Invitation to Reflexive Sociology*, edited by Pierre Bourdieu & Loic Wacquant, 1–59. Chicago: The University of Chicago Press.

3

THE BODY IMPERATIVE

Morgan, a 21-year-old white woman majoring in communication, had long sandy brown hair, blue eyes, and a tall slender figure. She sauntered into our meeting, smartphone in hand, wearing an Amy Winehouse t-shirt, skinny jeans, and black leather ankle boots. An early adopter of social media, Morgan started using Facebook in middle school, quickly expanding into other sites, such as Instagram, Snapchat, and Twitter. Instagram was her favorite because it provided a space for creative expression and external validation.

Morgan's family moved from a suburban town in New Jersey to Austin, Texas, when she was 16, a difficult transition that resulted in her feeling depressed and isolated. Morgan coped by retreating into social media. She found Instagram especially freeing as a teenager because she could easily portray herself and her life as fun and highly social even while she felt insecure and lonely. She used Instagram to impress new friends in Austin and show off her exciting life and accomplishments to the New Jersey friends she had left behind. As a teenager, Morgan said she lacked athletic skill and "book smarts" so she highlighted her looks, which was easy to do on Instagram, a site designed for sharing images. Morgan learned early on how to get positive attention online—photos of herself looking happy and showing off her body resulted in many likes. In contrast, posts that highlighted her political beliefs or philosophical musings did not receive much attention.

In an effort to balance her need for validation and attention with her desire to express her authentic self, Morgan began pairing her serious thoughts and feelings with sexy photos, a practice that continued into college. Most of the posts we saw from Morgan on Instagram highlighted her slim figure in a bikini or some other revealing outfit paired with a caption about the superficial nature of social media or a political commentary. For example, one Instagram photo

DOI: 10.4324/9781003182047-4

featured her in a skimpy swimsuit with a lengthy caption about the meaning of likes and instant gratification that ended with, "Know the difference between who likes you and who likes your photos. The phrase 'social media' is an oxymoron if you think about it." This post got more than 100 likes.

On Independence Day, Morgan posted a photo of herself in a revealing red, white, and blue swimsuit with a margarita in one hand and a cigarette in the other. The caption, a 320-word rant about contemporary politics, began with the caveat, "This feels like the equivalent of pouring gasoline all over my reputation, but here goes!" She went on to write:

> Today, I saw a lot of posts from people my age about how horrible the U.S. is. I love that we live in a country where people can say that. Things are f*cked right now. . . A hashtag won't change that, even political rallies won't change it. . . I have become increasingly frustrated with the identity politics my generation has fallen for. I don't care what color, gender, religion, sex or anything you aspire to. You are my equal. We are all Americans. Let's stop agreeing to terms and conditions. Let's come together and vote!

Feedback focused almost exclusively on her physical appearance and included flame emojis, heart eyes, and comments such as, "You look like a snack wrapped in our flag," and "Gasoline has never smelled so alluring."

Increasingly, Morgan felt trapped by the narrow social conventions that rewarded physical attractiveness on Instagram. She wanted to use Instagram as a platform for sharing who she really was, a self she expressed in her captions. Yet, she believed that the only way for her posts to get attention was to show off her body. Morgan valued and strived for authenticity, which meant honestly sharing her thoughts and creatively expressing herself in a way that focused on her personality and intellect rather than her physical appearance. In terms of social media, Morgan defined authenticity as, "Posting about what you want to share and what makes sense in your life as opposed to posting for other people or for likes." As much as Morgan hated the concept of posting for others, she could not help but edit her photos to appear more attractive, and she cared a lot about the number of likes her posts received. On the one hand, she spoke fiercely of the importance of pursuing authenticity in life. On the other hand, she told us she deleted posts that got fewer than 100 likes.

Morgan's vignette illustrates the choice that some young women face in establishing their identity and popularity online. Insecure about her intelligence, Morgan used what she perceived to be her "main asset"—her attractive body (Figure 3.1).

However, she struggled with her body-revealing Instagram posts because they interfered with her presentation of an authentic self. Morgan's dilemma was not unique; many women struggled with the imperative to self-construct

FIGURE 3.1 Morgan poses in a bikini in calm, turquoise water. Looking off into the distance, she appears aloof and distant. With her face partially obscured, the viewer's gaze is directed toward her body.

their own gendered and sexual identities along cultural norms for femininity. This meant showing your body, regardless of how you felt about your physical form.

While social media provides an opportunity for women to be creators of their own content, the posting process can be problematic. Communications researcher Stephanie Davis explains that young women's posts embracing their femininity and sexuality can be empowering, but also run the risk of being "quickly transformed into sites of hostile surveillance via the male gaze."[1] Though Morgan did not speak to this directly, the objectification of self that troubles her is partially rooted in this form of surveillance.

In this chapter, we examine the impact of social media on young women and men in relation to body image and sense of self. Accordingly, we explore a range of issues concerning body image, including popular discourse about ideal body types, the ubiquity of social comparison, gender differences, and the impact of the body positivity movement on body acceptance. We highlight several key themes that emerge in Morgan's story—authenticity, self-branding, surveillance, and the arduous work of beauty and gendered identity. Most of the narratives focus on references to Instagram, the most visual and curated site we studied.

We draw on individual interviews as well as focus group discussions comprised of all women groups and mixed gender groups. In our previous research, we have found that conducting group discussions among women friends is a particularly useful methodology when discussing body image, as participants often shared their emergent thoughts on this sensitive topic more openly among friends than in one-on-one interviews.[2] The discussions that ensued among women who knew each other well elicited natural speech and mirrored the kinds of conversations they might have in everyday life. Personal stories narrated by one woman can inspire others and serve as a springboard for friends in the group to share their own experiences.

Background to Social Media and Body Image

Prior to the emergence of digital social media, images of beauty and advertising for products promising to enhance one's appearance were pervasive in traditional media, such as television, glossy fashion magazines, and newspapers. These images and advertisements were replete with subtle and overt messages on how viewers, particularly women, should look, and the ads changed infrequently (i.e., once a month) with the publication of a new magazine. Fast forward to today's media environment, where people are interactive consumers and producers of highly curated, rapidly changing posts. Emerging adults are bombarded throughout the day with posts from friends, social media influencers, and advertisers, all of which serve as sources of comparison and reminders of how they should look. Additionally, feedback mechanisms, such as likes and comments, make it all too obvious which body ideals and body "assets" people consider attractive.

Important gender differences have emerged in the body image literature with regard to adolescents and emerging adults and their social media use. Research has shown that many women engage with social media specifically to compare themselves to others.[3] These comparisons at the site of the body begin in adolescence. Studies among teens report that girls are more likely to engage in social comparison and seek feedback on how they look on social media than boys.[4] Girls also spend more time than boys do curating their online image and getting help from friends in this endeavor.[5]

Studies have linked frequent Instagram use to greater self-objectification (i.e., thinking of your body as an object for others to gaze upon), especially when the user engages with celebrity culture.[6] Perhaps unsurprisingly, the more images we are exposed to, the greater the possibility for concern over our own body. Social media promotes thinness and dieting behavior through idealized images of "perfect" women.[7] Posting photos of one's self and viewing and commenting on others' photos have been shown to be particularly harmful to young women's sense of self as compared to men.[8]

An abundance of research points to higher body dissatisfaction in direct relation to time spent on social media, meaning the more time you spend online, the more likely that you will have bodily concerns. While most studies focus on young women's body image, an emerging literature documents that men also experience dissatisfaction with their bodies and engage in negative body talk (i.e., making disparaging remarks about their own body size and shape).[9] Giving voice frequently to one's bodily concerns is associated with disordered eating and greater body dissatisfaction among men.[10]

Studies conducted by psychologists have found that regardless of race, frequent exposure to social media among women results in dissatisfaction with one's weight and increased body surveillance.[11] In contrast, several qualitative studies have found that Black and Latina women have more flexible beauty ideals; they reject the thin ideal and value a curvaceous body, including having a larger butt as an important cultural aesthetic.[12] More nuanced research is needed on how social media use impacts body image among Black, Latina, and Asian women.[13]

Many psychology studies on social media use among college students expose participants to media content, like Facebook or Instagram posts, under experimental conditions in order to assess their response. For example, research that seeks to understand the impact of social media on body image has exposed young women to a series of Instagram posts and then asks participants to respond to questions about body dissatisfaction, social comparison, and their current mood. Most of these studies find that appearance comparisons on social media make women feel badly about their own bodies and put them in a negative mood.[14]

As anthropologists, the limitations of this methodology were apparent to us; how a person responds to posts of a stranger (or a celebrity) is different than their response might be to a friend's post. Clearly, responding to a hypothetical post in an experimental setting is quite different from experiencing feedback on your own post. As one of our participants explained:

> It's a lot easier to brush off comparisons to someone like a celebrity who has a team of people helping them look amazing. It's a lot harder to ignore comparisons to your friends who you know don't have anyone helping them when they look amazing.

In addition, findings from experimental studies tell us little about how these posts affect a viewer over time; the effect of seeing a stranger's post in an artificial setting may be short-lived, whereas comparisons to a friend's post may continue to bother you for an extended period.

Social media influencers—who are most commonly women—play an important role in beauty, fashion, and fitness posts and blogs. These women engage in visual narration of their personal lives while advertising specific brands. Influencers script their Instagram posts in such a way as to appear natural, non-commercial, and authentic.[15] Some emerging adults model themselves after Instagram influencers and have become a "promotional apparatus" for brands.[16] Many others are "aspirational entrepreneurs" who hope that they may become influencers in the near future.[17] As popular writer Jia Tolentino explains, "Social media has supercharged the propensity to regard one's personal identity as a potential source of profit—and, especially for young women, to regard one's body this way, too."[18] She writes that for women who have natural assets, it seems obvious to "think of your body the way that a McKinsey consultant would think about a corporation: identify underperforming sectors and remake them."[19] This is the strategy employed in the opening vignette about Morgan, who capitalizes on and reorients her audience to her looks to maximize online popularity.

Neoliberal and Post-feminist Approaches to the Body

Neoliberal governance operates through the embodied actions of free subjects. Rather than being externally imposed on people, health and a well-conceived self-presentation have become a moral duty of the individual.[20] Of central importance to a post-feminist "sensibility" is the idea that women have agency and the power to determine their own self-presentation; however, women are also expected to self-surveil and carefully manage their behavior.[21] Gender studies researcher Catherine Rottenberg differentiates the earlier feminist movement, which was dedicated to women's liberation, to the contemporary era of post-feminism, rooted in the "norms of neoliberalism," which frames liberation as the work of individuals rather than a collective of women working in solidarity toward a united goal of equality.[22]

Cultural theorist Rosalind Gill aptly characterizes the complexities of post-feminist approaches to the body on social media, explaining, "Notions of autonomy, choice, and self-improvement sit side-by-side with surveillance, discipline, and the vilification of those who make the wrong choices."[23] As such, the post-feminist context reframes compliance with gender-appropriate beauty regimes as "an expression of empowerment, choice, and self-worth."[24] Here, it is important to recognize that the notion of "choice" more closely resembles an "emergent mode of regulation" that appears to be about personal presentation of self, but can also be seen as obfuscating discussions of gender-based body inequality.[25] If we think back to Morgan's vignette, we recognize that she chose to perform femininity in culturally prescribed ways, while, at the same time, she felt deeply critical of her own behavior. We explore this contradiction more broadly in other students' narratives.

Body Image Ideals in the Age of Instagram

In focus group discussions, we asked young women to describe the current body ideal among their peers. Initially, they explained that their ideal woman was thin, tall, and curvy, defined as an hourglass shape similar to a coke bottle.[26] Following an active discussion among group members, they decided that body ideals for women on social media had expanded and it was no longer an imperative to be super thin. As one woman explained:

> People with more volume to their body are being hailed and people are trying to get that look now. So slim thick is a thing. People want that. I don't know. . . I feel like it's not just stick thin that everybody is striving for now.

Slim thick as a preferred body type for college-aged women emerged frequently in focus group discussions and individual interviews. Kristen, a self-described nature lover who taught yoga and spent her free time rock climbing, attributed the rise of the slim thick shape to the posts of celebrity Kim Kardashian.

> She's thick in all the right places but her waist is skinny and she's got skinny legs, you know. It's like guys want the thick thighs and ass but they don't want the big belly and arms, you know what I mean? It's stupid. Big breasts, but everything else, suck it back in.

Hailey, an anthropology major and sorority member, described the slim thick body she observed on social media fitness sites:

> I just keep on noticing everyone working towards getting that big butt and the toned stomach. Like, a big butt and a toned stomach is what you need to be perfect. And I follow a lot of Instagram fitness programs. They do a lot of, "You got to do glutes, and you got to do leg days." They're also working towards getting that toned big butt all the time. And they're bettering themselves but they're also, like, in the back of their mind, thinking about what other people want to see as well.

Hailey's narrative speaks to the body imperative for women obtainable only through repeated, targeted workouts. While she refers to this bodywork as a means to enhance her fitness, she is clearly cognizant of the desirability of the slim thick body type as a way to impress others. She reframes the hard work involved as a positive choice that will result in noticeable improvements in her body shape.

Despite the difficulty in achieving a slim thick body, Instagram posts are replete with selfies of women posing in cropped tops and yoga pants, in angles that attempt to accentuate their big butt and large rounded thighs, small waist, and flat stomach. Countless videos demonstrate exercises that can help move one's body shape closer to this ideal—like doing repetitive squats with weights. Many of our participants regularly watched other women's workout posts on Instagram, although few women in our study had developed a regular slim thick exercise routine themselves. Considering the difficulty in achieving this body shape, it seemed that rather than being an expansion of body ideals, women's awareness of the slim thick imperative through frequent Instagram posts resulted in frustration and dissatisfaction with their own bodies.

Millennial women, inspired by Kim Kardashian's body, have helped fuel a boom in plastic surgery for the Brazilian butt lift.[27] According to a survey by the International Society of Aesthetic Plastic Surgery, the number of butt lifts performed globally since 2015 has grown by 78 percent.[28] Indeed, it is the fastest-growing cosmetic surgery in the world. Leading surgeons, both in the U.K. and in the U.S., link this phenomenal growth to celebrity posts (e.g., Kim Kardashian, Jennifer Lopez, and Nicki Minaj) on social media that "have popularized the beauty of feminine curves."[29] One British aesthetic plastic surgeon described the highly desired body on Instagram as, "beach-ball buttocks . . . a bottom so scrutinized, so emulated, so monetized, that it no longer feels like a body part, but its own high-concept venture."[30] While the college women we interviewed were not having Brazilian butt lifts, their narratives certainly reveal awareness of this body ideal. Interestingly, cosmetic augmentation among Black women has increased significantly over the past decade.[31]

Although the slim thick imperative has been popular for several years, it has not completely replaced the thin body ideal. For most women, there was a strongly voiced concern not to look fat online. Chloe, a petite woman who described herself as "naturally thin," had spent a lot of time thinking about the effects of social media.

> People, of course, want to look skinnier in photos. Like, my friend was sucking in when she takes a photo. It's like everyone always wants to look skinny. Nobody ever wants to look fat on social media. But it's like if you are fat in real life, then there's nothing you can do about it.

For Chloe, it was not just a desire to look skinny that was guiding women's body shape ideals and their posting habits but also the desire and need to conform to "whatever fad is in for the female body." At present, she reminded us, the preferred body type had "evolved into people having thick bottoms and skinny waists . . . having a bell-shaped body, whereas it used to be just skinny in general. It kind of evolves with each generation." Her observation was important because it emphasized the increasing difficulty that women face in each generation to meet societal expectations of beauty. This is particularly true in the age of social media, which exposes women to a flood of imagery throughout each day.

Inspiration and "Exoticization" of Beauty on Social Media

Rather than viewing social media as a space for reinforcing narrow beauty ideals, Kayla, an unassuming journalism major who hid her figure under a baggy t-shirt and jeans, believed that ideas were expanding, as it was now possible "to see posts about somebody, like, a world away—which is insane—and you're going to get inspired from that." Other women in this focus group also commented that "different types of beauty" were emerging online, and that they increasingly saw "more color in how people are being represented."

As one woman in the group explained, "Like, a lot of Instagram girls, they're not like your typical kinds of beauty anymore, they're more . . . I don't want to use the word exotic because that's weird, but they're just not conventional beauty anymore." Thus, on the positive side, these women observed that the range of people—in terms of body type and skin color—was continually expanding online, so "you find people who are representing you." However, they were quick to point out that it depended on what sites you were looking at and which celebrities you followed.

Another woman expanded on this idea, noting how beauty standards on social media were changing and evolving, and how "different cultures were coming into play." Writer Jia Tolentino has described the rise of an "exotic Instagram Face" which is "a young face. . . with poreless skin and plump, high cheekbones . . . catlike eyes and long, cartoonish lashes, a small neat nose and full, lush lips." She further describes this face as "distinctly white but ambiguously ethnic."[32] One of the L.A.-based makeup artists whom Tolentino interviewed described this "exotic Instagram face" as comprised of "an overly tan skin tone, a South Asian influence with the brows and eye shape, an African-American influence with the lips, a Caucasian influence with the nose, a cheek structure that is predominantly Native American and Middle Eastern."[33] This makeup artist believed that in the increasingly visual world that we live in, "people want to upgrade the way they relate to it." The college students we interviewed observed this beauty look on social media and were adept at using the tools available on Instagram for manipulating their appearance.

"Comparison Is the Thief of Happiness"

We asked students how spending time on social media was affecting how they and their friends felt about their own body image. Kayla talked about how looking at posts online and drawing comparisons is "definitely a big factor in how you see yourself." She went on to explain:

> You see all the posts about the Victoria's Secret fashion show and all these models and they're beautiful, and you're like, I don't look at all like that.

I don't know, it kind of makes you be like, "That sucks for me." I wish I could have won that lottery.

Kayla's friend added that seeing super thin beautiful models puts pressure on you "to look, dress, eat or act a certain way . . . like how you see the Instagram models." Kayla went on to describe the feelings of insecurity that arose from these comparisons:

> It's kind of like all this comparison is the thief of happiness and that's essentially what social media is boiled down to. It's going to be a comparison game just by its nature. All these people on there and then you're putting your stuff on there, so it's going to be like, "Okay, one of these things isn't like the other."

We hear a frustration and resignation in Kayla's voice as she compares herself to models with whom she cannot match up. Her insightful comment—that comparison is the thief of happiness—is clear in indicting pervasive media images as a causal agent in her dissatisfaction with self.

Brianna, a focus group participant who wore yoga pants and a tank top to the discussion, said she likes to wear workout clothes because they are comfortable and show off her curves. She explained how her comparisons to other women on various platforms made her feel about herself:

> When it comes to social media and body image, there's always going to be someone prettier and skinnier than you are. I feel like sometimes when a boyfriend or girlfriend likes another picture of someone else that's not you, you look at the person, you see how they look—their face, body, hair, or the life that they live—and you compare yourself. I feel like social media makes you compare yourself. If you're okay with how you look, you're like "Oh, okay, that's fine." Then there's other people that compare themselves and then they'll work out, or people that are, "Oh, I need to look different" and they'll drastically change. I feel like it puts a certain image in our head, and we have to follow it.

Brianna's description of body comparison underscores the inevitability of seeing other women online who may make you feel badly about yourself because you do not measure up to how they look. What is particularly poignant in her narrative is that these micro-comparisons and evaluations of oneself go beyond outward appearance of face, body, and hair to an imaginary of how the "other woman's" life is constructed. The woman with the seemingly "perfect" body has—by extension—a perfect life.[34] Few are immune to the impact of these comparisons; while some can accept themselves for who they are, others feel they must take action to change themselves.

Feminist cultural theorist Angela McRobbie has discussed the idea of "the perfect," which places emphasis on the individual and equates "female success with the illusion of control, with the idea of 'the perfect.'"[35] In her analysis, the notion of the perfect is a heightened form of self-regulation. She asserts, "The constant calculations and the sense of 'being in control' have the effect of seemingly putting the woman in charge of her affairs."[36] However, McRobbie states that in the aspiration toward the perfect, a woman experiences ". . . a constant benchmarking of the self, a highly standardized mode of self-assessment, a calculation of one's assets, a fear of possible losses."[37] The idea that a woman with a perfect body lives a perfect life intensifies competition between women; it also results in women thinking that their own perceived flaws need to be improved.

Women of all body sizes experienced the insidious nature of comparisons at the site of the body. For example, Natasha described herself as having been thin when she entered high school. Since that time, she was diagnosed with a serious illness, and had gained 40 pounds due to steroid medications she was prescribed. Natasha observed that the ideal girl she saw online was "usually some skinny blond, happy chick." She went on to differentiate herself from that image:

> That's not who I am (laughs). And that's not what 80 percent of the girls that I know are, and I feel like that has a huge effect on whatever I do and how I feel. If I see something like that or like Victoria's Secret models, I always feel so bad after I see a picture of them (laughs). And I have them on Instagram. I don't know why I do that to myself. But I feel the need to see the way they look, and that's how I'm supposed to look, and I always feel bad every time I see a picture of them. And I know there's a ton of girls that feel the same way, too.

The comment "That's how I'm supposed to look" underscores how she had internalized the Victoria's Secret body type. Despite the personal distress that Natasha experienced after looking at beautiful models on Instagram, she felt compelled to continue viewing their posts. As British philosopher Heather Widdows explains, even though most people today are image-literate, meaning that they know images have been altered, it does not change the way they internalize their content.[38] In other words, they still look at a picture of a beautiful model and embrace her beauty rather than focusing on the fact that her image has been digitally altered or enhanced. Natasha exemplifies this issue in her persistent dissatisfaction with self. Perhaps she continues to hope that one day she might be able to change and look like them.

Previous studies on social comparison and women's body image have found that women are more likely to make upward appearance comparisons (that is, comparisons to those who are more attractive) than lateral comparisons (comparing oneself to someone of equal appearance) or downward comparisons (comparing oneself to someone less attractive).[39] Upward appearance comparisons are amplified on social media and have the most negative impacts on women's body image, a point captured by Natasha's narrative.

For some women, constant social media exposure to other women's bodies that did not match their own just "seeped into their brain," making acceptance of their own body challenging and frustrating. Alexis explained how her own online comparisons led to her dissatisfaction with self:

> I compare myself to girls who post pictures in their bikinis on the beach, and I'm just like, "Wow!" I would never post a picture of myself in a bikini . . . because I feel I would compare myself to that. Like, am I skinny enough? Am I fit enough? Does my body look okay in a swimsuit? I compare myself to girls who post in bikinis and they're fit, they're skinny, they have the right body for that and . . . that makes me feel bad because people are like, "Oh, you should post pictures in your swimsuit." And I'm like, "No, I'm good."

In Alexis' narrative, we hear again how women who felt like their bodies did not match up to images they saw online were hesitant to participate fully in posting, particularly if they were not comfortable posting pictures in a bikini.

Alexis' friend, Alyssa, also a participant in the focus group, went on to describe how social media distorted her sense of self and body image, leading her to question what she liked about herself, particularly if it did not seem to match cultural ideals for beauty. In other words, if she did not post photos of herself in a bikini, maybe there was nothing attractive about her. She reflected, "It's really bullshit; at the same time, I fall into it every time." Finding space for self-acceptance was particularly challenging in the age of social media.

Morgan, featured in the vignette that opened this chapter, also recognized that her comparisons to other women on social media were problematic, albeit for different reasons.

> And the weird thing is, I don't look at guys' Instagram posts because they don't interest me. I look at girls. I look at how they look compared to me . . . I sometimes look at models or famous people, but . . . what interests me is when other people go on my Instagram, what do they see? How do I look compared to the other girls out there?

Frustrated with her own behavior, Morgan went on to say that nowadays she was posting less because she felt anxious each time she posted, as she worried how many likes she would get. With close to a 1,000 followers, she felt that she mostly projected herself as an object for others' consumption. In fact, as described earlier, when she posted the type of photos of herself that she liked, she got very few likes from others. "If I'm not a happy girl at a park or I'm not in a bikini, no one will like my post—and that's very depressing. And I wish I could let go of that, but it's hard." While she recognized that comparing herself to others was a futile activity, she continued to engage in it just like everyone else.

Likes serve as a powerful form of online *social capital* among youth, a highly valued measure of external validation and popularity.[40] However, gaining social capital, while validating and potentially useful in some ways, also had limitations. For Morgan, online popularity came at a high cost of prioritizing the desires of her imagined audience over her own, which ultimately felt unsatisfying. Through the feedback mechanisms of Instagram, Morgan had learned and internalized the harsh reality that her audience was not interested in learning about her, or even viewing her as a person; instead, they valued her for her attractive body. Despite the angst Morgan expressed during our interview about posting in a self-objectifying way, we observed that she continued to post provocative images highlighting her body on Instagram. In this case, the lure of online popularity was too strong to resist, even though the reward was superficial and ungratifying. Despite feeling that she needed to obtain maximum likes, Morgan observed:

> The people who have the most likes are the loneliest people. Because if you think about it, these beautiful girls who have their parents paying for them to be in college, and all their confirmation is on how they look. Their sense of identity must be so warped, you know, especially if these pictures that they're posting are Photoshopped.

Three points raised by Morgan are worth further consideration. First, she refers to the emptiness of likes, that is, the recognition that Instagram popularity is not real popularity—that girls who get the most likes are probably lonely. Second, she realizes that basing your sense of self on the number of likes you get is a disastrous proposition that can really "warp your identity." Even with this level of insight, Morgan continues to be online, to post, and to compare herself to others. Why? She recognizes that girls like herself are highly reliant on validation from others for their sense of self—a need that keeps her tethered to social media. A third point raised in her narrative and documented in many social media posts is the importance of showing maximum flesh in posts, be it in a bikini near a pool or at the beach, in a sports bra and shorts at the gym, or in lacy underwear in your bedroom. Morgan was clear that showing skin resulted in more likes.

Motivation to Change: Fit Talk

For some participants, seeing other women's posts about working out served as an inspiration to begin exercising, a short-term solution that enabled women to feel like they were taking charge of their bodies. As Chloe explained:

> There are times when I'm not feeling 100 percent happy about my body weight and I'll look at girls on social media that are fit and they're working out and I'm like, "I'm going to look like that." But my body is totally different and would never look exactly like those people. But it's definitely a kind of motivation to try to fit that image or get to that place.

This narrative of feeling motivated by other women's online images emerged in focus groups, where women expanded on the importance of looking "fit and healthy." Brianna explained:

> I feel like, nowadays, I guess the standard that people are looking for is girls that are fit because health is becoming a big thing. I feel that girls should have muscle but not a lot of muscle. . . . Some of my guy friends are like, "Oh, I want a girl that's fit but not too fit," and I'm like, "Well, what do you mean?" and they're just like, "Well, she can be tall and she can have nice thighs, nice arms, but she can't be, like, overly built."

Other women in the group nodded in agreement with this analysis—that it was important to be fit but not too strong. Being too strong (i.e., having muscles that were too large) was considered unfeminine. This issue is reminiscent of high school girls who chose not to run competitively for fear that their calf muscles would become too large.[41]

In her interview, Paige, an English major with short blond hair who described her figure as "straight up and down," said she felt inspired by a YouTuber that posts "a lot of stuff about her running routines and her yoga practices." Rather than comparing herself to this woman, Paige appreciated her talk about fitness because she approached it in such a way as to make it appear doable.

> I think the way that she addresses it is more in a "Hey, this is my personal progression" and not as much of a "Look at my body; this is how much I weigh." She never talks about weight; she just talks about "Look at this pose I can do now." So it's a little bit of the jealousy thing of comparing myself but she's mostly handling it in a positive way where it makes me inspired to do a run myself. And it's not in a self-deprecating way.

Paige noted that watching other women online did not have to result in negative comparisons and feeling bad about yourself. She believed that she needed to be aware of boundaries in making comparisons to others on social media. As she noted, "Like, it's a line you've got to be careful with." In other words, she recognized that comparisons could be lethal to her self-esteem, but they could also serve as motivation to work towards self-improvement.

Gender Differences: Female and Male Perspectives

While most participants agreed that women were more likely than men to compare themselves to others on social media, men were certainly not immune. As Nicholas, who posted frequently across his sites, explained:

> I feel that, especially for me, like, I could see a guy or anyone on social media with a really good body, and I look at myself and I'm like, "I could be there, but I'm not, and I'm lesser than them because of that." And that thought got placed into my head just from seeing something on social media. So I feel the more time you spend on social media, the more images, like, that you're exposed to, the more you'll feel bad about yourself if you're not necessarily in a place that you want to be.

Nicholas' quote highlights how little it can take to trigger negative feelings about one's own body—and leads us to consider how repeated social media exposure serves to magnify the impact of comparisons. He went on to discuss how this differed for women and men:

> I've noticed that it's definitely a bigger issue with girls, as typically it's always been. Guys don't necessarily care as much, I feel. I know I care a lot, but I know that a lot of my guy friends don't. But I know that a lot of girls are pressured to look a certain way on social media, and then portray that same aspect in real life. So, I know that for sure, especially with my girlfriends, that it has affected them more.

His observation is important because it supports a widely held notion among youth that women experience the greatest pressure, both online and offline, to meet cultural beauty ideals.

Daniel, who considered himself "a 6 on a scale of 1 to 10" in terms of attractiveness, offered a different opinion. He provided this numerical evaluation of himself independently of any question we asked. Daniel felt that comparing yourself to others was something that everyone did and emphasized that comparisons at the site of the body were not just a recent social media phenomenon.

> It's not just social media because it all roots back to pop culture and celebrities, and you know, "Why can't you look like Kim Kardashian?" or

"Why can't you have Nicki Minaj's butt?" Even if you don't have social media, even if you're not into pop culture at all, basically if you don't live under a rock you're going to be comparing yourself to others, because that's just the society we live in. And it sucks and I think about it all the time, but there's literally nothing you can do about that. Like, your friends and family can support you and love you, and no matter what, you're always going to have this image. I know this guy who I worked with and I would consider him super popular on Instagram, like, he gets 400, 500 likes on his photos. But he doesn't think he's popular and he had body image issues even though he's a really good-looking dude. I wish I looked like him, and he wishes he looked like someone else. And I'm sure the person he looks up to is having body image issues and wishes he looked like somebody else. So, like, every single person you ever meet is always going to have body image issues.

The inevitability of having body image issues that Daniel espouses is sobering, especially since he points to its historical roots, which, in his analysis, predates social media. The chain of body image dissatisfaction (meaning that everyone wants to look like someone else) that he expresses was especially common among gay men, but also emerged in discussions with other men and women in our study. However, while dissatisfaction with self at the site of the body is a long-standing issue, our interviews highlight how social media intensifies and amplifies these feelings.

Jordan and his male friends described how they experienced pressure to post attractive photos of themselves so that women using dating apps like Tinder would find them attractive and want to meet them. Tinder allows users to make a swiping motion on their phones to like or dislike other users; when both users swipe right, they "match," which means they can chat with each other. As Jordan explained (Figure 3.2):

If you're a guy, you want to show that you're muscular and show yourself on the beach or in the gym. . . . The pressure is there because you're doing it for the swipe. You want someone to swipe right on you so . . . there's direct competition there.

Although we did not explicitly ask about Tinder, discussions about dating/ hook up sites like this did surface spontaneously in several interviews.

When asked how spending time online affects how he and his friends feel about body image, Kevin, a psychology major and fraternity member, replied by first explaining that he was talking about "people in general," not he and his friends, who "weren't really affected by social media." Despite this claim, Kevin recognized that looking at others' posts led to lots of comparison among

FIGURE 3.2 This college student partially shows off his torso, embodying a casual and confident attitude. He gazes directly at the viewer, inviting them to look back.

men, "because they see all these super-hot girls with the hourglass or pear image and they're like, 'Oh, I wish I had that.'" He continued, "I mean with guys you see those huge body builder types who have muscles the size of my head and you're like, 'Oh, well I don't want that, but I do not want to look like me.'" Because he did not want to look like himself, a revealing comment blurted out almost as an afterthought, Kevin recognized the importance of posting attractive photos to try to make himself more appealing and more competitive in the social marketplace.

While women generally agreed that men were concerned about their posts being sufficiently attractive, they also described the "I don't care" attitude that was pervasive among male college students. In answer to a question about gender differences, social media, and body image, Brianna explained:

> For a girl, it's the same thing for guys, I guess. Like, if your girlfriend's liking a picture of a guy that has a bigger build than you do or a different style of clothing and you see that as a pattern, I feel like the guy's going

to want to hit the gym more and try to become bigger or, like, they'll try to dress differently. It's the same thing with girls. Like, they'll go and work out to lose weight, but also it depends if they care or not. Because I know some boys tend to not care as much as girls do when it comes to their image. . . . Boys are just kind of like, "Oh, whatever." And then sometimes girls feel the need to please other people and boys are just kind of like . . . some of them, not all of them are just like, "Oh, I don't care, this is me and that's it."

This notion that many guys are "like whatever, I don't care" was certainly something we heard repeated across interviews. Drawing a contrast between men and women, Carrie observed:

I think that girls our age care more about what everybody else thinks about them . . . other girls, but also catching the attention of guys. And guys kind of care more about what other guys think of them. There's this thing like, "Oh, do you lift? Do you work out?" and people put that on social media too, like guys working out or drinking a bunch of beers or whatever they're prioritizing. Whether it's their fraternity, their body, their school.

Some women opined that men's interest in body image—particularly having muscles—was more rooted in their desire to impress other men than women. As evidence, women described how men engage in comparison to others at the gym where they tried to "one up each other" with how much weight they could lift.

Our data reveals a pattern of intense interest in appearance among both women and men, although there were several key differences. For example, while most students agreed that men had more latitude in terms of body ideals as compared to women, a notable gender difference was that women sought approval from their friends on social media in terms of how they looked, whereas men were more reluctant to do so. Emiliano, who said his goal is to "get shredded" (i.e., have well-defined muscles), further clarified this:

Guys do ask each other how we look. I just don't think guys make it public that much. Because I think girls would ask it through text or social media more. Guys just say it one-on-one, you know. They don't make a big deal about it.

The idea that "guys say it one-on-one," meaning in interpersonal contexts rather than on social media, aligns with results of a college survey, which found that 75 percent of men could realistically imagine hearing a male friend complain about his body shape and size, and 25 percent believed that their male peers frequently engaged in body-related talk. Much of the negative body talk among men focused on needing to lose fat and gain muscle.[42]

Boulder Shoulders and Dad Bods

Despite the belief that men experienced less pressure to conform to a particular body type, some women agreed that an attractive body for a 20-something man was to have "boulder shoulders" (i.e., broad and muscular on top) coupled with six-pack abs. This body type showed that a man spent time in the gym and was concerned about how he looked. As we talked to more women, we realized that ideas about preferred body type often depended on the speaker. For example, when asked what body type she preferred in men, Olivia laughingly said, "I want them to be trim on top but have juicy thighs."

Another woman in the discussion described her ideal man as "having big shoulders but a skinny waist, not a six pack but, like, skinny enough, and a bigger butt because 'a dude booty' is making a comeback for guys." Other women described an attractive man as being "fit and strong," specifically having a broad chest, big muscles, and large arms. While we recognized that college men also had preferred body types that they personally found attractive in women, it is interesting that women respondents talked about their preferences without prompting. Personal preferences emerged in focus group discussions with women openly sharing their likes and dislikes.

While the muscular body type was certainly popular among men and visible on social media sites, we were surprised that some women showed little interest in dating a man with too much muscle definition. As one woman in a focus group explained, "Like, a guy who's really ripped, I'd be thinking, 'You look great, you did a great job, but please, keep a ten-foot radius around me.'" One of her friends added, "Yeah, don't get near me!" They agreed that this body type was too hard, rigid, and tight, and was not the type of body they would want to cuddle with or hug. Another reason for their disinterest in this male body type was that attaining a hard, muscular body required many hours spent in the gym. This meant time away from the relationship and signaled that a man was obsessed with himself and his appearance.

As an alternative to the hard, muscular body, women said that a "dad bod" was trending, and some found it desirable in a partner. Women described a dad bod as having a "little tummy pouch," which they considered an asset as it made the man "softer and cuddlier" than "gym rats" who had hard, muscular bodies. Women agreed that even if a man had a dad bod, it was important that he cared about his health. With regard to social media, Carrie explained:

> That's the kind of thing you'd see a girl post on Twitter, "Oh I like dad bods". . .but then the next post you'd see from her would be, like,

these big buff guys working out with their arms and abs, so it's kinda contradictory.

When asked if a "mom bod" was considered attractive for young women, college students laughed at the seeming absurdity of the question. We were told in no uncertain terms that a woman with body fat was not considered attractive.

A lot of girls don't want the mom bod until they're actually a mom. . . . Like, the skinny, fit girls may want to wear the mom jeans (i.e. high waist, loose fitting jeans) but they don't want the mom bod.

A dad bod, on the other hand, was desirable as it signaled that a man had potential as a long-term partner—"He'd be the dad who's there for his wife, for his kids, and who is financially stable and supportive."

Women also liked the idea of dating a man with a dad bod because most felt that their own bodies were far from perfect. They explained that being in a relationship with someone who "also had body flaws" would make them less self-conscious about how they looked. As Monique explained, "I feel like he'd be less critical of me if he's got, you know, some flaws or whatever." It also reduced the worry that other women might find him attractive as "the more fit you are, the more opportunities you'll have." Thus, a man with a dad bod was less of a risk overall as other women might be less attracted to him. In interviews, some women expressed reticence about partnering with a really good looking guy who might have lots of other options and would leave them.

In contrast, men we interviewed did not express this concern. While having an attractive body shape was clearly important for women and men, their thinking about attractiveness and who made a good partner varied significantly. Many of the women we interviewed believed that while looks were initially important in attraction, upon settling into a relationship they cared less about a man's appearance and more about how he behaved toward them. One young woman explained that looks were important, but "if they're nice and they stay nice it's what keeps girls there. . . . It's about them being authentic."

Hailey articulated an alternative reason for the acceptance of the dad bod. She observed that a big part of the fraternity lifestyle was consuming alcohol, which could easily result in a dad bod. She believed that some fraternity members did not want to expend the energy it took to work out because the shape and size of their body was not as important to them as maintaining their social status within the fraternity and their perceived loyalty to their brothers. While it was socially acceptable, even desirable, for fraternity guys to eschew becoming a gym rat, our data indicate that it was not an option for women whose body image expectations remained narrow, difficult to achieve, yet important to pursue.

Having the Self-confidence to Post

Media researcher Sarah Banet-Weiser discusses a key element of popular feminism—the imperative for girls and women to be self-confident, particularly at the site of the body. Highlighting a critical paradox in this imperative, she notes, "Even as the average U.S. teenage girl is flooded with images of the 'perfect' female body, she is also inundated with what seems like the opposite of that perfection: exhortations that she should love herself for who she is."[43]

Messages about the importance of accepting oneself and one's body, regardless of body size and shape, are relentlessly circulated on social media, and they surfaced prominently in the voices of college women whom we interviewed. Our respondents were painfully aware of this "double think," which they attempted to navigate through skillful editing and positive comments about themselves. Under that façade, however, we heard echoes of their dissatisfaction at not being able to meet cultural beauty standards.

For many participants, a consequence of frequently comparing oneself to others' bodies was an erosion of self-confidence and a hesitancy to post pictures of themselves. Shelby, who spent a lot of time scrolling through her sites but rarely posted, told us that showing your whole body required a lot of confidence, and depending on how you felt about yourself, you limited what you would be willing to show. When asked how body image affects posting habits, she explained that it was not about *how much* you post, as it was about *how* you post.

> If you're comfortable with your body, you'll post full body. If you're not, you'll crop it. If you don't like it, you just won't post it. 'Cause that's something that people are gonna come look at you and you're automatically getting judged. Not meant necessarily in a bad way, but you're getting evaluated by whoever's watching your pictures. So if you don't like it, you don't want others to see your flaws. . . . But you also have the people who are very confident and go almost naked. So, like, it's just how proud of yourself you are.

Having self-confidence to post full body shots required a certain degree of acceptance and sense of pride in one's body. Clearly, not all women possessed this level of assurance, a fact that was obvious among friends.

In talking about her friend who rarely posted photos of herself alone, Aliyah said:

> It's a big deal because everybody knows she doesn't really post or when she posts, it's just of her and her friends . . . so that way her self-image isn't associated with her likes. 'Cause it's very sad when you post something of yourself and you don't get as many likes or as many comments.

Thus, posting photos with friends was a strategy deployed to improve a woman's chances for attracting attention. Posting group photos also lessened feelings of embarrassment and disappointment from getting too few likes.

Natasha, the woman introduced earlier who had gained 40 pounds due to steroid medications, similarly described her hesitancy in posting pictures of herself, a feeling she shared with her fiancé whom she said also had a larger physique.

> I don't really post pictures of my full body or of my face really because I'm not too comfortable with what I look like. And I know my fiancé doesn't do that either because one, he's a guy, and two, he's also like chubbier than he would like to be. So he doesn't really post pictures either. And I know that whenever I try to take a picture of us together, we usually both decide on a good picture before we post anything. I believe body image does have a huge impact on what you post.

She went on to discuss how she thought posting was much more problematic for women who did not conform to the cultural stereotype of the ideal thin body, as compared to men. One of the concerns was that others viewing a large woman's post might make negative comments.

> I know this one girl who is really big, but she's positive about it. . . . Like, she loves who she is. She posts pictures of her face, but she doesn't post pictures of her body even though she says she's body positive. I think that has a whole lot to do with this—if she did post her whole body what would people say? I feel if you're not very comfortable with who you are and what you look like and then you post about it online, someone's gonna have something to say and it's gonna affect you in some way. I feel like you've got to be very confident to be posting a picture of yourself. Like, you know, you have these super pretty, super skinny girls posting about themselves every day 'cause they know they look good. They know that they're within the social norm of what they're supposed to look like. . . . They have a nice body so they flaunt it. I guess it's fine, but for me personally, I've never really liked the way I looked.

Three important points surface here. First, we see clearly in Natasha's quote that self-confidence is a prerequisite to posting full body pictures on social media. Thus, despite the importance of posting to retain a presence on social media, for many women this is a fraught experience. Second, one needs to be careful in posting as it might lead to unforeseen consequences. Making comments on someone's posts was far easier when they were not physically present—that is, when you do not have to look at the person you are speaking about. This anonymity gives rise to unfettered comments in ways that would rarely occur in offline contexts, especially among adults. Third, the notion that women are more accepting of their bodies in the age of the body positivity movement has limitations, for even a woman who espouses a body positive perspective needs to be careful, a point we return to in a later section of this chapter.

Men also reported a hesitancy to post and the need for self-confidence in posting. Daniel, who called himself "scrawny" and felt self-conscious about his body, explained that men who felt confident about their bodies were more likely to post photos of themselves. Since Daniel was not fully comfortable with how he looked, he restricted the type of photos he was willing to share on Instagram.

> I don't post photos at the beach or without a shirt on 'cause I'm still body-conscious on how I look. Like, how my chest looks because it doesn't look like a lot of the other gay guys, so I'm just like, "Damn. Oh well." Clearly, most people that have abs and have a nice body are going to post shirtless photos on a weekly basis. And the people that don't have that type of body aren't going to post. In my opinion, that roots back to popularity and looking good and the brutal-ness of popularity and attractiveness. The better you look, the more likes you're going to get. You're going to post more shirtless photos. You're going to be more confident in yourself.

Daniel's comment shows how he has adapted to his perceived limitations, and the scaffolding of self-confidence required in the digital age.

Cody, a gaming enthusiast with fluffy brown hair and thick glasses, reported that when he sees men posting numerous selfies on Instagram, he is unsure if this signals self-confidence to show their bodies or if they are just vain and seeking attention. He went on to describe how other men's posts made him feel about his own body:

> It kind of affects my self-confidence, and I know it affects other people's self-confidence, where it's always the hot people with six-packs who love to post self-portraits of very aesthetically pleasing things. Like, either they're posing nude, but in a not revealing way, or, like, shirtless. . . . I feel like Instagram is the biggest culprit of FOMO, like, fear of missing out, where people think they see that your life is way happier than it actually is in real life.

Cody went on to discuss how looking at other people's posts made him feel a pressure to make sure that what he posted was aesthetically pleasing, properly framed, and that filters were used to enhance the shot. His comment highlights that comparisons to others' posts are not simply about how someone else looks, but also refers to how they present their photos and how they live their lives.

Fishing for Compliments on Social Media

In interviews, we explored whether people put themselves down on social media to get compliments on how they looked, a strategy we had identified in face-to-face conversations. Earlier research identified that many young women complain about their body weight to friends (exclaiming, "I'm so fat!"), which typically prompted the response, "Oh no you're not!"[44] This ritual, "fat talk," occurred frequently among friends throughout the day. Engaging in fat talk indexed personal and cultural concerns about weight. Saying "I'm so fat" was more than just an observation about how a young woman looks or feels. It is a call for support from her peers, an affirmation that she is in fact not fat, and that things are not as bad as they might seem.[45] In recent years, a plethora of studies confirm that fat talk remains a powerful and frequent conversational speech form among women and increasingly among men.[46] Some researchers refer to this phenomenon as "negative body talk," a broader term meant to acknowledge that fat talk extends beyond explicit comments about body fat.[47]

We asked our participants if some form of fat talk (or negative body talk) existed on social media. Amber agreed that she heard fat talk a lot among her peers, adding, "That's insecurities—they want people to tell them they look good." While she felt this happened more in person, she went on to describe how this exchange worked on social media:

> I don't think a girl's gonna post a picture and say, "Oh, I look so fat in this photo." But I have seen lately that girls will post a selfie and they'll say something like, "Thought it was cute, but I might delete it later" and then people will be, "No, don't delete it, you look so good." I don't know why, but I've seen that a lot. I've also seen a lot of posts making fun of that.

Other students similarly commented on this phrase, "Thought I looked cute, might delete later" and slight variations. Aliyah described an interchange with a friend whom she questioned about using this phrase as a caption for her photos. Her friend responded, "It's for people to comment and say 'No, don't take it down. It looks great,' or 'You look really nice in this picture.'" Aliyah went on to compare this to people who posted vague remarks on social media, like, "I had a terrible day," without providing any context about what had happened. Announcing to others that you had a terrible day was an indirect way of inviting people to comment and ask questions about what had occurred. Similarly, self-deprecating comments opened the door for positive responses that refuted your negative self-image.

Another attempt at getting a compliment on social media was to say, "Oh, didn't want to try today" even though the person posting looked like they had carefully applied makeup and styled their hair. This type of comment annoyed

Heather, and, at least in her mind, she would question them: "Really? You didn't want to try? Not even for an hour?" In her estimation, women who posted like that were doing it to attract the attention of men. "They just want guys to comment and be like, 'Oh, let me take you out, let's go do something.'" Shelby similarly explained that a girl might post a beautiful picture of herself with a specific complaint like, "I hate my lips" or "I wanted to post this picture but I really hate my eyes, but posted it anyway." In such cases, it was clear that the desired response was positive feedback that, in fact, you looked great.

Some women expressed a heightened sensitivity to body-focused feedback on social media, recognizing that it reflected women's deep need for validation. For example, one woman explained:

> I mean, maybe it's just because I am insufferably a bleeding heart, but even if I know it's just looking for a compliment, I'm still going to say, "You look wonderful, I love your bod" . . . because I do the same thing. I need it, too. I'm not gonna deny it for someone. And well, especially because other people who are out there whose pictures get a lot more attention, they're going to get so much love, they're going to get so much hate . . . I do what I can to put positivity out there. I know that they're just fishing for it, but, like, it's not my place to deny it. That doesn't mean I comment on every single one, but you know.

Her empathy and compassion for other women her age was notable and rooted in her awareness of her own need for positivity from her friends about her appearance. In face-to-face communication, multiple meanings of a comment like "I'm so fat" or specific complaints about one's body parts emerge—it can be a call for support from friends as well as a way to bond with other women, to show that you have bodily concerns in the same way they do. This negative body talk can serve as a leveling device that makes it clear you do not feel more attractive than your friends do. In contrast, in the impersonal realm of social media, body talk that indicates dissatisfaction with self ("I'll delete this later") are oft times seen as annoying and an obvious tactic for getting likes.

Body Positivity

In recent years, body positivity posts have grown exponentially on Instagram. A Google search reveals that the hashtag # bodypositive has over 16 million posts on Instagram and the hashtag #bodypositivity has over 9 million posts. The body positivity movement serves as a counterweight to posts of thin women flaunting their flat stomachs and thigh gaps.[48] The focus of this movement, which has its roots in the fat liberation movement, is about accepting one's body (including fat rolls, cellulite, acne, scars, stretch marks, disabled bodies, etc.) and rejecting narrowly defined and largely unobtainable body ideals. In principle, the body positivity movement challenges assumptions that fat bodies are not active and fit and recognizes that women can be healthy and beautiful at any size.

Some researchers have questioned whether the emphasis placed on "loving one's body" reinforces the cultural preoccupation with appearance, albeit in a repackaged format that still begins and ends with image.[49] From this perspective, the body positivity movement continues to privilege how one looks over other attributes (e.g., personality, intelligence, sense of humor). Other critics argue that Instagram influencers have commodified body positivity posts in their efforts to create and post an identity coherent with the brand they are representing. These influencers, paid by companies to promote and endorse specific products, receive training on how to post images and captions that appear authentic despite their artificiality and co-constructed branded identity.[50]

The views of Gen Z consumers are critical to companies, as this cohort currently represents about $150 billion dollars in spending power.[51] A new ethos has emerged in the past few years wherein people use consumption as a means to express their deeply held beliefs. Fashion companies, for example, are showing signs of being *woke* (defined as becoming aware of societal injustices). In an effort to show they are woke, fashion retailers have increasingly used the word *feminist* on their homepages: This usage increased by a factor of five between 2016 and 2018.[52] While companies pay lip service to feminism, the issue of plus-sizes reveals a deeper reality.

In recent years, despite the seeming inclusion of plus-sizes in the clothing sector, many fashion brands sell no size-inclusive clothing, even when they feature a plus-sized model in their online advertisements. For example, when Everlane launched a new underwear line, they featured a curvy, larger size model in their ad campaign in an effort to appear inclusive, although they did not actually sell plus-sized underwear. Other companies, such as Madewell, have faced criticism for deceptive ads featuring plus-sized women modeling their jeans in provocative poses. These ads attract plus-sized consumers who then cannot find the product in their size.[53] Such practices give the appearance of creating inclusive clothing lines when in reality they fail to do so.

Recent evidence suggests the clothing industry is beginning to take the plus-size market more seriously after facing criticism from consumers. Athleta, a women's active wear brand, has recently rolled out a major plan for plus-sized customers; within the next year, the number of styles available in extended sizing will exceed 500. They will also provide training to their employees on body positivity language and plus-size fit. There is clearly a financial incentive here; Athleta's plus-sized customers shop twice as frequently and spend almost 90 percent more than their other customers.[54]

This brings us to an important question: How did college students whom we interviewed view the body positivity movement? Perhaps unsurprisingly, their responses reveal a range of opinions. Some women did feel more comfortable in their skin because of the movement. One woman explained, "I've been seeing a lot on Twitter lately, like people tweeting, 'Oh, I finally love myself' even if my body type is not the ideal." Given this development, she believed the evolution of acceptability was occurring for both men and women.

While some women opined that the body positivity movement conferred some benefits in terms of normalizing a larger body size, other women were skeptical that the plus-sized models they saw online were "really plus-size women." As Olivia, a confident woman who considered herself plus-sized, explained:

> For a long time, I was following, and it was a mistake, a lot of plus-sized models, because I was like, "I need to see more girls like me, I need to be looking at more positive representation of bodies, but even though they're bigger, they're still a shape that my body isn't, you know." Everyone calls Ashley Graham the perfect plus-sized model because she has the perfect curves. . . . She's bigger but she has the perfect waist to hip ratio and she has a really rigorous fitness routine.

Receiving agreement from her friends in the focus group, Olivia continued to expand on her feelings: "Plus-sized models—even if they're 200 pounds—have weight that is distributed in a way where they still have a perfect hourglass." These women believed that plus-sized models on social media were either heavily edited or were wearing shapewear that padded their hips in such a way as to make them look fuller and shapelier in the desirable places. Thus, even within the body positivity movement, there were specific expectations for women's bodies.

Reflecting for a moment on the issue, Olivia added, "It's really hard to find authentic images because everyone's afraid to post them. And the people that do get shamed so hard for it." For example, one of Olivia's friends recounted seeing larger models who received multiple hate messages online, with comments like, "Oh you're so fat, why are you even a model?" or if they were featured doing exercise, a shaming comment would appear: "There's a lot of girls who are way fitter than you are. You don't even look that good." These comments highlight the backlash to the body positivity movement and call into question the acceptability of larger body size.

Conversely, this group of friends also expressed annoyance and outright anger at the many posts of plus-sized people (not models) who posted themselves exercising, which they felt was "just a way to show people they're healthy." As one woman in the group noted:

> It makes me feel like shit because I'm here at Taco Bell eating and doing my homework, and I feel that I'm not allowed to have this body because I don't have the excuse that I work out and still look like this.

In other words, plus-sized women who pictured themselves exercising made other large women look bad, as if they were not trying hard enough to change their appearance. Working on your body through exercise regimens made it appear that you really cared and understood how you "should look"—even if you had not achieved it "yet."

Olivia, with confirmation from her friends, railed at what she termed transformation posts, which she was "totally sick of seeing":

> I mean, they're really bad right now because it's summer and everyone's talking about beach bods. . . . It's before and after pictures, like you would see in an infomercial but people are tweeting them of their own accord. When you see it on social media, it feels more realistic, it feels more authentic, and so it makes you feel like, "Well, they can do it, so why am I not doing it?" And that's been the worst for me. I really hate transformation weight loss.

For Olivia, transformation posts—where women showed how they looked before their diets and workouts and how they looked now—were offensive precisely because they felt like the antithesis of body acceptance. Further, because it was a real person's post on social media and not an infomercial, it seemed "more authentic," thus increasing the pressure for her to engage in weight loss activities. One woman in the group described a friend who "uses Instagram like an accountability for her progress in weight loss." Others agreed that they had seen many "thinspiration" and "fitspiration" posts and felt offended by how it seemed to be a requirement to work on your weight and fitness.

Women in our study who did not fit the thin ideal expressed frustration with skinnier women who participated in body positivity talk. Olivia said that she was "really sick of people who post comments like, 'Oh I'm being body positive, I'm loving all my curves,' and it's a skinny girl just sitting in an unflattering position and has, like, a little roll." Comments like these are reminiscent of thin women who would engage in fat talk, a behavior that angered other women who would sometimes respond with piercing, silent stares. Researchers have explored body comments among women of all sizes, although they typically have not discussed this in relation to social media.[55] Our ethnographic findings reveal the type of posts that appear on social media in relation to body size and online communicative styles.

"You Better Love Your Body!"

Another important point that emerged was that larger sized women felt like it was no longer acceptable to express negative feelings on social media about how they looked. Olivia explained:

> So, we have the body positive movement, right? So now every girl is supposed to abide by the idea of love your body, love yourself, everybody is

perfect, like that's what you're supposed to believe. Because that's the common ideology now, it feels like you're not allowed to talk about what you don't like. . . . If I post, "God, I really hate my stomach," then someone's gonna immediately say, "Your body is perfect, love your body." You're not allowed to voice your feelings about not liking your body because it's all about body positivity and love your body and so it's like an imperative.

Thus, even in a time when body image expectations appear to be expanding, an element of control remains in place, particularly in relation to popular discourse about appearance.

The extent to which social media was reinforcing a narrow ideal of attractiveness was discussed and questioned by several students. During a mixed-gender focus group discussion on this topic, Dylan recognized that, paradoxically, there was still an ideal "that you should look like this," even as the body positivity movement was going strong. Interestingly, he and his friends believed that the movement was increasing the pressure on individuals to show they felt confident about themselves. A woman in the group noted, "Yeah, if you're not hot, you have to at least be proud that you're not, like, conventionally hot. So it still puts a lot of pressure on the way that you look, no matter what." Dylan added, "Nowadays, women are supposed to value their own sexy larger body. . . . It's like body positivity so love your rolls. Like, you can take pictures in your underwear just like anybody else."

These friends went on to say that, given the pressure to be perceived positively by peers, you had to have something going for you—"Like, if you're ugly, you've got to be funny," or "You could be either pretty or you can be cool." Emma explained:

> Like, I was fat growing up, so I had to develop a personality that I was fine with. And now I'm not really at the age where I can just totally neglect my appearance. I have to find some sort of balance, and I don't want to. I don't know. It's easier for people that have looks as kind of, like, their thing . . . to navigate social media, because that's a large part of what it is.

According to Emma and her friends, people who were good looking and had bodies that met cultural body ideals could more easily leverage this asset to get followers on social media. However, those who did not feel so attractive needed to explore and develop other avenues upon which they could receive positive feedback. To be clear, this was more difficult in a largely visual medium like Instagram where "If you're not attractive, no one will even bother to look at your captions." Emma believed that it was much harder on social media to play up other strengths that you might have, like your sense of humor, intelligence, personality traits, or anything about you that was not appearance related. Whereas "real life" allows for multiple aspects of the self to be seen, appreciated, and explored, social media, particularly Instagram, privileged one's outer appearance above all else.

Emma felt that body positivity as a movement was mainly targeted at women and that despite a greater acceptance of fat bodies, she was still seeing a lot of messages to "lose weight, be fit, be skinny." Dylan added that although the movement has done "a good job helping women realize that larger women are valid too, a lot of straight men still preferred conventionally attractive women, sexually and physically." He concluded by stating, "Despite the fact that the body positivity movement has been effective among women, I don't think it's been as effective on men." In other words, while some women were changing and becoming more accepting of their larger body shape, men's attitudes about preferred body size for women were slow to follow.

Students recognized that there was an expansion of beauty ideals, and that, for the most part, "People are more accepting of plus-size models or people of color . . . and for guys, there's more feminine looking guys being celebrated." However, they were also cognizant of a counter current, visible on social media through hateful speech and negative feedback that reinforced long-standing narrow beauty ideals.

Summary

While women have long been judged for their appearance, the social media age appears to have intensified their body self-consciousness and dissatisfaction due to increased comparison to others and a heightened awareness of other's evaluations of how they look. To a certain extent, these findings also apply to men, although most students agreed that women were more concerned with their appearance and were more sensitive to comments by others. The feedback that college students, both female and male, received on their posts—measured by the number of likes and comments—either enhanced their self-confidence or resulted in feelings of fear about posting in the future. One's "like metrics" became a barometer of self-worth.

Cultural anthropologist Daniel Miller and his colleagues have discussed how social media reinforces the production of normative gender roles through its feedback mechanism.[56] In other words, self-presentation that aligns with dominant gendered perceptions of how women and men should look and behave is rewarded with likes and positive comments. In our research, we found that Instagram is yet another space where women encounter pressure to create an identity that conforms to narrowly defined feminine ideals. While ostensibly "just posting fun moments," women described the arduous work of creating and posting their best selves (i.e., one that hid their perceived flaws) in light of an imagined audience that was ready to scrutinize and comment on their bodies. The gendered work of beauty that women performed required continuous self-surveillance and monitoring. For most, this was a fraught experience.

Narratives about the body confirm that women compared themselves to images of other women they considered more attractive (e.g., Victoria's Secret models, thin women posing in bikinis). Notably, women of all sizes experienced the insidious nature of comparisons at the site of the body. Overwhelmingly, this resulted in negative feelings about their own bodies. Although most, if not all, of the students recognized that such comparisons were an unhealthy practice, they found it difficult, if not impossible, to abstain from making them.

In light of the body positivity movement, messages about the importance of accepting oneself and one's body, regardless of size and shape, circulate continually on social media sites. These positive messages coexisted with personal desires to show one's authentic, unfiltered body online. Nonetheless, students understood this to be a risky practice. Whereas "real life" allowed for multiple aspects of the self to be seen and appreciated, social media, particularly Instagram, privileged one's outer appearance above all else. Despite the frustration that many students expressed on the topic of social media and body image, being online remained a central feature of emerging adults' lives.

Notes

1 Davis 2018, 3.
2 Taylor and Nichter 2017a, 2017b.
3 Haferkamp et al. 2012.
4 Nesi and Prinstein 2015; Twenge and Martin 2020.
5 Yau and Reich 2018.
6 Fardouly, Willburger, and Vartanian 2017; Frederickson and Roberts 1997.
7 Perloff 2014.
8 Meier and Gray 2014.
9 Engeln, Sladek, and Waldron 2013.
10 Ibid.; Sladek, Engeln, and Miller 2014.
11 Mills et al. 2018; Tiggemann and Slater 2013.
12 Capodilupo 2015; Hicks 2018; Lamb and Plocha 2015; McClure 2017; Nichter 2000.
13 Fardouly and Vartanian 2015; Howard et al. 2017.
14 Fardouly and Vartanian 2015; Hogue and Mills 2019.
15 Banet-Weiser 2012.
16 Carah and Shaul 2016.
17 Duffy and Hund 2015.
18 Tolentino 2019, 2.
19 Ibid., 2.
20 Cairns and Johnston 2015.
21 Gill and Scharff 2013, 4.
22 Rottenberg 2014.
23 Gill 2007, 163; see also Davis 2018.
24 Cairns and Johnston 2015, 159.
25 Ibid.; McRobbie 2009, 51.
26 Anderson-Fye 2004.
27 Bursztynsky 2019.

28 Elmhurst 2021; International Society of Aesthetic Plastic Surgery 2020.
29 Elmhurst 2021.
30 Ibid.
31 Epperson 2018; Hilliard 2020.
32 Tolentino 2019.
33 Ibid.
34 Jackson and Vares 2015; Nichter 2000; Taylor 2016; Widdows 2018.
35 McRobbie 2015, 4.
36 Ibid., 9.
37 Ibid., 10.
38 Widdows 2018.
39 Leahey and Crowther 2008; Leahey, Crowther, and Ciesla 2011; Hogue and Mills 2019.
40 Bourdieu [1972] 1977.
41 Taylor 2016.
42 Engeln, Sladek, and Waldron 2013.
43 Banet-Weiser 2018, 72.
44 Nichter 2000.
45 Ibid.
46 Greenhalgh 2015; Mills and Fuller-Tyszkiewicz 2018; Shannon and Mills 2015; Sladek, Salk, and Engeln 2018; Sturtz Sreetharan et al. 2019.
47 Engeln-Maddox, Salk, and Miller 2012.
48 Salam 2017.
49 Cohen et al. 2019a, 2019b; Webb et al. 2017.
50 Cwynar-Horta 2016.
51 Amed et al. 2019.
52 Ibid.
53 Mull 2018; Peters 2018.
54 Tovar 2021.
55 Greenhalgh 2015; Nichter 2000; Shannon and Mills 2015.
56 Miller et al. 2016.

References

Amed, Imran, Anita Balchandani, Marco Beltrami, Achim Berg, Saskia Hedrich, and Felik Rolkens. 2019. "The Influence of 'Woke' Consumers on Fashion." *McKinsey & Company*, February 12, 2019. https://www.mckinsey.com/industries/retail/our-insights/the-influence-of-woke-consumers-on-fashion#.

Anderson-Fye, Eileen P. 2004. "A 'Coca-Cola' Shape: Cultural Change, Body Image, and Eating Disorders in San Andres, Belize." *Culture, Medicine and Psychiatry* 28 (4): 561–95.

Banet-Weiser, Sarah. 2012. *Authentic: The Politics of Ambivalence in a Brand Culture*. New York: New York University Press.

Banet-Weiser, Sarah. 2018. *Empowered: Popular Feminism and Popular Misogyny*. Durham, NC: Duke University Press.

Bourdieu, Pierre. 1977. *Outline of a Theory of Practice*. Translated by Richard Nice. Cambridge: Cambridge University Press.

Bursztynsky, Jessica. 2019. "Instagram Vanity Drives Record Numbers of Brazilian Butt Lifts as Millennials Fuel Plastic Surgery Boom." *NBC Health and Science*, March 19, 2019. https://www.cnbc.com/2019/03/19/millennials-fuel-plastic-surgery-boom-record-butt-procedures.

Cairns, Kate, and Josée Johnston. 2015. "Choosing Health: Embodied Neoliberalism, Postfeminism, and the 'Do-Diet.'" *Theory and Society* 44 (2): 153–175.

Capodilupo, Christina M. 2015. "One Size Does Not Fit All: Using Variables Other than the Thin Ideal to Understand Black Women's Body Image." *Cultural Diversity and Ethnic Minority Psychology* 21 (2): 268–278.

Carah, Nicholas, and Michelle Shaul. 2016. "Brands and Instagram: Point, Tap, Swipe, Glance." *Mobile Media & Communication* 4 (1): 69–84.

Cohen, Rachel, Jasmine Fardouly, Toby Newton-John, and Amy Slater. 2019a. "#BoPo on Instagram: An Experimental Investigation of the Effects of Viewing Body Positive Content on Young Women's Mood and Body Image." *New Media & Society* 21 (7): 1546–1564.

Cohen, Rachel, Lauren Irwin, Toby Newton-John, and Amy Slater. 2019b. "#bodypositivity: A Content Analysis of Body Positive Accounts on Instagram." *Body Image* 29: 47–57.

Cwynar-Horta, Jessica. 2016. "The Commodification of the Body Positive Movement on Instagram." *Stream: Interdisciplinary Journal of Communication* 8 (2): 36–56.

Davis, Stephanie E. 2018. "Objectification, Sexualization, and Misrepresentation: Social Media and the College Experience." *Social Media + Society* 4 (3): 1–9.

Duffy, Brooke Erin, and Emily Hund. 2015. "'Having it all' on Social Media: Entrepreneurial Femininity and Self-Branding among Fashion Bloggers." *Social Media + Society* 1 (2): 1–11.

Elmhurst, Sophie. 2021. "Brazilian Butt Lift: Behind the World's Most Dangerous Cosmetic Surgery." *The Guardian*, February 9, 2021. https://www.theguardian.com/news/2021/feb/09/brazilian-butt-lift-worlds-most-dangerous-cosmetic-surgery.

Engeln, Renee, Michael R. Sladek, and Heather Waldron. 2013. "Body Talk among College Men: Content, Correlates, and Effects." *Body Image* 10 (3): 300–308.

Engeln-Maddox, Renee, Rachel H. Salk, and Steven A. Miller. 2012. "Assessing Women's Negative Commentary on their Own Bodies: A Psychometric Investigation of the Negative Body Talk Scale." *Psychology of Women Quarterly* 36 (2): 162–178.

Epperson, Jennifer. 2018. "Why Black Women are Increasingly Seeking Plastic Surgery." *Lenny*, May 15, 2018. https://www.lennyletter.com/story/kim-kardashian-black-women-plastic-surgery.

Fardouly, Jasmine, Byrdie K. Willburger, and Lenny R. Vartanian. 2017. "Instagram Use and Young Women's Body Image Concerns and Self-Objectification: Testing Mediational Pathways." *New Media & Society* 20: 1380–1395.

Fardouly, Jasmine, and Lenny R. Vartanian. 2015. "Negative Comparisons about One's Appearance Mediate the Relationship between Facebook Usage and Body Image Concerns." *Body Image* 12: 82–88.

Gill, Rosalind. 2009. "Beyond the Sexualization of Culture Thesis: An Intersectional Analysis of 'Sixpacks,' 'Midriffs' and 'Hot Lesbians' in Advertising." *Sexualities* 12 (2): 137–160.

Gill, Rosalind, and Christina Scharff. 2013. "Introduction." In *New Femininities: Postfeminism, Neoliberalism and Subjectivity*, edited by Rosalind Gill and Christina Scharff, 1–17. Basingstoke, UK: Palgrave Macmillan.

Greenhalgh, Susan. 2015. *Fat-Talk Nation: The Human Costs of America's War on Fat.* Ithaca, NY: Cornell University Press.

Grigoriadis, Vanessa. 2021. "The Beauty of 78.5 Million Followers: How Social Media Stars like Addison Rae Gave the Cosmetics Industry a Makeover." *The New York Times*, March 23, 2021. https://www.nytimes.com/2021/03/23/magazine/addison-rae-beauty-industry.html.

Haferkamp, Nina, Sabrina C. Eimler, Anna-Margarita Papadakis, and Jana Vanessa Kruck. 2012. "Men Are from Mars, Women Are from Venus? Examining Gender Differences in Self-Presentation on Social Networking Sites." *Cyberpsychology, Behavior, and Social Networking* 15 (2): 91–98.

Hicks, Adora Burdette. 2018. "Black Beauty, White Standards: A Phenomenological Study of Black American Women's Perceptions of Body Image at a PWI." PhD diss. University of Alabama. Retrieved from http://ir.ua.edu/handle/123456789/5261.

Hilliard, Chloe. 2020. "The New Black Body: My Case for Equal-Opportunity Cosmetic Enhancements." *The Atlantic*, January 28, 2020. https://www.theatlantic.com/health/archive/2020/01/new-black-body-cosmetic-surgery/605575/.

Hogue, Jacqueline V., and Jennifer S. Mills. 2019. "The Effects of Active Social Media Engagement with Peers on Body Image in Young Women." *Body Image* 28: 1–5.

Howard, Lindsay M., Kristin E. Heron, Rachel I. MacIntyre, Taryn A. Myers, and Robin S. Everhart. 2017. "Is Use of Social Networking Sites Associated with Young Women's Body Dissatisfaction and Disordered Eating? A Look at Black–White Racial Differences." *Body Image* 23: 109–113.

International Society of Aesthetic Plastic Surgery. 2020. "Global Survey on Aesthetic/Cosmetic Procedures, 2019." December 8, 2020. https://www.isaps.org/wp-content/uploads/2020/12/ISAPS-Global-Survey-2019-Press-Release-English.pdf.

Jackson, Sue, and Tiina Vares. 2015. "'Perfect Skin,' 'Pretty Skinny': Girls' Embodied Identities and Post-Feminist Popular Culture." *Journal of Gender Studies* 24 (3): 347–360.

Lamb, Sharon, and Aleksandra Plocha. 2015. "Pride and Sexiness: Girls of Color Discuss Race, Body Image, and Sexualization." *Girlhood Studies* 8 (2): 86–102.

Leahey, Tricia M., and Janis H. Crowther. 2008. "An Ecological Momentary Assessment of Comparison Target as a Moderator of the Effects of Appearance-Focused Social Comparisons." *Body Image* 5 (3): 307–11.

Leahey, Tricia M., Janis H. Crowther, and Jeffrey A. Ciesla. 2011. "An Ecological Momentary Assessment of the Effects of Weight and Shape Social Comparisons on Women with Eating Pathology, High Body Dissatisfaction, and Low Body Dissatisfaction." *Behavior Therapy* 42 (2): 197–210.

Lloréns, Hilda. 2013. "Latina Bodies in the Era of Elective Aesthetic Surgery." *Latino Studies* 11 (4): 547–569.

McClure, Stephanie M. 2017. "Symbolic Body Capital of an 'Other' Kind: African American Females as a Bracketed Subunit in Female Body Valuation." In *Fat Planet: Obesity, Culture, and Symbolic Body Capital*, edited by Eileen P. Anderson-Fye and Alexandra Brewis, 97–124. Albuquerque and Santa Fe: School for Advanced Research Press and University of New Mexico Press.

McRobbie, Angela. 2009. *The Aftermath of Feminism: Gender, Culture and Social Change.* London: Sage Press.

McRobbie, Angela. 2015. "Notes on the Perfect: Competitive Femininity in Neoliberal Times." *Australian Feminist Studies* 30 (83): 3–20.

Meier, Evelyn P., and James Gray. 2014. "Facebook Photo Activity Associated with Body Image Disturbance in Adolescent Girls." *Cyberpsychology, Behavior and Social Networking* 17 (4): 199–206.

Miller, Daniel, Elisabetta Costa, Nell Haynes, Tom McDonald, Razvan Nicolescu, Jolynna Sinanan, Juliano Spyer, Shriram Venkatraman, and Xinyuan Wang. 2016. *How the World Changed Social Media.* Vol. 1. London: UCL Press.

Mills, Jacqueline, and Matthew Fuller-Tyszkiewicz. 2018. "Nature and Consequences of Positively-Intended Fat Talk in Daily Life." *Body Image* 26: 38–49.

Mills, Jennifer S., Sarah Musto, Lindsay Williams, and Marika Tiggemann. 2018. "'Selfie' Harm: Effects on Mood and Body Image in Young Women." *Body Image* 27: 86–92.

Mull, Amanda. 2018. "Body Positivity is a Scam: How a Movement Intended to Lift up Women Really Just Limits their Acceptable Emotions. Again." *Racked on Vox*, June 5, 2018. https://www.vox.com/2018/6/5/17236212/body-positivity-scam-dove-campaign-ads.

Nesi, Jacqueline, and Mitchell J. Prinstein. 2015. "Using Social Media for Social Comparison and Feedback-Seeking: Gender and Popularity Moderate Associations with Depressive Symptoms." *Journal of Abnormal Child Psychology* 43 (8): 1427–1438.

Nichter, Mimi. 2000. *Fat Talk: What Girls and Their Parents Say About Dieting.* Cambridge, MA: Harvard University Press.

Perloff, Richard M. 2014. "Social Media Effects on Young Women's Body Image Concerns: Theoretical Perspectives and an Agenda for Research." *Sex Roles: A Journal of Research* 71 (11–12): 363–377.

Peters, Lauren Downing. 2018. "When Brands Use Plus-Size Models and Don't Make Plus-Size Clothes." *Racked on Vox*, June 5, 2018. https://www.vox.com/2018/6/5/17236466/size-appropriation-brands-clothes-plus-size.

Rottenberg, Catherine. 2014. "The Rise of Neoliberal Feminism." *Cultural studies* 28 (3): 418–437.

Salam, Maya. 2017. "Why 'Radical Body Love' is Thriving on Instagram." *New York Times*, June 9, 2017. https://www.nytimes.com/2017/06/09/style/body-positive-instagram.html.

Schooler, Deborah. 2008. "Real Women Have Curves: A Longitudinal Investigation of TV and the Body Image Development in Latina Adolescents." *Journal of Adolescent Research* 23 (2): 132–153.

Shannon, Amy, and Jennifer S. Mills. 2015. "Correlates, Causes, and Consequences of Fat Talk: A Review." *Body Image* 15: 158–172.

Sladek, Michael R., Rachel H. Salk, and Renee Engeln. 2018. "Negative Body Talk Measures for Asian, Latina (o), and White Women and Men: Measurement Equivalence and Associations with Ethnic-Racial Identity." *Body Image* 25: 66–77.

Sladek, Michael R., Renee Engeln, and Steven A. Miller. 2014. "Development and Validation of the Male Body Talk Scale: A Psychometric Investigation." *Body Image* 11 (3): 233–244.

Sturtz Sreetharan, Cindi L., Gina Agostini, Alexandra A. Brewis, and Amber Wutich. 2019. "Fat Talk: A Citizen Sociolinguistic Approach." *Journal of Sociolinguistics* 23 (3): 263–283.

Taylor, Nicole. 2016. *Schooled on Fat: What Teens Tell Us about Gender, Body Image, and Obesity.* New York: Routledge Press.

Taylor, Nicole. 2017. "Fat is a Linguistic Issue: Discursive Negotiation of Power, Identity, and the Gendered Body among Youth." In *Fat Planet: Obesity, Culture, and Symbolic Body Capital*, edited by Eileen P. Anderson-Fye and Alexandra Brewis, 125–148. Albuquerque, NM and Santa Fe, NM: School for Advanced Research Press and University of New Mexico Press.

Taylor, Nicole, and Mimi Nichter. 2017a. "Body Image: Supporting Healthy Behaviors on College Campuses." In *Further Wellness Issues for Higher Education: How to Promote Student Health During and After College*, edited by David S. Anderson, 19–37. New York: Routledge Press.

Taylor, Nicole, and Mimi Nichter. 2017b. "Studying Body Image and Food Consumption Practices." In *Food Culture: Anthropology, Linguistics and Food Studies*, edited by Janet Chrzan and John Brett, 58–69. New York: Berghahn Books.

Tiggemann, Marika, and Amy Slater. 2013. "NetGirls: The Internet, Facebook, and Body Image Concern in Adolescent Girls." *International Journal of Eating Disorders* 46 (6): 630–633.

Tiggemann, Marika, and Amy Slater. 2014. "NetTweens: The Internet and Body Image Concerns in Preteenage Girls." *The Journal of Early Adolescence* 34 (5): 606–620.

Tolentino, Jia. 2019. "The Age of Instagram Face: How Social Media, FaceTune, and Plastic Surgery Created a Single, Cyborgian Look." *The New Yorker*, December 12, 2019. https://www.newyorker.com/culture/decade-in-review/the-age-of-instagram-face.

Tovar, Virgie. 2021. "Athleta to Train Employees on Body Positive Language and Plus-Size Fit." *ForbesWomen*, January 21, 2021.

Yau, Joanna C., and Stephanie M. Reich. 2018. "Are the Qualities of Adolescents' Offline Friendships Present in Digital Interactions?" *Adolescent Research Review* 3 (3): 339–355.

Webb, Jennifer B., Erin R. Vinoski, Adrienne S. Bonar, Alexandria E. Davies, and Lena Etzel. 2017. "Fat is Fashionable and Fit: A Comparative Content Analysis of Fatspiration and Health at Every Size® Instagram Images." *Body Image* 22: 53–64.

Widdows, Heather. 2018. *Perfect Me*. Princeton, NJ: Princeton University Press.

4

THE POSITIVITY IMPERATIVE

Jayden, a tall, lanky Latino man, turned up at our meeting in an oversized black hoodie, jeans, and sneakers. A 19-year-old business major, he was soft-spoken, sitting slightly hunched over and making intermittent eye contact. When asked about social media, Jayden said he uses Instagram, Facebook, Snapchat, and Twitter. He posted on all four sites, but his favorite was Snapchat because it felt like a place where he could be himself without worrying about likes. On Snapchat, Jayden could see how many people and who had viewed his posts, but there is no mechanism for his friends to like or comment on posts. Sometimes friends would send him a DM (direct message) with a comment, but since they had to make a special effort to send a message, he did not expect to receive many.

Jayden had a conflicted relationship with social media. He had recently watched a video in his communications class about the downside of social media that made him more aware of how spending time online frames our sense of reality. He talked at length about how social media encourages us to compare ourselves to others in terms of attractiveness, body image, lifestyle, and adventure in ways that harm self-esteem. Jayden also had a lot to say about authenticity, which prompted us to ask what that word meant to him. He explained, "Social media is inauthentic because you can't express all sides of yourself, and you can't share your full range of emotions. It requires that you cultivate your image, that you be positive and fun all the time." He added that the feedback you get in the form of comments and likes gives you information about what people want to see and influences what you are willing to share.

Jayden avoided posting sad content. Even on Snapchat where he felt more freedom to be authentic, Jayden explained that he expresses all of his emotions except for sadness. He showed us examples of happy, funny, frustrated,

DOI: 10.4324/9781003182047-5

and angry posts. One Snapchat story was a video of Jayden ranting about his annoying roommate. In another video, he expressed excitement about getting a good grade on his history exam. He also showed us stories he prepared but never posted because he felt like they were too sad. One such story featured a photo of Jayden with a melancholy expression and the caption, "Not ready to leave Houston." While he felt it was okay to post mildly sad content, he felt his post about leaving Houston had crossed a line.

We asked what a mildly sad post would look like, and he replied that a photo where he is looking off into the distance with a vague caption like "Had better days" would be appropriate. Jayden explained that social media is an escape from the difficulties of everyday life, and that interjecting your sadness into someone else's feed ruined their experience. When Jayden wanted to communicate to his friends that he feels sad, he just stops posting for a while. Since he was so active on social media, when his friends did not see him post for a few hours, they would reach out through the direct message feature to ask if he is okay.

Jayden's narrative highlights several key themes that emerged in our study: social norms and tacit rules for posting; the struggle for authenticity on social media; and the many works of digital multiples, identity, and maintaining social relationships in online worlds. Jayden was not alone in his sentiments; students consistently described a social norm requiring that they show only positive emotions online, especially on Instagram. Another man captured this norm succinctly: "It's always about looking perfect, like I'm having a good moment; it's always me enjoying life…. Like, me on social media is perfect, but me in real life is not perfect."

This raised several questions for our research. Was the focus on positivity an imperative that had intensified in the era of social media? How did norms and expectations of positivity differ across online contexts? Further, given the importance of appearing upbeat, how and to what extent did young people express their negative emotions online? In this chapter, we address these questions, focusing primarily on Instagram. We also describe how other sites, such as Finsta (fake Instagram), Twitter, and Snapchat functioned as "emotional overflow" spaces where expression of sadness, anger, anxiety, and negativity were more acceptable. Finally, we discuss what students had to say about the imperative to portray a one-dimensional happy self, and we consider the impact of keeping negative feelings inside.

In her book on positive thinking, social commentator Barbara Ehrenreich explores the centrality of positivity in American culture.[1] Ehrenreich notes that a key component of positivity is optimism, which she defines as "a cognitive stance, a conscious expectation, which presumably anyone can develop through practice."[2] Optimism has long been a part of the American dream that posits hard work as a path to achievement and movement up the economic and social ladder. In late capitalism, consumer culture encourages individuals to strive for and aspire for more than they currently have. Positive thinking reinforces the idea that we deserve more if only we are willing to go after it, to work for it. Given this perspective, individuals bear personal responsibility for their successes and failures.

In today's social media environment, a belief in the value of hard work persists, albeit in new forms. The burden of working hard has shifted from laboring within formal structures (e.g., an industrial workplace) to a focus on creative self-enterprise. People are encouraged to invest time, energy, and capital in creating an imagined future that includes calculated strategies of branding the self to garner maximum attention.[3] The number of followers one has on social media is powerful evidence, visible to all, of one's social and cultural capital, which can be transformed into a career track (e.g., monetary or material capital).

Positive self-promotion on Instagram is a strategy employed by many emerging adults, particularly women, who cultivate their self-brand through positive affect, bodily display, and exuding "passion" about their activities.[4] Banet-Weiser explains that in the current economy of visibility, where visibility is the path to empowerment, women invest in "the desire to become a corporatized, consumable (popular) body."[5] She further notes, "For women and girls, the business of the self has largely meant focusing on personal attitude adjustment," meaning taking responsibility for exuding confidence and a positive outlook.[6]

This is not to say that the majority of college students we interviewed were involved in active entrepreneurial activities. Most were not. Rather, we suggest that elements of the cultural imperative to appear upbeat and passionate about one's life were pervasive across narratives. The positivity imperative has become seamlessly embedded into what Bourdieu refers to as *habitus*—cultural patterning that becomes second nature, internalized, and viewed as a natural part of existence.[7]

Previous research confirms a positivity bias on social media, that is, a tendency to post positive rather than negative affect.[8] This is particularly true on platforms like Instagram and Facebook as compared with Twitter, which allows for a wider range of emotions.[9] In Western cultures, rules for appropriate display of emotion favor the expression of positive emotions and the suppression of negative affect, particularly in the company of acquaintances and strangers.[10] It is only recently that researchers have turned quantitative attention to emotional expressions on social media.[11] To date, little ethnographic research has focused on this topic.[12]

Despite the gleeful display of positive affect on social media, nationwide statistics on the mental health of emerging adults portrays a different picture. Over the past decade, serious mental health concerns among this age cohort, including depression, anxiety, suicidal ideation, and self-injury, have all risen in prevalence and severity. Results of a ten-year study among 155,000 college students nationwide reveal that the percentage of students with lifetime diagnoses increased from 22 percent in 2007 to 36 percent by 2017; rates of treatment increased from 19 percent to 34 percent across these years. Thus, over this period, rates of diagnosed mental health conditions, including depression and suicidality, increased by almost two-thirds, with over one-third of college students reporting a diagnosed condition in 2016–2017.[13] The rates of emotional distress reported by college students in a recent nationwide survey ($n = 67,000$) found that 22 percent of students "felt overwhelming anxiety" in the past year and 20 percent "felt so depressed it was difficult to function."[14] Across the U.S., college counseling centers are struggling to meet the mental health needs of their students.[15]

What do we know about the impact of social media use on the mental health of emerging adults? Several large-scale studies suggest associations between time spent on social media and increased symptoms of depression and anxiety as well as lower psychological well-being.[16] Other studies report that frequent social media users report less happiness and more feelings of loneliness and social isolation.[17] Psychologist Jean Twenge suggests that frequent digital media use may affect psychological well-being because it displaces engagement in other behaviors more beneficial for happiness and mental health, such as in-person social interaction, exercising, and spending time outdoors.[18]

As a backdrop, the rise in a broad range of mental health concerns among emerging adults stands in stark contrast to the upbeat and happy presentation of self frequently seen online. In this chapter, we explore the positive presentation of self on social media and then turn to a discussion of how students presented online when they were feeling "less than perfect."

"Living the Life" on Instagram

In interviews, participants talked about tacit rules that influenced how they post and interact on Instagram, including an expectation that posts represent only the most exciting, adventurous moments. This sentiment was captured with the popular phrase, "living my best life," and was often included as a hashtag (#livingmybestlife). This catchall phrase was commonly represented through images of important milestones (e.g., graduation, awards, 21st birthday celebrations), having fun with friends (e.g., at a concert, party, or seasonal event), and adventurous activities or vacations (e.g., overlooking the Grand Canyon, splashing playfully in the ocean).

One study that analyzed social media posts divided the adventure category into two components: daring adventures, where a person is participating in a physically challenging event (e.g., rock climbing, running a marathon), or location adventures that occur in an "exotic" locale (e.g., a beach, the Louvre). Each makes its own statement about how a person is experiencing their best life; the daring adventure celebrates risk-taking, and the location adventure signals exploration. Both are important cultural values, especially for emerging adults, who are in the process of developing their identity and often engage in risk-taking to show they are living on the edge. Both images invite viewers to imagine the experience for themselves, perhaps with some degree of envy.[19]

In our interviews, we asked participants what kind of posts made them think someone was living their best life. Brody, a 21-year-old recent college graduate who worked as a yoga and meditation teacher, explained that living your best life is "kind of that living in the moment thing . . . to act boldly." He gave an example of "going on a trip, posing for grandiose pictures, like on the top of a mountain." When asked what being on top of a mountain says about someone, Brody said, "That they are going out and, like, exploring life, seeing all that it has to offer and really engaging life. They're adventurous and willing to go out and find new places and expand themselves in that way." Brody's analysis confirms and extends the study discussed above.

In a focus group discussion, a group of friends explained that the goal of posting is to "look like you're living this great life, like you don't have a single worry, like you can do whatever you want." An example given was "beautiful sunset photos" with captions that read "Loving the life in Maui," or "Living my best life in the Caribbean." These posts highlight the importance of the present in contemporary culture, with little connection to the past or future.[20] An emphasis on the present keeps posts light, without reference to a deeper context. Further, the person posting presents themselves as carefree and in possession of sufficient resources to do "whatever they want." It is noteworthy that many of the students in our study were working hard to support their college tuition and living expenses.

Regardless of what a person's day-to-day life actually looked like, it was important to cultivate an online image that showed your life was far from ordinary. Daniel explained:

> When you're living your average life, it's not too exciting. I'm not gonna get a picture of when I'm in class and be like, "Oh yeah, worked hard." Or, like, sleeping, or doing homework at the library, like, you do these things every single day, and none of them are exciting. So I'm not gonna post a photo of that on Instagram.

Daniel went on to describe the perceived tedium of everyday life:

> Like, people will wake up, they might go to the gym, go to work, they'll work from eight to five, they'll go home, they'll make dinner, they'll watch, like, a T.V. show, and then they'll go to bed. And it repeats every single day, Monday through Friday. And then on Saturday and Sunday, they might do something worth posting about.

Though the college students we interviewed did not work eight to five jobs, they spent their weekdays juggling classes, work, and studying. In the evenings, some exercised, and most watched television and spent hours scrolling through their social media to unwind from the day.

So how do these college students create online personas that make it appear that they are always socializing, having adventures, partying, and enjoying life when they only occasionally engage in these kinds of activities? Brody described a popular strategy:

> I know plenty of people who get a group of friends together on the weekend, get dressed up and go out, take all of these pictures, and then edit them so that they have things to share on social media from the weekend. So that you can show you're living your best life.

Amber, a business major from a coastal town, exemplified this strategy. When she returned home on college breaks, she and her friends engaged in hours long photo shoots of each other on the beach in bikinis, and she posted those photos throughout the break. She said that even though she spends plenty of time just hanging out in her house with her family, people think she has glamorous beach vacations when she is on break because of the way she posts on social media.

How to Avoid Looking Boring

Anthony, an outgoing sophomore who seldom posted, confirmed that he only shared happy moments on social media and talked about people he knew whose sole reason for going to parties was to appear to have an active social life.

> They secretly don't do anything, they just stand in the corner and post just to let people know they were there . . . to live up to the expectation that other people may have put on them, or to not look boring.

There are two important points here: First, Anthony articulates an expectation that if you are a college student, you are partying. Of course, many students do not fit this stereotype. However, given the imperative to show that you are living your best life, Anthony recognized that you could just go to a party, take photos, and not even interact with anyone. A second related point is that not having something to post could make you seem boring, like someone who had nothing to do. To appear boring is to reveal an absence of momentum or flow in your life—as if your life were standing still. A boring person is out of sync with the rhythms of social life.[21] An antidote to appearing boring was to post pictures of yourself at parties, which affirmed your identity as someone who had friends and knew how to have fun.

Heather, a self-described introvert, told us she usually preferred to stay at home, although she did go out sometimes. She explained the strategy she adopted to appear to have an active social life:

> I don't always post the pictures when I go out right away, because I like saving them. So, if I'm bored, I'll just post a picture. So, it's like, "Oh, she has a life. She's not just sitting at home."

Again, we see how giving others the impression that you are going out and having fun makes it clear that you are not a boring person, nor are you bored with your life.

Brian, an introspective and articulate student, equated boring with "being normal." As a result, he projected himself "as being always happy or always having a good time, always doing something adventurous, always having these great experiences." For example, if he posts that he is out to lunch with a friend, the caption would have to indicate that it is an exceptional lunch, like with a friend he had not seen in years as opposed to an ordinary lunch with a friend from his current, daily life. Not only would Brian appear boring if he posted himself doing "ordinary" things, he also risks alienating his friends and followers who would be uninterested in viewing posts that are sub-standard and fall beneath well-established expectations for presentations of self.

College students who are in a phase of experimentation with self-image can post photos of themselves in party settings to "play with" and embrace new identities. Anthropologist Peter Stromberg, drawing on the work of Dutch cultural historian Johan Huizinga, has written on the significance of play as a cultural phenomenon.[22] Huizinga describes play as an activity that entails a stepping out of real life into a temporary sphere of activity. "Play begins, and then at a certain moment it is 'over.' It plays itself to an end."[23] We can understand social media posts within this purview as it allows people to step out of the everyday to highlight or play at another identity, which they embrace for a delimited time. Perhaps because it is time bound, pictures of an altered self—such as a typically shy person surrounded by a group at a party—are acceptable to viewers. One's digital multiple provides an opportunity to present a self who is bolder and more fun loving than the offline self.

Laughter and Big Smiles

Students consistently described a social norm requiring that people exude happiness and laughter online. We confirmed this imperative by observing the commonality of posts featuring our participants laughing with others (Figure 4.1).

FIGURE 4.1 In this photo, Daniel captures the essense of the positivity imperative. Smiling and laughing, he exudes a sense of joy and excitement. His placement in front of a colorful graffitied wall accentuates his blue shirt.

Chloe, a communication major who repeatedly expressed excitement about participating in our study, explained:

> Like, with my friends and the whole capturing the laughter and stuff, it's definitely like you want to portray this idea that we're happy people. Like, we're happy friends, we always laugh like this and we always look like this when we laugh.

This portrayal of happiness and laugher sometimes extended beyond friendships to include family. For example, Andre, an animated theater major, posted a picture of himself with his family at his college graduation in which they were all laughing with their heads thrown back. Andre had clearly staged the photo; his mother and father looked a little uncomfortable, though they were playing along. He summed up the phenomenon of "capturing laughter" and happiness with the phrase, "Good vibes attract people." In other words, positivity attracts success, measurable by the number of likes received.

While extroverted students seemed to post open displays of laughter with ease, some shy students expressed sensitivity and discomfort with such displays. Brian had a subdued and serious demeanor during the interview. Thus, it was noteworthy when he said, "I have a tendency to always make, like, a happy or excited face, because I do think, for whatever reason, people respond to that burst of energy that comes out of the photo." It was difficult to imagine Brian appearing excited based on his affect in real life. Yet, true to his word, he wore a big smile and appeared excited in his posts, most of which focused on his participation in political events.

Brian clearly understood and had internalized what he called "the unspoken code of Instagram," explaining that "it would be weird if you made a post and you weren't happy or excited." Even so, he felt conflicted about participating in such a highly cultivated online world. He talked at length about the fake nature of people's online personas, and he struggled with a desire to be the same person across contexts, which he referred to as "authenticity."

> Instagram is . . . inauthentic in the sense that every post shows people happy and excited about life . . . and it doesn't reflect real life. Like if someone from another planet came and looked at Instagram and tried to formulate what life is like in the United States, they would assume that everyone's always happy and that everyone has their lives, like, put together. And there's no sadness. There's no awkwardness in life. People never get mad. It's really limited to expressing one emotion.

Despite this, Brian enjoyed sharing his experiences online and seeing what his friends were doing. This helped him feel more connected to people. Thus, he was a reluctant participant in the positivity imperative. The unified positive public image he described on Instagram greatly simplifies what he terms "real life" by airbrushing the messiness of everyday experience. College students did not want to appear complicated; they knew that others were not interested in the difficult aspects of their lives—those moments of awkwardness, anger, and sadness. The positive happy self is also the uncomplicated self who appears simply to enjoy life.

Similarly, Mariana, a reserved woman with a serious demeanor, explained that she grew up in a "rough neighborhood." As a result, she was reluctant to open up to people and slow to make new friends. She showed little affect during the interview, explaining that where she is from, expressing emotion is a sign of weakness that others can take advantage of or "use against you." Yet, during the interview, Mariana said, "Instagram is more of a happy place. My posts are usually very happy, excited or just like warm, very presentable, you know." Her posts were, in fact, happy and warm; in them, she was always smiling or making a playful kissing face at the camera. In one photo, Mariana smiles as she poses on the beach in a swimsuit and sunglasses. The caption reads, "So excited for my summer to start." Another photo features her and two girlfriends, all smiling with their arms wrapped around each other in front of an artistic graffiti style painted wall. The caption reads, "Happy to call you my friends." In an Instagram story, Mariana is singing along to a pop song with a halo of hearts floating over her head. The caption reads, "I'm obsessed with this song lol." These posts are striking because they do not resemble either Mariana's description of her personality or her offline demeanor.

The concept of digital multiples is at play here even within the seemingly one-dimensional happy person who appears on Instagram. For example, Mateo described himself as silly, playful, and always smiling. In the interview, his demeanor was easy going and casual. However, he said that online he showed two personas, both highly social and more polished. In posts with his girlfriend, he smiled sweetly and wrote "cheesy" captions about being in love. In posts with his guy friends, he aimed for a tough, "gangsta" look. For example, in one post he and a friend are at a club standing side by side in suits, each holding a cigar. Their expression is straight-faced and serious. His Instagram features several photos like this one. However, the vast majority of Mateo's posts with friends on Instagram show them all smiling or laughing with their arms around each other. In several photos featuring Mateo alone while on vacation in Italy, he is smiling as he looks up into the sunny sky, or his arms are outstretched, fingers spread wide, as he beams at the camera. Most of his Instagram posts exude a sense of fun, adventure, and excitement (Figure 4.2).

Mateo's description of his various online personas is important because it allows us to consider the gendered component of the positivity imperative in relation to digital multiples. In posts with his girlfriend, Mateo expresses love and enthusiasm about their relationship; in contrast, with his male friends, he projects himself as a tough guy. This reminds us that while emerging adults commonly display positivity online, they are far from monolithic in their behavior. Regardless of which persona he posted on Instagram, Mateo emphasized that his online self was "his perfect self" who enjoys life and projects confidence—a confidence that sometimes eludes him in his everyday life. In both his romantic posts and his "gangsta" posts, Mateo projects a simplified public image where there is one constant: He is always having a good time. What his posts hide is the labor required to both create and maintain these divergent selves.

So how does seeing all this positivity make viewers feel? Research in offline contexts has found that laughter is effective in eliciting a behavioral response; that is, the act of laughing or smiling broadly often results in others experiencing positive affect.[24] Laughter is contagious; research shows that when someone laughs, others in the surrounding environment immediately experience pleasure.[25] What do we know about the response to laughter in online contexts? Some researchers have found that emotional contagion does occur online— much like offline—and suggest that seeing positive posts on social media can evoke positive emotions among viewers.[26]

FIGURE 4.2 Here, Mateo's post exemplifies adventure and the excitement of traveling abroad. He poses in front of a church in Italy, possibly evoking a sense of envy or inspiration for his Instagram followers.

On the other hand, researchers who study social media from a social comparison perspective find that browsing other people's positive posts has negative effects on mood as it can evoke jealousy and feelings that others are living a better life than you are.[27] At present, much of what we know about people's emotional response to posts is based on experimental studies or survey research. Therefore, to explore this issue further, we asked students in interviews what emotions they felt when they scrolled through social media.

"It Stresses Me Out"

Most students told us they felt stressed while looking at other people's posts. When asked specifically what it was that stressed her out, Morgan, a self-described social media cynic, offered a litany of reasons: "Seeing people out doing things, seeing people have closer relationships than I have, seeing people move farther in life, seeing people prettier than me, seeing people happier than me, seeing people going out on adventures and doing things." While Morgan recognized that what people posted was fake, she spent a great deal of time online viewing others' posts and posting about herself; she needed "the hearts" from others for validation.

Similarly, Chloe talked about how she had "to validate her existence to be on social media," meaning that she couldn't just "be living her life" but had to make it appear to be larger than life because everyone else did. She described the feeling as:

> a weird sense of inferiority, because you just don't feel like you're part of this giant loop . . . that everyone else is a part of . . . and then you feel weird trying to tap into it, because you feel like you're trying really hard to get people to notice you or something.

Like so many other students, she understood that she needed to live up to a fake standard. In terms of identity management, emerging adults recognized that social media posts did not reflect offline life, yet many felt pressured to create their own fake content to compete. Engaging in this identity work helped them fit in and was a means to manage social relationships.

Another emotion that many students experienced on social media was jealousy. As one woman expressed:

> 'Cause it's like you're seeing everybody else's highlight reel, and you're like, "What am I doing with my life when it's perfectly fine?" I know that I'm bettering myself, getting an education. I'm doing a lot of great things in my life and my mom reminds me of that constantly. But, I mean, you see that, and it's jealousy, and it's terrible but it's there. You feel those things, and you're like, why can't I do this? Like, why can't I be on vacation, why can't I be getting engaged with a rock on my finger, like, you know . . . with all those things. Um, it sucks but it's there.

Her friend in the focus group confirmed that she also felt that way. For her, the jealousy was particularly intense when seeing friends who got into the college she had always planned to attend—until she did not get in. Another source of jealousy was seeing others traveling—getting to go to places where you wanted to go someday.

A recent study among college students examined the impact of social media use on students' emotional state. Eighty students completed a brief survey multiple times throughout a ten-day period on their most recent use of Facebook, Instagram, and Twitter. They reported how long they were online, what they were doing (e.g., scrolling, posting), and how they felt immediately afterward. Results reveal that the longer the students had been online, the greater their negative affect. Although the authors did not interview students, they attribute greater negative affect to social comparison. Observing others' posts about "living their best life," these students may have concluded that their own life was seriously lacking.[28]

While many studies confirm the heightened negative affect that people can experience after being online, our interviews provided further insight into this outcome. Students described how viewing others' positive posts resulted in a more nuanced response, dependent on several factors, including one's mood and mental state that day and whether the person was a close friend or a stranger. In other words, it was not simply viewing posts that made you feel that you were inadequate—not all posts elicit a similar response. We need to consider the social context within which students view online content. As one woman explained:

> Sometimes it makes me feel kind of inspired like, "Oh man, I want to go do something like that." But if I'm already in a worse mental state, or if I feel like that's not something that's attainable for me, then it's like upsetting and, like, maybe kinda stressful because it's like, "Well, I could be doing that, but I'm just sitting here in my room eating, like, a bag of Doritos."

Her friend in the focus group agreed that while social media invited comparison, it could also result in feeling happy for others and inspired. For example, if a friend from high school was studying something different from you and "interested in different stuff," you might think their post was "cool."

Olivia explained that the closer a post got to her own life experience, the more salient the comparison.

> If someone from the radio station where I work, who works in a really similar environment to me, or someone who's in one of my major classes and we're in a really similar place in our life, if they get to do something really awesome and incredible, that feels like a punch to the gut. Because it's like why didn't I do it? Why couldn't I do it?

At that point, her friend, Paige, an English major, confirmed this frustration, recalling how she felt when other students posted about getting their stories published in the college literary magazine. At that time, she chided herself saying, "Why haven't I done that yet?"

In a similar vein, Mateo described how seeing his friend's post about his team winning a soccer title had saddened him as he compared himself to his friend and was forced to come to terms with own decisions and fears. Mateo had turned down a soccer scholarship to that college because it was over a 1,000 miles away from home, and he believed that would be challenging for him. He had been an avid soccer player his whole life and deeply regretted giving up his dream of playing for a first-rate college team. His friend's soccer posts served as a constant reminder that he was missing out.

Some students could not articulate what they felt when scrolling. As Gavin explained, "Honestly, most of the time if I'm on Instagram, I'll just mindlessly flip through and not even really pay attention to what I'm seeing. I don't even know what kind of emotion that would be."

His friends in the focus group agreed, explaining that sometimes they felt bored or empty when on Instagram. Gavin expanded, "Empty, yes. That's a good word for it. Because you don't really feel anything, you just, you're like a robot flipping through, looking at things."

Through these examples, we see the range of emotions—sadness, jealousy, competition, inspiration, emptiness, boredom—that arise from viewing posts. Again, it is important to recognize that social comparison leads to different feelings depending on context. Factors such as the closeness of the relationship to the one posting, or the similarity in life experience, also affect one's emotional response. While this is not entirely surprising—and would be similar in offline relationships—social media does amplify and intensify the emotive responses of viewers, in large part due to the time spent online and the overwhelming number of comparisons one can make to others while scrolling. For many, the result of these comparisons was, as one student articulated, an "internal self-pressure to, like, have your shit together."

Expressing Negative Emotions Online

Because of the positivity imperative, many students downplayed and expressed hesitation to post about their negative emotions—including sadness, anger, disappointment, and worry. In some ways, this made sense because in our offline lives, we have all experienced running into someone you know when you are feeling down and out. In this situation, we may have observed ourselves answering the question, "How are you doing?" with a pre-emptive, "Just fine. Everything's great," knowing that our response was far from the truth. Therefore, it was not all together surprising that students were hesitant to reveal their emotional upheavals online.

While social media can facilitate communication and encourage emotional self-expression, some research has found that people consider "overly emotional" posts—a concept that is not well defined—a violation of appropriate behavioral norms.[29] Other studies have found that individuals do post both positive and negative emotional expressions online, although positive posts remain far more common.[30]

At present, few ethnographic studies have explored the reasons why young adults hesitate to post negative feelings online. Our interviews explored the following issues: How does a person's audience typically respond to a post expressing negative feelings? Do students have strategies for appropriate posting when sad or upset? What is the effect of showing one side of your emotional self (e.g., your happy side) to your online audience? We turn first to some of the reasons that students provided for not posting negative emotions and then move on to consider responses to the other questions.

"It's Nobody's Business"

A common reason for not posting sad or negative emotions was a widespread notion that it was none of anyone's business, especially when this related to something everyone experienced, like grades. Sofia, an education major who mostly posted selfies that featured her big smile, explained:

> Social media is the happy side. When I'm mad or sad I won't post about it. Like, for example, if I get a good grade, I'll post it. But if I get a bad grade, I won't post it (laughs).

Sofia elaborated by saying, "When I'm going through a tough time, like, I won't put my business out there."

Andre explained that he would not share anything about himself that was too personal, like when his grandmother was very ill or had just passed away. Similar to Sofia, his rationale was that his personal affairs were not anyone's business but his own. Even during his grandmother's illness, he recalled, "I didn't even do the whole 'pray for my Grandma . . . send me positive vibes' type thing." Andre preferred to share sad events with those who were close to him. As he explained, "I'll end up just texting my sister or I'll text my best friend because I have a strong support system in my interpersonal life." He expanded on other reasons for keeping his innermost feelings off social media:

> I won't post about negative things not because I don't think it's important but because I just don't think it's anyone's business . . . I just don't want to burden anyone else with my problems. And, like, the bottom line is that no one cares, like, just no one will care. And the thing is if you do care, then you would know what was happening already. I don't need to post that on social media, you know.

Andre recognizes that posting his problems would impose a burden on his friends who are online mostly for their own entertainment, not to deal with his personal issues. He also felt that he did not want to add his problems to a world already filled with so much negativity. "That's my burden to deal with, not other peoples'," he noted. Additionally, Andre believed that even if you have many followers (as he did with over 1,800), no one is really too concerned about what you are going through.

In his narrative, Cody drew a comparison between what people did online in terms of filtering out negative feelings from their posts to how people behaved offline in a public space, like a restaurant.

> Like, you're not going to let the person next to you in the line at Chick-fil-A know that you're having a mental breakdown. It's socially unacceptable, and maybe that's an extension of why I don't do it online, because I'm like, "It's nobody's business." Not that I necessarily care about over-sharing, just more like no one cares to help you normally. They're like, "Oh, well that's sad, but, like, it's not my problem, or it's none of my business, or I don't know that person that well."

Cody's observation that it was socially unacceptable to share one's mental health status with others aligns with research on the topic. Findings from a quantitative study among college students found that participants who had mental health concerns felt shame, believed that they were judged by others, and were embarrassed to seek treatment.[31]

As professors, however, we have both observed that students are increasingly willing to speak openly about their own mental health diagnoses and treatment. Recent research seems to confirm this trend among college students; a survey conducted among 33,000 college students across the U.S. found that 94 percent of students said they would not judge someone for seeking help for mental health issues. Nonetheless, about half of students surveyed believed that others might think poorly of them if they sought help, revealing the sensitivity of students to perceived stigma.[32] In one study conducted on a college campus, having mental health problems like depression or anxiety and seeking support indicated that one did not have their life together, or that they were a weak person who could not manage their own life. These perceptions made students hesitant to seek help from mental health professionals.[33]

Chloe referred to the indifference she perceived in response to her sad posts as "the mentality of nobody cares." When she posted something sad, she felt that "nobody cares about me because they will not respond, or keep tabs on me, so I'm like ok, then they don't want to be bothered and they don't care so I won't try to update them or whatever." Chloe went on to say that the lack of response on social media did not diminish her sense of self-worth, because she still had friends whom she could talk to in person. She differentiated herself from others who appeared not have any "real" friends, explaining:

> There's people that use social media because they literally have no friends in real life, so they just, like, let it rip on their social media, and they're just sharing their day, sharing their feelings, and sometimes it's comical because it's like those people don't talk to anybody. But they're like, I have virtual friends, so I'm just gonna share with them. But I've never

been that person, don't want to be. I like having face-to-face conversations with people.

In fact, many participants shared Chloe's belief that people who posted their sadness and emotional pain on social media lacked friends "in real life." The logic here was that if you had friends, surely you would prefer to share these intimate details of your life with them in face-to-face communication rather than posting it online for all to see.

The Risk of Showing Vulnerability

Another reason students cited for not posting sad or negative emotions on social media was concern that others might interpret it as a cry for help or attention. Cody observed:

> It's kind of sad that we feel like we can't tell each other that we're sad. Part of the reason why I don't post about feeling sad is because a lot of people get this vibe that the person is attention seeking and they just want somebody to talk to. And maybe that is what they're doing, but at the same time, they might not have anybody to talk to, so maybe they are attention seeking, but not in a selfish way, and they're doing it because they need somebody to talk to. There's so many, like, intricacies to this, it's so complicated, what you do and don't do online, and it's so different for everybody.

Cody went on to explain that while he thought it was important to be vulnerable, he had taught himself "the standard of what is allowed and what isn't" (on social media), so there was no way he was going to "spill his life out on Twitter." To the extent possible, he conformed to the standard of socially appropriate posting norms. It is worth noting that while students considered it acceptable, and indeed admirable, to call attention to how you are living your best life, they considered it unacceptable to call attention to the downturns in your life, even if temporary. This is another reminder that the easy-going, uncomplicated self is the gold standard of online life.

Several people said that they did not want others to pity them, and nobody wanted to be perceived as needy. Nicholas, a frequent poster, described himself as a person who "struggled with loss of immediate family members, loss of pets, loss of friends, depression, self-loathing, self-doubt, literally anything that you can think of, I've dealt with." He provided a powerful narrative about selectively sharing emotions on social media:

> If I'm going through a hard time, if I'm sad or upset, I typically will not post about it on social media, or even really brush on the topic. So

anything like that, if it's super personal, dealing with family, I won't post about that. . . . I literally remember times when I was crying and then five seconds later I'll retweet something funny or I'll tweet something funny myself. Knowing that I just cried, like, five minutes ago, because I'm in devastation over something.

Nicholas's description of crying and yet posting something funny seemed contradictory, so we asked him to explain why he would engage in what seemed like a "cover-up" of his feelings.

I guess because I just don't want anyone to know, I just don't want anyone to ask if I'm okay or feel that I'm not okay. 'Cause I've had experiences before, like, on and off social media where I've been too open, and it's not taken well by others. So, I just don't want anyone to think I'm being overdramatic, or I need help when I'm okay, I'm just going through something. . . . I just don't want to be seen in a negative light.

Nicholas believed that showing vulnerability online signaled weakness. This issue emerged when we asked how his posts changed when he was going through a hard time.

I think I try my best not to let them change. Even if I'm going through a horrible time in my life, I still try to stay true to my feed and post a happy memory. Because in a way, I'm not being disingenuous because I was happy in that picture. But I try my best not to post any sad pictures, because you don't want people to see that you're weak. It's definitely a thing with social media, especially since so many people follow you that you don't know. How would they react to something that's personal to you if they don't really know you? They might feel that you're being overdramatic. And weakness is definitely a thing. For so long, people feel that when someone shows emotion, you're weak, you're not strong. You can't deal with things like others can.

He went on to say that because everyone was using social media now, some of the cultural notions of appropriate behavior in the offline world—like always appearing strong, not weak—had now filtered into the world of social media.

Steven, a senior who was engaged to his girlfriend and headed for the Marines after graduation, discussed the gendered component of showing weakness and vulnerability, observing how this was particularly important for men.

I think some guys view feelings or emotions as vulnerability and guys hate being vulnerable. Societally, it's more acceptable to be vulnerable if you're a female, which is why in sexual assault cases, most guys who have been assaulted will never say anything. Because it's shaming to them. Guys don't like to be open. It makes them feel like they're weak.

He went on to describe how his own emotional health and his ability to show vulnerability with others had greatly improved from being in a serious romantic relationship.

The importance of not showing vulnerability on social media emerged as a norm shared by both the person posting and their audience, whose reaction could complicate things. As Mariana explained, if she posted that she was feeling sad or depressed, "People will either be overly concerned or they'll think I'm doing it for attention, you know." Not wanting either outcome, she explained that she never shared her real feelings because it served little purpose: "Telling someone, like what are they gonna do?" She was also concerned that posting could enhance her own vulnerability in terms of intensifying what she was feeling, as she was putting it out there for everyone to see. Talking about it could make it worse.

Brian wrestled with the dilemma of wanting to be authentic—defined as being able to share with others that he was having a bad day or going through a period of sadness—and not wanting to do this online in a public forum. While he recognized that he and others could break the norm and be vulnerable by posting feelings other than "I'm so happy," or "Look at me, my life is great," he was aware that the majority of people would not do that as it entailed social risk, meaning that it could result in losing followers or friends. He believed that more people spoke authentically in face-to-face conversation, in terms of both sharing their own problems and showing heightened empathy toward others who were going through a difficult period. He explained, "Online, I feel like there's no space in a majority of social media platforms to share the more vulnerable parts of life."

Focusing on the Audience

Digital multiples are at play here in the commonplace decision of many emerging adults not to disclose their problems online. We hear in participants' voices how they have internalized the norms of appropriate behavior, which dictate the necessity to project strength and not weakness. As a result, many students compartmentalized their emotions, strategically managing their online self to appear upbeat and carefree, while their offline self remained troubled. Some felt that this online persona would be more palatable to their audience and more in line with perceived cultural norms. For example, Morgan, a junior communication major who described herself as "tense, uptight, and scared of being judged," explained that on social media she presented herself as a "unique free spirited person," which was quite the opposite of the conformist she considered herself to be in her daily life. Morgan hid her anxiety in posts because she believed that would help her fit in better with her peers.

> I try and post things that other people find relatable because so often social media is fake happiness. Look I made Dean's List, look people are getting engaged, look at all these wonderful things happening in people's lives. So sometimes, I try and post things that make people laugh or make people feel positive. . . . I also put myself in the best light. I try and hide my loneliness and my isolation and a lot of my anxiety right now. I'm trying to figure out what I want to do and who I want to be. I realize how much I hate my major . . . and I don't really talk about that. You got to fake it till you make it is what I'm learning. And, um, social media is a really, really good tool to fake it, you know.

Because much of her audience were followers whom she did not know well, it was possible for her "to fake it till she makes it"—that is, put on a happy, together face until such time that she might actually feel that way. Morgan's relative anonymity from her audience benefitted the carefree image she had cultivated, effectively masking her real emotions from public view.

Students emphasized the importance of knowing your audience and being clear about what you were willing to show them; most agreed that they did not want to show others their personal turmoil. Many echoed the sentiment that their audience "would not be able to handle your problems" or "it would be a lot for my friends to see." Students described being uncomfortable when they saw others going through a hard time and suffering. One woman recalled seeing an Instagram post of someone's grandfather who was in the hospital dying. While she felt badly for the person and her family, she did not know how to respond. "I just thought the idea of liking it on Instagram was weird because it's something sad." In her opinion, this type of post was inappropriate because it caused discomfort for the audience and because, "It was just people's way of getting attention." In fact, according to several participants, a post had gone viral on Twitter depicting someone's grandparent lying dead in a hospital bed as a way of sharing the person's sadness and sense of loss. Those who brought up this post in interviews did so to underscore how inappropriate it was, all exclaiming emphatically that it had "crossed a line." If posting about a sad emotion or experience was not acceptable, then posting a depiction of death and all the sadness it encompassed was a major violation of social media norms.

Mindlessly scrolling through sites was a common way for students to pass time and feel entertained. Viewed through a lens of relaxation and pleasure, someone who posts a message that signals distress is failing their audience, intruding on their personal time, and changing their mood. In part, this is because there is not a recognized cultural norm of how to respond. Students raised many questions about emotional, sad posts that popped up on their feed (e.g., "I'm just struggling right now"), primarily because they wondered what they were supposed to do with this information. Now what, they asked? How am I supposed to deal with this? Should I reach out to the person? Should I worry about them? Are they manipulating people? Are they crying out for attention? Are they just being funny? These types of questions disrupted the power of the audience to be indifferent to other people's feelings, infringing on the act of mindlessly scrolling. Thus, students viewed posts that expressed or alluded to sadness and emotional upheavals as an imposition on other's time and space.

Researcher Donna Freitas interviewed and surveyed college students at several universities around the U.S. and identified similar responses to what we found about posting unhappy emotions online.[34] In a survey, she asked students to respond to the statement, "I am open about my emotions on social media." Only 19 percent of students agreed; over 75 percent disagreed. One woman in her sample described how others "just want to see you conform. . . . People believe that if you're happy, then everything is good, so you don't have to do anything."[35] Freitas writes:

> If everyone plays along and pretends that all is well, then the "audience" gets to feel at ease, even apathetic about everything they see. . . . Viewers get to remain just that—passive viewers, scrolling through their feed and nodding their heads and never really having to engage anyone on a level that is real.[36]

To be clear, while some people expressed annoyance or apathy at posts that displayed personal struggles, others expressed greater sensitivity. One student, for example, recognized that while many people would not feel drawn to help someone who expressed emotional hurt online, he felt compelled to reach out and help in some way. "It doesn't have to be a big over the top thing. It can be something small because that may be all someone needs."

Strategies for Posting When Upset

So, if college students are largely conforming to the imperative to post happy images of themselves, are there ways to turn emotions considered unpalatable into something more acceptable? From interviews and observations of students' social media, we identified a range of strategies, many of them with the purpose of eliciting a response, albeit indirectly. Chelsea, a freshman who described herself as artsy, was typically reticent when it came to posting something emotionally difficult because she recognized that her feelings were probably temporary, but her posts could be permanent. She also did not want others to see her as a needy person.

> Sometimes I have a problem posting when I'm upset because I do want somebody to reach out but (laughs) I'm a little bit crazy in that sense. I

don't like directly asking for help. I kind of expect others to get the hint. So, I'll do that a lot, but I think other people do it as well.

One commonly used strategy for indirectly signaling that you are going through a difficult time on social media was to joke about it. One woman explained:

> Whenever I got upset I'd put on this one filter and I'd be like, "I'm upset part 30 and I'm upset part 31" and I just went on like that. It was half a joke, but I was actually upset each time I posted. But it was funny to me, so I just kept on going with it. It made me feel better even though I was still upset.

When asked how people responded, she explained that she got likes, but people would not reach out to her until they met in person when they might ask, "Hey what's wrong?" In her response, she minimized her real feelings of being upset. "I would say something like, 'Oh I just, I dropped my cup of water on myself or whatever. It wasn't anything serious ever.'" By framing her emotional upset in humor, she avoided talking about her issues.

Some women talked about seeing lots of "casual suicide jokes" or people posting offhanded comments like "Oh, I have so much homework, I'm gonna go jump off a cliff." While they realized these were jokes, they recognized that when you posted in that way "all the time, it does, like, get in your head." Another concern was that stating an intent to self-harm could trigger someone else who was feeling stressed to take action. They recalled how people used to post a smiley emoji with a gun next to it, a symbol indicating that someone was shooting their self in the head. The gun emoji was changed to a water pistol a few years back.

Some people framed their stress or sadness by posting a meme. For Diego, a self-described rapper who took pride in his unique sense of style, memes coupled with a motivational quote posted by others were helpful in his own mood regulation. As he noted, "It's just like, say you're having a bad day and then you read one, and you're like, well that's pretty good, so . . . ," indicating that it lifted his spirits and could change his perspective on what he was going through.

Another participant who spoke about memes was Aliyah, a freshman who described herself as socially anxious. Aliyah provided an example of a friend who posted a picture of a three-year-old girl crying, with a caption that read, "Me when I found out that I have two tests tomorrow and three homework assignments due that I haven't done yet." When asked what the caption said to her, Aliyah replied:

> That she's stressed out. But of course, it's just more dramatic online when you post a meme and a dramatic caption. I mean, she doesn't really have three homework assignments and two tests, but it still tells you, "I'm stressed out and I want to rant about it."

Another strategy was to post about a difficult experience once you had moved past it, and then reframe it as a "life lesson" or a "great feat" that you had overcome. To this end, some people posted inspirational quotes to index what they had gained from the hardship they experienced. Chelsea described how she posted when she felt like she was "fighting depression":

> I don't think my posts change in a noticeable way. I feel like when I'm going through something tough, I just want to figure out why or what I can do to resolve it. So, I do a lot of thinking. You know, I feel if I can bring myself out of it a little bit and come back with a lesson, I like to share that. I don't think that's very noticeable to others because it doesn't really come across in a sappy way or anything. But it's just like, okay, I realize this, and it helps me so maybe it could help somebody else.

The advantage of this approach was that by posting at the conclusion of her experience, Chelsea spared her audience the need for involvement, as she had already resolved the situation. Chelsea also recognized that this strategy allowed her to talk around issues like depression but "not like flat out say that I have these things." A general rule was that viewers did not like off-putting topics, like learning that someone was depressed.

In accord with Chelsea's comment, there was a widely held idea that it was okay to post about sadness if you felt your insight might be of use to others, especially those who would be reluctant to share their own vulnerability. Andre typically did not post when he was upset but made an exception for something that might help others.

> If something sad happened and I think that this might help someone else who may not want to speak out about it and will find comfort in it, I will post it. You know what I mean? If it's something like, "Oh I didn't get the part in the play," and I think that that's gonna help someone else, I will post it.

Extending the idea of the life lesson approach to emotional posting, Kristen, a self-described nature lover who taught yoga, critically observed that when someone posts an inspirational quote and talks a little bit about their experience, it truncates the actual vulnerability that one feels. "It kind of nips it in the bud," she explained, "In real life we're not always resolving our issues in a 30 second readable post." She compared this compression of experience to television programs, which had to "wrap up" within a short time frame, explaining:

> A lot of people's idea about posting is you want someone to know everything about you in just one post. So you have to have the beginning,

middle and end—and that follows all the ranges and emotions that you're allowed to post. It's like you have to resolve it.

Nicholas also alluded to the importance of the resolution in posting something sad, noting how you need to "have a happy note at the end. Just to always let them know that you're still good, you're doing fine. 'Cause you have to, like, display the best you are on social media, your best life."

Another strategy that allowed people to communicate sadness indirectly was to post an artsy picture of themselves, particularly on Instagram. As Mariana described, to do this effectively, the photo needed to be black and white with the person looking wistfully into the distance, evoking a solitary self, a sense of loneliness. Another type of photo that evoked sadness was posting a picture in bed, under the covers. Posts of this kind were an evasive technique that helped the individual present real feelings in a masked manner. Designed to pique a modicum of concern from one's audience, this evocative approach to posting often included a vague caption, such as "Had better days," or "Today's not my day." This was a way of further signaling distress, allowing a person to express that they were having a hard time but were not comfortable saying so directly. The "vague caption strategy," created to elicit concern from the audience, is well recognized and has been termed "vaguebooking." Urban dictionary defines this as "an intentionally vague Facebook status update that prompts friends to ask what's going on or is possibly a cry for help."

Going Silent

Participants explained that they would just go quiet when they were experiencing emotional upheaval. Going quiet (or "going ghost") indicated to others that something was wrong, oft times prompting them to reach out. As Jayden, the student featured in our opening vignette, noted:

> People are just like, "Oh, he hasn't posted in a while." That's a big deal on Snapchat. Like, I have a friend who posts a lot every day. If I know that he hasn't posted in, like, two days, I'll think, "Oh, something's wrong, so I need to go ahead and check on him." So I'll snap him, "Like what's wrong, you haven't posted anything in a while?"

He and others explained that after a while, the person would re-engage online providing a vague reason for why they had stopped posting. "I think it just picks back up whenever you're feeling fine again." When silent, typically close friends observed your absence, rather than the broader audience.

Going silent rather than sharing your negative feelings was a somewhat risky approach, because one needs to be continually present on social media to maintain a following. Nicholas expressed concern that he could lose followers over lack of content if he did not post "for a really long time," which he defined as "like four days." He felt that people would notice his absence and would question, "Like, where did he go?" Nicholas explained:

> There's pressure to stay active on social media for sure. Like, sometimes you just will not be in the mood to post, you don't have content to post because you've been going through hardships in your life to where you're not out and about like you would usually be as much. So, but there's still pressure to post, to maintain followers, to maintain image.

With a large audience expecting to see his latest posts, Nicholas speculated that going silent could result in undesirable consequences. Not only would viewers wonder about his absence, but also they might also find others to follow.

Alternative Spaces for Emotional Expression

Some of the students we interviewed told us about alternate social media forums where it was acceptable to express emotional difficulties, including Finsta ("fake" Instagram accounts), Twitter, and Snapchat. We came to think of these sites as emotional overflow spaces, that is, a safe space where negative emotions not typically seen on Instagram could be expressed. Though few of our participants admitted to having Finsta accounts themselves, many had these accounts in middle and high school that they had since deleted, and some had college friends and significant others with these accounts. Finsta accounts are set up to be anonymous, with a fake name and profile picture and privacy settings enabled, making it difficult to find the person by searching their name on Instagram.

Generally, people allowed only a small group of close friends to follow their Finsta accounts. Anthony described Finsta as a "locked vault" that only a few people have access to, explaining, "It's a way to express yourself without the whole world seeing it." Students told us Finsta is a place for any content you don't want everyone on Instagram to see, including things that are funny, silly, risqué (e.g., partying, engaging in sexual behavior), and emotionally vulnerable. It is a place for expressing one's unfiltered self on Instagram. Diego explained that he has friends who share their sadness and difficult experiences on their Finsta accounts. For example, he had recently seen Finsta posts by friends featuring a photo of a blank piece of paper or themselves along with a lengthy paragraph about how their day went and how they were feeling. He said, "Finsta is for people who are too scared to, like, post who they really are on their real Instagram. I feel like they don't wanna show people the real them."

Steven felt that people who post on Finsta "come off as really depressing." He provided examples of emotional posts he has seen on friends' Finsta accounts:

Just about, like, their problems, like, how hard life is, and "this is really difficult for me right now, and I feel like I have no one to talk to." And then their regular Instagram is more like typical Instagram, like all the good things in their life.

Steven was highly critical of the practice of expressing drastically different sides of oneself on different social media platforms, to the extent that he refused to follow his girlfriend's Finsta. He explained, "I feel like it's like a personality disorder thing, like, where these people have their negative side on their Finsta, and not negative necessarily, but realistic, I guess, like closer to how they're actually feeling." Hailey, an anthropology major who brought her ferret to the focus group discussion, described Finsta as a "free for all." She said:

> I don't like the term, "fake Instagram" because it's not fake. It's a real account. They made the account so they can be, like, real and express their feelings. Like, that's the real person, versus the account that they show everyone else.

Students' use of Finsta provides an example of digital multiples, referring to how students intentionally cultivate their personas differently across social media platforms. As "everyone" knows, Instagram is a place to show your happy self, your best life self. Finsta, on the other hand, is a space for expressing emotions that would be unwelcome on Instagram. Hailey challenges the idea that Finsta is fake because she sees it as a space where people can share their true emotional state. Others, like Steven, felt uncomfortable with the divergent identities that appeared on different platforms. In fact, he felt so troubled by the divergent digital multiples he observed on his girlfriend's Instagram and Finsta accounts that he refused to even look at her Finsta account. It did not match his sense of who she was.

Several women participating in a focus group pointed out that many negative and sad feelings turned up on Finsta, but they were easy to dismiss. One participant, Carrie, offered the following example:

> I saw one of my friends on her Finsta straight up say, "Oh, I haven't taken my anti-depressants for this amount of time. Let's see how this goes," kind of thing. And, you know, it's framed in a way that's like, "Ha, ha, we'll see how my life goes." But that's a serious thing, like she's taking those pills for a reason. And, like, this is something that's important, and, like, impacts her day-to-day life, but it's framed in a way that's like, "You only live once, like, whatever."

Carrie's reflection on her friend's light-hearted presentation of such a serious issue captures the levity of mental health dilemmas that have come to characterize the social media era. Emerging adulthood is a time when people engage in risk-taking as a way to display the different sides of themselves. Particularly for women, showing that they could live on the edge and be carefree about their health could be a statement of empowerment.

Twitter

Like Finsta, Twitter was an online space where "anything goes." Nicholas said, "I feel that frustration, anger, sadness, and happiness are portrayed a lot through Twitter. You can convey emotion through Twitter. That's what I see the most." Twitter was a space for expressing emotions by re-tweeting widely recognized cultural artifacts, like memes, song lyrics, or lines of popular poetry. For example, Natasha, an education major who maintained an active presence across her sites, described Twitter as a place for doing things, like:

> re-tweeting common things, like, how I feel. Like, if I'm having a bad day I post how much I want wine or how much I want to just lay in bed or something. Or I'll re-tweet memes of something that I'm feeling at the moment that other people were feeling, too. I think that's pretty cool, so I just re-tweet and let everybody know I'm feeling the same thing (laughs).

Diego not only posts his sad emotions on Twitter when he is having a tough day; he also describes himself as a "sad boy" on Twitter, embracing the emotion as part of his online identity:

> There's this thing called "sad boy hours," where it's a time between 2 and 4 a.m., where you're just lonely and sad. Being a "sad boy" means that you're a very sensitive boy. I'm a sensitive boy in real life, so I do sensitive stuff on social media, I guess.

As an example, he described a Halloween picture that he posted of a kid dressed up in costume with a caption that read, "I don't wanna grow up." Diego saw the sad boy hours as a Twitter community where he could freely express his sad emotions with others who could relate. Urban dictionary defines sad boy hours as "the act of young and independent men who come together to talk about their depression."

In one sense, expressing emotion through memes and lyrics serves as a distancing strategy, like "vaguebooking," in that you are revealing something about yourself indirectly through another person's words and images. Also, the words and images are decontextualized, which can obscure their meaning, inviting multiple interpretations. However, re-tweeting emotional expressions through memes and lyrics was also a statement about shared emotional experiences. Every person who re-tweets a poignant meme or song lyric signals that they can relate to what the original person who posted was feeling and experiencing. Re-tweeting allowed students to feel like they are part of a larger community who share similar feelings.

Though Finsta and Twitter both serve as emotional overflow sites, there is a major difference worth noting: Finsta is private and Twitter is public. Even though Twitter users can choose to make their profiles private, the students we interviewed all had public accounts and took for granted that this was the norm. We wondered what it was about Twitter—especially given its public and sometimes volatile nature—that invited emotionally vulnerable posts. Nicholas explained:

> It's really interesting to see 'cause I could be reading something so personal, someone sharing their story, or a family story, alcohol, drugs, depression, school, immigration, being gay, everything. Like, literally so many issues go on Twitter, and it's such personal things to read. And you forget that you're just reading it off of a username. Like, you don't even know this person, but you know so much about their story because of what they're choosing to put out there.

Even though Twitter is not truly anonymous unless you set up a fake account or make your account private, which was not common among our participants, students seemed to feel a false sense of anonymity because of how the site functions. On a public Twitter account, anyone can follow another person without their permission, which means it is normal for total strangers to connect on the site. In addition, it is common for people who are active on Twitter to tweet and re-tweet multiple times throughout the day, which quickly buries posts in their feed. Chances are good that if someone has not seen your tweet within an hour or two of posting, they will probably never see it. The rapid posting culture of Twitter lowers the stakes and impact of a post, which may contribute to people feeling freer to share the full range of their emotions on the site.

Snapchat

Students had less to say about Snapchat than Finsta or Twitter as a space for emotional overflow, but it is worth discussing briefly. Participants likened Snapchat to Twitter in the sense that both are spaces where people share sad emotions and difficult experiences. As Nicholas explained:

> Like, I've noticed that with friends who post on Snapchat or Twitter, like, they just broke up with their boyfriend, so it's nothing but sad posts. Like, "I can't believe he did this," "When will I feel okay again?" Or, like, "another sleepless night," or "this and that," and you're like, okay, well, this person is obviously going through something that is affecting them.

One woman explained, "Sometimes on Snapchat I'll post just, like, a black picture and have words, like, 'Today's not my day,' or something like that. I think Twitter is similar. People do that as well on there." Another woman told us that Snapchat and Twitter are similar in that both are places where people will "post anything." She explained, "They'll be like, 'Oh yeah, having a bad day.' I'll post, like, 'Guys, I just failed a test, okay, cool, bye.'"

Because students perceived Snapchat as a personal, intimate space, they felt comfortable revealing vulnerabilities. The impermanent nature of Snapchat posts emboldened many people to share personal aspects of themselves they would not normally share online, including sadness. As Diego explained:

> As for Snapchat, it's just, it's personal, like people who I talk to, who I know personally. . . . I'll send them, like, ugly pictures of me, and stuff like that. I can be personal on Snapchat and post feelings there.

Jayden used Snapchat to share the more mundane, day-to-day experiences that included a fuller range of emotions. He said his posts reflected his mood of the day. For example, during final exams when he feels stressed, he will post a series of selfies throughout the day where he looks tired. If he is in an upbeat mood, then he will share funny posts all day long. Upon reflection, he noted that several of his friends have daily mood themes on Snapchat as well, especially "that theme of having a bad day."

> Yesterday one of my friends posted that her dress was torn by the door. And then she's talking about how her eyeliner had messed up when she rubbed her eye, or something like that. She just showed how bad her day was going through Snapchat.

Like Finsta, most students who used Snapchat restricted their followers to close friends. However, some allowed people outside of their intimate offline circle to follow them on Snapchat, and they had to work a little harder at managing their image. Most did this by posting generic, emotionally even keel content to their Snapchat stories for all to see, and direct messaging anything emotionally revealing, personal, or vulnerable to their close circle of friends.

Chelsea employed a slightly different strategy. She posted everything to her story, which compelled her to manage her Snapchat identity in a similar way to how she managed her Instagram identity. Chelsea told us she vents and complains a lot on Snapchat.

> I've been having a hard time finding a job recently. And I'll just post a video, it's like, "I'm so tired of this," you know. Venting, sort of. Like, "Can you believe the shit day I've had because of, like, this and this?" But I put a funny twist on it so it's not, like angry. I try to make it light.

In line with posting norms on Snapchat, Chelsea felt freer to express her sadness and frustration. Yet, she also felt pressure to keep it light because her followers represent both close friends and acquaintances.

Mental Health as a Joke on Social Media

Steven expressed concern about how mental health issues appeared on social media, observing that Twitter posts had "degraded mental health as far as, like, the seriousness of it." He went on to explain, "Words like *college student* and *depression* or *college student* and *anxiety* have just hundreds or thousands of shares, and there's almost, like, a comedic side to it, like people are trying to make it a joke." When asked to expand on his thoughts, Steven said:

> It's not like they're making fun of people who are actually depressed, but if you were to look at a post about depression on Twitter, you would think, "Wow, there's like 12 million people who are depressed who are college students," which is just not true. It's just something where people feel like they belong all together, and they associate with each other. We're all going through something. . . . I don't know if my generation is just not as apt to deal with things that come their way or if there really are that many people who feel like they're depressed. Mental health is joked about on Twitter a lot. It gets shares and retweets and followers and favorites.

When asked to provide an example of the kind of posts he was talking about, he offered, "Oh, I thought I did well on my test and I got it back and it was, like, a 60 and now I'm going home to kill myself." He went on to explain:

> We all know you're not—at least, I hope you're not—going to go home and kill yourself, but there's people who actually do feel that way. If you're that person and you're seeing 300,000 people laugh at that situation, it's just not healthy. A lot of people don't really know how to articulate themselves, or how to have conversations with people in real life. I feel like those are the people who thrive on Twitter, the people who just aren't capable of having healthy human interaction, or they just don't know norms, that you just don't say that. Because that's not right, you know?

Steven highlights two important points about social media: First, some college students refer to their own mental health in such a flippant manner (e.g., "I got a bad grade so I'll kill myself") that it trivializes the suffering of those who might be at risk for committing suicide. In the online world, there is little opportunity to evaluate if the speaker is serious or not. While this type of comment might be dismissed as a joke when uttered in a passing conversation with a friend—or be followed up by questions to determine its veracity—in the online context, one's audience cannot evaluate the sincerity of the threat. Perhaps because such a comment is difficult to interpret, others make light of it as a distancing strategy. Second, Steven believes that many people "aren't capable of having conversations," implying that people his age are losing the ability to openly discuss their feelings. This concern, discussed earlier, emerged from the narratives of many college students.

A recent article in a college newspaper explored the impact of mental health jokes on campus, especially at a time when so many are experiencing anxiety and depression.[37] The author describes two popular posts exemplifying mental health jokes that circulated on a college meme page. One is an Instagram post stating that death is an escape from the burden of student loan debt, and the second is a Tumblr meme featuring a sleeping cartoon character with the caption, "Me going to sleep at 3 a.m. knowing my suicidal thoughts are getting progressively worse and I'm doing nothing to stop them."[38] It is clear that these types of posts appear on many social media sites (Twitter, Finsta, and Tumblr, to name a few). While humor has long been considered a coping mechanism that can have benefits, dark humor can also normalize and trivialize suicidal thoughts, making it difficult to distinguish when someone is "just joking" and when they are in need of help. As Steven noted, social media has desensitized young people to the point where seeing a post like "I'm going to kill myself so I won't have to take this exam" hardly raises an eyebrow.

Consequences of the Positivity Imperative

For most students we spoke with, a one-dimensional portrayal of a happy self did not adequately reflect the emotional vicissitudes of their everyday offline lives. Some participants were able to articulate how this dilemma played out in their lives, recognizing how it differed depending on the site. Cody explained:

> Any social media—no matter what you post—it's always edited because you're thinking of the best way to get those feelings out, and then it's reducing this three dimensional person into this two dimensional thought that can be interpreted in so many different ways, you know? So, like, even on Twitter when I'm making stupid jokes, or everyone is making a joke about being depressed or whatever, like, that's such a loaded message, and it's so deep for everyone, and it just kind of turns it into this, like, "I'll be okay, whatever." You know what I mean? And then on Facebook it's like you just don't even acknowledge that kind of stuff. You just say, like, everything in life is fine. It's kind of like when people ask, "How are you?" and the socially acceptable response is either "good" or "okay."

Although Cody acknowledges how site-specific norms determine presentation of self, his comments also highlight the complexity of emotional experience, specifically how an online context can smooth over the nuanced range of emotional expression. At the same time, he acknowledges that most people hide their deeper emotions and vulnerability offline as well.

Brody observed that the need to self-present as a happy, upbeat person was having serious consequences for his generation. From his perspective, "When you're online you're always interacting with partial people . . . things that they have determined that you get to see about them with the things that you have determined they get to see about you." Using a baseball analogy, he went on to say, "There are no curveballs if you get to plan everything in advance." Because of these highly curated presentations of self, Brody believed that young people had difficulty engaging in spontaneous conversations where they lacked control over the interchange.

> So even just face-to-face interactions that go beyond, "Hey, how are you doing?" are something people don't do often. It definitely bolsters social anxieties because it's like, I don't show any of these people my vulnerabilities. I can't hide that shit in real life, what if it comes out? And so better than having that come out and having somebody see that and identify me with that thing, I just, like, won't talk to people. I'll just sit here.

He recognizes that since the element of control is absent in interpersonal interactions, people experience more discomfort and social anxiety when they are talking to people offline. His depiction of "partial people"—that is, people who allow others to see only a part of themselves—is an apt and powerful description given the culturally appropriate norm of always posting positive.

Kristen conjectured that a potential outcome of suppressing negative feelings online was that it becomes increasingly difficult to share these feelings with others in offline contexts. She thought that, at most, people had one friend that they reached out to, but that, in general, most people suppressed their feelings. When asked to explain this observation, she said:

> I think it really boils down to a fear of intimacy. People are just really scared to connect if they don't have the opportunities to connect. So, if they're suppressing their feelings and they are constantly telling themselves their feelings are invalid if they're not this way (happy) and they feel like they can't even talk to somebody about it, then they're losing that practice of talking through it. So, in the long run, you're really hurting yourself, you're kind of numbing yourself in a sense. . . . I think you can't help but build up that subconscious distinction between what's acceptable and what's not because you're placing a lot more value on sharing positive

things than you are on the non-shareables. I think in the long run you're gonna reaffirm, reaffirm, and reaffirm to the point of really suppressing what's not happy.

Kristen's concern is that, over the long term, not sharing the range of your emotions might desensitize you to your real feelings. The distinction between what she terms "sharables" and "non-sharables" is useful for our discussion because it aptly captures the dichotomy between what is culturally appropriate to post and what is not. In Kristen's analysis, the cultural emphasis on the "sharables" leads to a continual use of this "muscle," and at the same time, our ability to discuss our deeper (non-happy) feelings diminishes as that muscle memory weakens and erodes. It is a sobering analysis of her generation.

Summary

In interviews, most students described the pressure they experienced to appear happy and excited in their posts, even during times of personal emotional upheaval. Repeatedly, we heard about the mandate to show that you were "living your best life," and students described numerous strategies for doing so even when their life was dull. Given the positivity imperative, it has become more important than ever to conceal the fluctuations of one's daily emotional life. Students spoke openly about the fake nature of people's cultivated online presentation of self but remained active participants themselves. Across social media sites, the work and purpose of digital multiples was a repackaging of emotional expression to present an airbrushed emotional self, where culturally undesirable internal states (e.g., anger, frustration, anxiety, sadness) were flattened and smoothed out, if not entirely erased. This process was similar to erasing one's perceived external flaws, such as blemishes or body fat.

Why did emerging adults do this? Many students, both women and men, expressed concern that others would see them as weak or vulnerable. They worried that posting about their emotional struggles might make them appear needy, that they were asking others to take care of them. This would require emotional labor on the part of their audience, who they perceived to be largely unequipped (and unwilling) to take on a task of this nature. Further, it was deemed culturally inappropriate to impose on one's friends and followers who were online to mindlessly scroll through sites for their own entertainment. Ultimately, showing need and vulnerability could lead to a loss of followers, and was thus a risky venture. While not revealing one's emotional problems to others is certainly not unique to the age of social media, it does carry distinctive challenges in this historical moment. Because of a limited and premediated presentation of self in online settings, emerging adults may feel increasingly uncomfortable showing vulnerability in offline settings where there is little opportunity to preplan and curate one's self.

Psychologist Sherry Turkle has painted a sobering picture of how excessive time on social media can lead to reduced intimacy, empathy, and self-reflection among youth. Turkle concludes that young people feel isolated and fearful of face-to-face interaction because they spend so much time online.[39] Our interviews with emerging adults did not fully confirm Turkle's observations. While the cultural norms of social media certainly contributed to emerging adults hiding their vulnerabilities and emotional struggles, we found that most students were acutely aware of this dilemma and were interested in talking about it. They wrestled with the imperative to present an authentic self while masking their feelings. Rather than having reduced self-reflection, students valued the opportunity to examine and reflect upon the differences between communications across contexts.

Notes

1 Ehrenreich 2009.
2 Ibid., 4.
3 Duffy and Hund 2015; Marwick 2013.
4 Banet-Weiser 2012.
5 Banet-Weiser 2018, 88.
6 Ibid., 77.
7 Bourdieu 1984.
8 Reinecke and Trepte 2014.
9 Waterloo et al. 2018.
10 Brotheridge and Grandey 2002.
11 Waterloo et al. 2018; Wirz et al. 2021.
12 Ross 2019.
13 Lipson, Lattie, and Eisenberg 2019.
14 American College Health Association 2019.
15 LeViness et al. 2019.
16 Shakya and Christakis 2017; Twenge and Campbell 2018; Wirtz et al. 2021.
17 Primack et al. 2017; Twenge, Martin, and Campbell 2018.
18 Twenge 2019.
19 Goodnow 2016.
20 Ibid.
21 Brissett and Snow 1993; Hall 1983.
22 Huizinga 1955; Stromberg 2009.
23 Huizinga 1955, 104.
24 Gervais and Wilson 2005.
25 Owren and Bachorowski 2003.
26 Tandoc, Ferrucci, and Duffy 2015.
27 de Vries et al. 2018.
28 Wirtz et al. 2021.
29 Lambert 2016.
30 Lin, Tov, and Qui 2014; Waterloo et al. 2018.
31 Crumb et al. 2019; Gagnon, Gelinas, and Friesen 2017.
32 McAlpine 2021.
33 Crumb et al. 2019.
34 Freitas 2017.
35 Ibid., 68.

36 Ibid., 68.
37 Azad 2020.
38 Ibid.
39 Turkle 2015.

References

American College Health Association. 2019. *American College Health Association-National College Health Assessment II: Reference Group Executive Summary Spring 2019.* Silver Spring, MD: American College Health Association.

Azad, Kimla. 2020. "The Quad: Looking into the Impacts of Mental Health Jokes among College Students." *Daily Bruin,* University of California, Los Angeles, March 12, 2020.

Banet-Weiser, Sarah. 2012. *Authentic: The Politics of Ambivalence in a Brand Culture.* New York: New York University Press.

Banet-Weiser, Sarah. 2018. *Empowered: Popular Feminism and Popular Misogyny.* Durham, NC: Duke University Press.

Bourdieu, Pierre. 1984. *Distinction: A Social Critique of the Judgement of Taste.* Cambridge, MA: Harvard University Press.

Brissett, Dennis, and Robert Snow. 1993. "Boredom: Where the Future Isn't." *Symbolic Interaction* 16 (3): 237–256.

Brotheridge, Céleste M., and Alicia A. Grandey. 2002. "Emotional Labor and Burnout: Comparing Two Perspectives of 'People Work.'" *Journal of Vocational Behavior* 60: 17–39.

Crumb, Loni, Allison Crowe, Paige Averett, Janee A. Harris, and Courtney Dart. 2019. "'Look Like You Have It Together': Examining Mental Illness Stigma and Help Seeking Among Diverse Emerging Adults." *Emerging Adulthood* 6 (12): 121–132.

de Vries, Dian A., Marthe Möller, Marieke S. Wieringa, Anniek W. Eigenraam, and Kirsten Hamelink. 2018. "Social Comparison as the Thief of Joy: Emotional Consequences of Viewing Strangers' Instagram Posts." *Media Psychology* 21 (2): 222–245.

Duffy, Brooke Erin, and Emily Hund. 2015. "'Having it all' on Social Media: Entrepreneurial Femininity and Self-Branding among Fashion Bloggers." *Social Media + Society* 1 (2): 1–11.

Ehrenreich, Barbara. 2009. *Smile or Die: How Positive Thinking Fooled America and the World.* London: Granta Publications.

Freitas, Donna. 2017. *The Happiness Effect: How Social Media is Driving a Generation to Appear Perfect at Any Cost.* New York: Oxford University Press.

Gagnon, Michelle M., Bethany L. Gelinas, and Lindsay N. Friesen. 2017. "Mental Health Literacy in Emerging Adults in a University Setting: Distinctions between Symptom Awareness and Appraisal." *Journal of Adolescent Research* 32: 642–664.

Gervais, Matthew, and David Sloan Wilson. 2005. "The Evolution and Functions of Laughter and Humor: A Synthetic Approach." *The Quarterly Review of Biology* 80 (4): 395–430.

Goodnow, Trischa. 2016. "The Selfie Moment: The Rhetorical Implications of Digital Self Portraiture for Culture." In *In the Beginning Was the Image: The Omnipresence of Pictures: Time, Truth, Tradition,* edited by Benedek András and Veszelszki Ágnes, 123–130. Frankfurt am Main: Peter Lang.

Hall, Edward. 1983. *The Dance of Life*. Garden City, NY: Anchor/Doubleday.

Huizinga, Johan. 1955. "Nature and Significance of Play as a Cultural Phenomenon." In *The Game Design Reader: A Rules of Play Anthology*, edited by Katie Salen and Eric Zimmerman, 96–121. Cambridge: MIT Press, 2005.

Lambert, Alex. 2016. "Intimacy and Social Capital on Facebook: Beyond the Psychological Perspective." *New Media & Society* 18 (11): 1–17.

LeViness, Peter, Kim Gorman, Lynn Braun, Linda Koenig, and Carolyn Bershad. 2019. *The Association for University and College Counseling Center Directors Annual Survey: 2019*. Indianapolis: Association for University and College Counseling Center Directors. www.auccd.org/director-surveys-public.

Lin, Han, William Tov, and Lin Qiu. 2014. "Emotional Disclosure on Social Networking Sites: The Role of Network Structure and Psychological Needs." *Computers in Human Behavior* 41 (1): 342–350.

Lipson, Sarah K., Emily G. Lattie, and Daniel Eisenberg. 2019. "Increased Rates of Mental Health Service Utilization by U.S. College Students: 10-Year Population-Level Trends (2007–2017)." *Psychiatric Services* 70 (1): 60–63.

Marwick, Alice. 2013. *Status Update: Celebrity, Publicity, and Branding in the Social Media Age*. New Haven, CT: Yale University Press.

McAlpine, Kat J. 2021. "Depression, Anxiety, and Loneliness are Peaking in College Students." *The Brink: Pioneering Research from Boston University*, February 2, 2021.

Owren, Michael, and Jo-Anne Bachorowski. 2003. "Reconsidering the Evolution of Nonlinguistic Communication: The Case of Laughter." *Journal of Nonverbal Behavior* 27: 183–200.

Primack, Brian A., Ariel Shensa, César G. Escobar-Viera, Erica L. Barrett, Jaime E. Sidani, Jason B. Colditz, and A. Everette James. 2017. "Use of Multiple Social Media Platforms and Symptoms of Depression and Anxiety: A Nationally-Representative Study among U.S. Young Adults." *Computers in Human Behavior* 69: 1–9.

Reinecke, Leonard, and Sabine Trepte. 2014. "Authenticity and Well-Being on Social Network Sites: A Two-Wave Longitudinal Study on the Effects of Online Authenticity and the Positivity Bias in SNS Communication." *Computers in Human Behavior* 30 (1): 95–102.

Ross, Scott. 2019. "Being Real on Fake Instagram: Likes, Images, and Media Ideologies of Value." *Journal of Linguistic Anthropology* 29 (3): 359–374.

Shakya, Holly, and Nicholas Christakis. 2017. "Association of Facebook Use with Compromised Well-Being: A Longitudinal Study." *American Journal of Epidemiology* 185 (3): 203–211.

Stromberg, Peter. 2009. *Caught in Play: How Entertainment Works on You*. Stanford, CA: Stanford University Press.

Tandoc, Edson, Jr., Patrick Ferrucci, and Margaret Duffy. 2015. "Facebook Use, Envy, and Depression among College Students: Is Facebooking Depressing?" *Computers in Human Behavior* 43: 139–146.

Turkle, Sherry. 2015. *Reclaiming Conversation: The Power of Talk in a Digital Age*. London: Penguin Books.

Twenge, Jean. 2019. "The Sad State of Happiness in the United States and the Role of Digital Media." In *World Happiness Report*, edited by John Helliwell, R. Richard Layard, and Jeffrey Sachs. New York: Sustainable Development Solutions Network. https://worldhappiness.report/ed/2019/.

Twenge, Jean, Gabrielle N. Martin, and W. Keith Campbell. 2018. "Decreases in Psychological Well-Being among American Adolescents after 2012 and Links to Screen Time during the Rise of Smartphone Technology." *Emotion* 18 (6): 765–780.

Twenge, Jean, and W. Keith Campbell. 2018. "Associations between Screen Time and Lower Psychological Well-Being among Children and Adolescents: Evidence from a Population Based Study." *Preventive Medicine Reports* 12: 271–283.

Waterloo, Sophie, Susanne Baumgartner, Jochen Peter, and Patti Valkenburg. 2018. "Norms of Online Expressions of Emotion: Comparing Facebook, Twitter, Instagram, and Whatsapp." *New Media and Society* 20 (5): 1813–1831.

Wirz, Derrick, Amanda Tucker, Chloe Briggs, and Alexander Schoemann. 2021. "How and Why Social Media Affect Subjective Well-Being: Multi-Site Use and Social Comparison as Predictors of Change across Time." *Journal of Happiness Studies* 22: 1673–1691.

5

COVID-19

Emergent Imperatives

In the midst of writing this book, Covid-19 emerged as a global pandemic, disrupting every aspect of our daily lives. This chapter explores social media use during a period of sudden, life-altering social change. We focus on how Covid-19, a global pandemic that killed approximately 4.6 million people worldwide and 660,000 people in the U.S. within the span of 18 months, changed the way people interact online.[1]

This chapter addresses the following questions: How did the pandemic affect college students' engagement with social media? Did social media serve a different purpose now that it was their only, or at least, primary way of interacting with friends? In terms of posting, how did the pandemic influence social norms—what did it mean to post with or without a mask, and how did people feel about party pics and other images of social gatherings? To explore these questions, we gathered data about students' experiences with social media during the first year of the Covid-19 pandemic. Over the course of two semesters, we asked 40 students in upper division anthropology classes to reflect on these questions and observe interactions of their friends online. Students shared their accounts with us through a series of approximately 130 narrative essays, which we analyzed for emergent themes. Although these students represent only a small slice of campus life, their narratives provide a window into emerging adult experiences during this intense period of social change.

Covid-19 was not the only life-altering event of 2020; it occurred within a broader convergence of social and political events, which resulted in a deadly, emotionally wrought year of constant upheaval. Other major news stories, including the Black Lives Matter protests, two presidential impeachments in less than one month, and a violent attempt to overturn the presidential election results, permeated social media feeds across all platforms. Even Instagram became

DOI: 10.4324/9781003182047-6

an outlet for political expression, a content shift that would have been inconceivable prior to 2020. This socio-political context converged with Covid-19 to influence both the content students viewed and the ways in which they posted and interacted with friends online. These major events contributed to a sense of anxious uncertainty that students sought to both understand and escape through social media.

Though we acknowledge that an integrated analysis of how the major social justice, political, and health events of 2020 influenced the way college students experienced social media, given the focus of our book, a deep dive into politics and social issues that occurred in tandem with the pandemic is beyond the scope of our analysis. Instead, we focus on themes we have explored throughout this book as they relate to Covid-19, including shifts in how students experienced social media, online social norms, surveillance, social comparison, and the resulting emotional effects.

Covid-19 in Context

On Saturday, March 11, 2020, the World Health Organization declared Covid-19 a pandemic. Soon after, communities all over the world went into lockdown as many people quarantined at home in order to stop the spread of the virus. We had to rethink everything, including how to bring groceries into our homes safely, connect with friends and family, work, and learn. People canceled any activity that necessitated leaving their homes and socializing in close proximity with others, including travel plans, parties and social gatherings, graduation ceremonies, going to restaurants and bars, concerts, and other events.

That weekend in March marked the beginning of spring break at the university where we conducted this research project. By mid-week, university leaders announced they had decided to extend spring break by an additional seven days in order to allow time to plan. Early the following week, we learned that all classes would go online for the remainder of the semester and students living on campus would need to move out by the end of the week. Many students headed back to their childhood homes to live with their parents. Classes remained virtual through the first summer session. During the second summer session, only a handful of classes transitioned to an in-person model that included masks, social distancing, hand sanitizer, and sophisticated air filtration systems.

University administration grappled all summer long with impossible decisions about how to meet the conflicting needs of students (and faculty) who were afraid to attend in-person classes and students who demanded a "normal" college experience. The 2020–2021 academic year included a mix of in-person, online, and hybrid style classes. "Zoom," a cloud-based video conferencing platform, became a primary form of communication and a daily routine for many. In fall of 2021, as we neared completion of this book, the Covid-19 dashboard that tracks daily cases on campus remained a prominent link on the university's homepage; testing kiosks located on campus had become a seamless part of the university landscape; Covid-19 vaccines continued to be offered on campus; and the university began an incentive program to encourage hesitant students, faculty, and staff to get vaccinated.

The events of 2020 drastically changed how college students engaged with social media in terms of which sites they frequented, how they posted, what they saw on their feeds, and how they felt about others' posts. Quarantined at home with minimal in-person social contact, many students spent more time than ever scrolling through social media, where they alternately sought out news to make sense of the chaos and mindless entertainment to escape it. They posted less and paid more attention to how close together people stood and whether they wore masks properly when scrolling through their friends' posts.

Recent research suggests that college students have been at heightened risk to poor mental health outcomes during the pandemic.[2] Studies have found increased levels of stress, anxiety, and depressive symptoms among those aged 18–24, with students reporting feelings of being overwhelmed, isolated, and lonely. One study of first year college students found that the prevalence of moderate-severe anxiety increased from 18 percent to 25 percent within four months of the onset of the pandemic; the prevalence of moderate-severe depression increased from 22 percent to 32 percent during this time. White, female, and sexual/gender minority students were at highest risk for increased symptoms of depression.[3]

Notably, almost 70 percent of college presidents report that mental health among students during the pandemic currently ranks among their top concerns.[4] Some of the mental health issues on campus may be due to the difficulties in learning online, concerns about loved ones contracting Covid-19, and financial struggles.[5] At present, little is known about whether social media use has changed during Covid-19 and the extent to which it may serve as a stressor or helpful distraction for students during a time of isolation.

Changes in Social Media Use

College students said their time on social media drastically increased when the pandemic started. Many moved home to live with their parents. Those who stayed in town to complete the spring semester online were stuck in their apartments with nowhere to go and no way to socialize safely with friends in person. Anxious and bored, they turned to social media. Most reported spending anywhere between 6 and 10 hours a day on their sites. One woman who wrote that she began spending about 30 hours a week on social media after the pandemic started, exclaimed, "That's like having a part-time job!" She went on to explain:

> I've always known that Instagram wasn't great for my mental health but having to quarantine due to Covid-19 made my screen time really spike.

> I would wake up in the morning and scroll through Instagram for about an hour, close the app and then reopen it soon after to start all over again.

Our qualitative data align with findings from large-scale surveys. A recent study among more than 2,500 college students across 7 U.S. colleges found that their mean screen time during the pandemic was 7.74 hours per day.[6]

Amelia, who described her sheltered childhood under the watchful eyes of overprotective parents, had fully embraced the freedom and independence of college life. Covid-19 forced her to move back in with her parents who were terrified of the virus. As a result, Amelia could only leave the house rarely and with her parents' permission. She described her daily quarantine routine:

> I have been in total quarantine since mid-March, only leaving my parents' house to go on drives or visit my friends from a distance in their front yards. My social media use has absolutely skyrocketed. According to my screen-time report, I spent 60 hours and 39 minutes on my phone last week, and half of that was on social networking. Twenty-one hours and 38 minutes of that was on Twitter alone.

Most students, especially those who had moved back home, expressed fear about catching the virus and infecting their parents or other elderly family members who were at greater risk for health complications. Recent data from 14 U.S. college campuses ($n = 18,764$) found that 65 percent of students reported concern about family members contracting Covid-19; 65 percent reported worry about how long the pandemic would last.[7] Similarly, in our study, many students wrote about struggling with the sudden transition from a life of independence and autonomy at college to one of rules and restrictions in their parents' home. Social media became a way to connect socially with friends, escape their new realities, and tune out their parents.

Early on, news about Covid-19 dominated students' social media feeds across platforms, exposing them to information about the pandemic for many hours a day. One student estimated that about 10 percent of her social media content was news related before the pandemic, as compared to 50 percent once the initial lockdown began. Ethan, a contemplative environmental studies major, wrote that he scrolled through his feed for hours on end, skimming one tragic headline after another, a practice widely referred to as "doom scrolling." He added, "I've become totally addicted to social media. I obsessively refresh my apps all day long because I'm worried I'll miss out on a major news story." Many students described a similar routine of constantly scrolling and refreshing their feeds as they stared anxiously into their phones all day long.

Many students who had not paid close attention to news before the pandemic became hyper-focused on news during the quarantine. For example, Isla, an avid follower of celebrity culture before the pandemic, wrote that she had developed a habit of checking the news as soon as she woke up and found herself scrolling for new headlines throughout the day. She explained, "I never would've thought I would ever voluntarily check the news out of necessity, but I can't help it since the pandemic doesn't seem to be slowing down anytime soon." The fear of missing out, popularly referred to as FOMO, had shifted focus overnight from fun activities and adventures to pandemic-related news about widespread death and illness. Constantly checking the news for updates became a compulsion, an imperative even. As Isla and many other students noted, they could not help but constantly refresh their feeds in search of the latest tragic story.

Claire, a junior psychology major and sorority member, described the dramatic shift in her Instagram feed at the beginning of the pandemic.

> Before Covid started, I loved Instagram and got a lot of joy from the site. It was my favorite site to be on, and I spent the majority of my time on social media scrolling through Instagram. I loved seeing friends who were all around the country and the world and what they were doing. I am someone who always wants to be traveling and exploring different places, so I like to live vicariously through the pictures people posted of their studies abroad and vacations all across the globe. I used it as a form of escape, a distraction. It was a brief period of my day where I could pretend I did not have papers due or an upcoming test. I could put myself in their shoes and temporarily satisfy my wanderlust. Once Covid hit, the entire app quickly became very political and totally focused on Covid-related news. No one was doing anything worth showing off. They could no longer pretend they had these amazing, perfect lives. Instagram very quickly became a site where people were posting about different political viewpoints, Covid-related or otherwise, and it completely filled my feed. Seeing all this information on the terrible state of our world became incredibly draining and depressing, as everyone was inside with nothing to look forward to or be excited about. It was a lot of negativity in an already very dark time.

Claire's description of how her Instagram feed and her experience with the site completely changed with Covid-19 powerfully illustrates the disruptive effects of the pandemic on everyday life. Instagram went from a site where Claire could experience adventure vicariously and escape into an aspirational mindset to one filled with grim reality and sobering stories about fear, death, and suffering. We can imagine how all of this negativity might have been particularly difficult for college students who were used to portraying their lives as positive online.

Monique, an anthropology major and 25-year-old single mom of two young children, wrote:

> At the beginning of the pandemic, my newsfeed on every social media account was flooded with information about Covid, which would range anywhere from symptoms to the rising numbers of deaths worldwide. It was really depressing sitting at home watching these deaths go through the roof and there really wasn't anything for us to do besides stay at home and wash our hands.

She explained that as an essential grocery store employee, she had to continue working, even during the lockdown. In her free time, Monique began scrolling through her social media feed to glean information about how to prevent and recover from Covid-19, a practice driven by fear and anxiety.

> Anytime someone posted a video on TikTok about how they had gotten Covid and recovered, I would look at their page and take notes on what they did to recover. I was terrified that I would get Covid at work and spread it to my children or my older family members.

Monique's mom and grandparents helped care for her young children while she worked and studied. She felt a lot of pressure to keep her family safe from the virus, especially since she was the only one in her family who continued to work outside of the home.

Monique described a routine where she checked Covid-19 statistics at the beginning and end of every day "to see how many people had become infected, how many had died, how many had recovered, and how bad the virus was here in my community." She explained that staying apprised of news helped her feel a sense of control. However, at a certain point, she realized that her hypervigilance about the virus, something outside of her control, was causing her to feel anxious, and so she stopped checking the news as frequently and began scrolling past Covid-related posts in search of lighter topics. Other students described a similar experience of "doom scrolling" early in the day before reaching an emotional threshold and turning to lighter content for distraction in the afternoon and evening.

In Chapter 4, we explored online social norms requiring positive self-expression. Pre-Covid-19, the idea that Instagram would become a site focused on news and serious content was unimaginable. Other sites such as Snapchat, Twitter, and Finsta (fake Instagram) served as emotional overflow sites where people felt freer to express sadness, anger, and frustration. News posts have always peppered people's Twitter and Facebook feeds, but had never appeared on Instagram, according to our participants. Before the pandemic, Instagram was a site populated with influencers, heavily filtered images, and easily recognizable self-branding, as well as a space for sharing adventures, travel, and big life moments. During 2020, a time when the pandemic converged with other major newsworthy social issues, the positivity imperative took a backseat to the unfiltered reality of everyday human trauma, with news stories dominating social media feeds.

Posting during the Pandemic

Though students' time on social media increased during the pandemic, posting decreased initially. Many said they stopped posting altogether, especially early on in the pandemic. Amelia wrote, "I don't post much anymore because I don't do anything. I have nothing to share," a reflection mirrored in many of the students' narratives. Robyn similarly explained, "I'm not hanging out with friends. I barely post. What would I even post about when I'm home with my parents all the time?" Bored and lacking interesting content to share, students said they constantly refreshed their apps hoping for something new to appear.

Many students had begun commenting more on posts and liking their friends' posts within seconds after they appeared, a practice considered taboo before the pandemic. Amelia noted:

> A trend I've noticed in myself and my friends on Twitter is that we're all anxiously refreshing our feeds waiting for new content to be posted, so we always end up liking someone's post a few seconds after they post it, making us seem like stalkers or weirdos.

She went on to explain that before the pandemic, she never really commented on posts, but now she does as a way to maintain a personal connection with her friends during the quarantine. It remains to be seen whether students will continue to respond instantaneously to posts, or whether pre-pandemic norms of strategically waiting, in order to appear busy, will once again take hold.

Those who continued posting did so sporadically, and the content of their posts and their feeds changed. Once the initial shock of the quarantine and pandemic wore off and people began to settle into their new routines, students said that posts shifted from nonstop news updates to the more mundane aspects of life at home, including newfound hobbies. Stephanie, a woman who described herself as a reluctant social media user before the pandemic, wrote that she fully embraced it during the pandemic as a way to stay connected with friends. She shared her observations of how posting behaviors had changed:

> Although some people continue to showcase luxuries and travel, most share recipes, new workouts, popular reads, jewelry making strategies, etc. My friends and I started using social media to share new ideas for DIY (do it yourself) projects. We posted ideas for painting, home décor, recipes, and body/face/hair care.

Stephanie, a sophomore geography major, also described the contrast in her close friend, Jill's posts before and during the pandemic:

> Before Covid, Jill frequently uploaded photos and short clips of her adventures downtown on the weekends. She would film her experiences at coffee shops with live music, spontaneous walks through nature parks, or shenanigans with her roommates on campus. Now that she has moved back home to live with her parents because of the pandemic, Jill posts entertaining videos of her dogs, solitary walks in her backyard and neighborhood, and craft projects she does out of boredom.

This trend toward posting crafts and mundane aspects of daily life emerged out of a convergence of boredom and frustration with news heavy social media content. Students began to find other ways to pass the time besides constantly refreshing their sites. Sharing snapshots of quarantine life on social media became a new posting norm, illustrating an evolution in online sociality as the pandemic continued.

Living Your Best Life during a Pandemic

In their essays, several students described how popular posts of "living your best life" had completely changed. Allison explained that her social media feed during the pandemic appeared to focus on "glamorizing ordinary tasks." She wrote:

> I used to see a lot of travel stuff, and now I feel like it's more like, "Look how cute my room is!" or like, "How I'm spending my time!". . . No one is going anywhere exciting, so I see people going to a park alone or with a friend or something. It's almost like people are trying to look like they're not trying. It's like, "Look at this candid photo my friend just took of me while we're walking," but it's actually a heavily edited photo that doesn't seem candid at all.

Mackenzie observed a similar trend, which she referred to as "fake candids":

> Any sort of fun is being blasted because it's not safe with Covid. . . Before the pandemic, people would only post if they were doing an event like, "Oh we're at Six Flags," or "Oh we're having a big brunch party." Now they're really stepping out for every small thing just to find content to post. They're like, "Oh my God, going to Target (laughs)!" They're glamorizing anything that they can.

She described Target photos as the new party post. Mackenzie reported that while the types of activities deemed post-worthy changed drastically during the pandemic, editing practices and the importance of looking good, which she described as "the cuteness factor," were still observable on social media, particularly among her women friends.

Despite the persistence of the editing imperative during Covid-19, some students noted that they found quarantine posts more relatable and authentic than the content they used to see highlighting the glamorous and adventurous moments of life. One woman wrote:

> Prior to quarantine, I mostly saw people flaunting their lives. People were posting pictures almost to brag about where they are going and what they are doing. It was almost like people were engaging in specific activities for the sole purpose of being able to post about it on social media. But after the stay-at-home orders were in place, I noticed that people posted more causal photos, like cooking or hanging out on the couch with their dog. These kinds of posts feel more personable and relatable.

Similarly, Ryan, a reluctant social media user, observed:

> With Covid, people seem to have become more authentic on social media. Since everyone had to self-isolate, it may have made them realize that there's no point in faking it anymore. There's no need to exaggerate their lives because we are all stuck at home.

In some ways, quarantine life was freeing. There was no longer an expectation of adventure or excitement, and no longer any pressure to live up to a highly cultivated online image. For the first time, it was okay to live an ordinary life. It is unclear whether this trend will persist or at least influence online social norms beyond the pandemic.

The Rise of TikTok during Quarantine

A few months into the quarantine, students became bored with posts about hobbies and daily routines at home. One woman noted, "Everyone's posts began to look the same; it was just them in their houses with absolutely nowhere to go." At this point in 2020, Black Lives Matter protests, sparked by the killing of Breonna Taylor and George Floyd by police, were occurring all over the world against systemic racism and police brutality. Students' social media feeds, now dominated by stories of these events on top of ongoing updates about the pandemic, were more anxiety provoking than ever. They expressed a sense of feeling overwhelmed and depressed by all that was happening in the world, and their go-to sites no longer offered any respite from harsh reality. One man wrote, "Getting on Twitter and Instagram was very draining and depressing to the point where I would avoid logging in. It was so bad that it could change your mood for the day or for the hour."

Many turned to TikTok in search of more entertaining content. TikTok is a video-sharing social media app that allows users to upload 15-second videos on any topic. Similar to Instagram, users can string together short videos to create a story, and feedback mechanisms include the heart emoji and comments. The app highlights trending videos and compiles data on what you like, suggesting content based on your interests. Overall, students reported spending more time on TikTok and shifting away from their other apps as the pandemic progressed. Many described TikTok as an escape from depressing news about Covid-19 and social injustice. They turned to TikTok for mindless entertainment and a sense of connection with others through humor.

Claire wrote that during the pandemic she stopped using Instagram and began spending most of her time on TikTok, a site she described as "a funny, creative distraction from the world."

> I found myself spending hours laughing at videos telling ridiculous retail stories of rude customers that I could relate to from my own work experience. It became a different kind of escape from reality. TikTok also did not make me as mad as other sites like Facebook or Snapchat, where people would post about Covid being a hoax or share videos of themselves hanging out, not wearing masks.

Claire, like most of our participants, desired escapism and relatability. Funny stories about work scenarios she experienced provided a much-needed sense of normalcy in a topsy-turvy world.

Grace, who reported spending 4–6 hours a day on TikTok during quarantine, described the app as "easy entertainment." She explained, "Once I'm on there I just keep scrolling through videos. TikTok keeps me entertained without comparing my quarantine routine to others. I started relying on it to keep myself distracted." She enjoyed the "For You" page, which "constantly adds new videos based on the posts you've already interacted with, so the second you like or comment on a post, the app immediately suggests similar videos for you to watch." For Grace, TikTok was a one-stop shop where she was continually amused because of its "never-ending content." Another benefit was that "there is such a wide array of groups and communities within a single platform you don't have to switch between platforms to receive all types of media."

Some women talked about the fun of "watching weird dancing videos and trying to learn them" so they could post themselves doing that dance. In fact, several women described spending hours practicing a popular dance video in preparation for posting their own version of it on TikTok. This active participatory component of TikTok appealed to students stuck at home in their childhood bedrooms.

Many students started using TikTok for the first time during the pandemic and quickly became hooked on the app. Zoe wrote that several of her friends kept insisting that she download TikTok, and she finally gave in to the pressure during quarantine to see what all of the hype was about. Zoe soon began spending about 3 hours a day scrolling through videos. She articulated the appeal of the app beyond entertainment:

> TikTok videos aren't just for comedic relief; they are also relatable and, at times, educational. Videos produced during the pandemic included satirical content involving Covid-19, including how schools handled the situation. TikTok showed kids moving back home, jokingly upset that they could not participate in the same activities as when they were away at university.

We see again how the familiarity and relatability of humorous skits offered a break from the stress of daily quarantine life.

Nathan, a junior anthropology major who had spent most of his time on Twitter before the pandemic, similarly reported that he downloaded TikTok during quarantine out of boredom. It quickly became his favorite site. Though Nathan struggled with how much time he spent on TikTok, he also felt like it provided a much-needed connection to the outside world during quarantine. He wrote, "TikTok has been another way for me to sort of cope with the loneliness of it all." Other students shared this sentiment. One woman similarly described how TikTok provided solace while living at home:

> Throughout quarantine, TikTok has become a way for me to engage with others while maintaining the safety of social distancing. Going from having constant interaction with friends and classmates on campus to being locked in my parents' house was definitely a major transition, and one that encouraged me to spend more time on TikTok.

In the blink of an eye, the role of social media for these emerging adults shifted from identity work and self-branding to providing a sense of community during isolating and uncertain times.

TikTok became so popular during the quarantine that students who had previously opted out felt pressure to download the app in order to understand the constant TikTok references among friends. For example, Avery, a marketing major who aspired to be an influencer, explained, "I downloaded it mostly to stay connected. . . I'm trying to keep up with my friends and understand it." She described a culture of TikTok marked by inside jokes about popular videos. Avery wrote, "My brother would tell a joke, and I'd be like, 'I don't get it,' and he's like, 'It's from TikTok, everybody knows it.'" She referred to this sort of insider TikTok knowledge as a "pop culture awareness." It is noteworthy that during a global pandemic when people were socially isolated, a shared culture formed around this social media app. Insider knowledge of TikTok culture, distributed almost entirely online, became a powerful form of social connection.

Not everyone became enamored with TikTok. Allison, for example, refused to download TikTok during the quarantine because she was afraid she would spend hours a day on the app like so many of her friends. Because she opted out, Allison felt excluded from many online conversations among her friends that focused on trending TikTok videos.

> During the pandemic, TikTok became so popular, all of my friends were constantly talking on social media about the videos they had seen on it. I didn't download that app and felt left out of all of that. It was interesting how not having just one app in your social media arsenal could drastically affect your ability to socialize with friends online.

Allison's commentary resonates with a key theme we have discussed throughout this book—the many works involved in maintaining an online life. It appears that fluency and active engagement in yet another social media site is now required among emerging adults.

Connection through Social Media Hobby Groups

Some students turned to hobby groups on social media as a way to connect virtually with others who shared their interests. For example, Elijah, a sophomore sociology major who moved in with his grandmother and became her primary caregiver during the pandemic, wrote that when he became bored with his friends' quarantine routine posts, he "revisited old hobbies, such as collecting vinyl records and retro video games, as well as starting new hobbies, like painting on canvas." He began searching for others with similar interests and friending them on social media. Elijah enjoyed the connections he made; as he accumulated more friends with shared interests, his social media feed began to reflect his new hobbies. He connected to artists who had similar styles to his own and found that social media could be a source for creative inspiration.

Zoe began watching bartending videos during quarantine and joined a local Facebook group that emerged after the start of the pandemic called Quarantined Beer Lovers. The site brought beer enthusiasts together to share beer-related pictures and memes, videos of themselves chugging beer, and recommendations for new beers to try. She wrote, "My drinking habits slightly increased while in quarantine, probably because my parents were in a different state, leaving me alone at home. Also, when my classes went online, I felt really isolated." Zoe described Quarantine Beer Lovers as "a place where likeminded people could drink and forget about everything going on around them." According to Zoe, the group quickly amassed more than 25,000 followers from all walks of life, including parents, working professionals, unemployed bartenders, and college students. She wrote, "In the group, I watched people connect with strangers over their love of alcohol. After the official lockdown ended, I saw people make plans to meet up in person with those they had connected with in the online group."

Zoe explained that many similar groups emerged across social media during the pandemic. For example, she described a group called Quarantine Karaoke that "became a global hub for music lovers craving a sense of community." With approximately 720,000 members at the height of quarantine, this group became a global online space where people posted videos of themselves singing favorite popular songs as well as songs they wrote. Zoe noted, "Across the world people used social media to unite."

Vanessa, an English major and self-described nerd, reported that she spent roughly 6–7 hours a day on social media during the pandemic, checking her phone approximately 200 times a day. After returning to her childhood home once classes went online in March of 2020, Vanessa began revisiting favorite shows, movies, and books from her early teen years. She quickly noticed that many of her friends were also "reminiscing about the days before we 'grew up.'" Vanessa referred to this phenomenon as "the Renaissance of the 90's/00's kid and the return of childhood classics, like *Avatar: The last Airbender, Friends, Twilight,* and *Harry Potter.*" Vanessa explained that she and her friends craved things that were familiar during an uncertain time, kind of like comfort foods.

> I was definitely detaching myself from reality, getting that small "high" of happiness instead of facing the pandemic. I depended on social media as an escape from worrying about my godparents who had contracted Covid-19 because they were essential workers or my constant fear that my grandparents, the most important people in my life, could possibly become ill with the virus.

Delving into her childhood interests helped Vanessa connect to a simpler time, thereby providing a mental and emotional break from worrying about the impact of Covid-19 on her family.

Entrepreneurship in the Time of Covid-19

Some students turned to entrepreneurial efforts during the pandemic, developing online businesses and promoting their skills as a way of making money and sharing their creative pursuits on social media. For example, Sierra admired the entrepreneurial spirit of several high school friends who had developed online businesses during the pandemic. She described one woman who developed an online cosmetics business inspired by looks from a Korean boy band. Another friend from her hometown started customizing shoes with pictures or patterns and selling them online. Both of these entrepreneurs came from families that could not financially support them through college, so Sierra was impressed that they were able to make money through creative endeavors during the pandemic. Her observation is noteworthy as financial stress, a known predictor of college mental health, increased significantly during the pandemic, with two-thirds of students reporting that their financial situation became more stressful as they lost employment during this time.[8]

Xavier, a music lover who aspired to work in the entertainment industry, spent time during the quarantine promoting his disk jockey sets. He wrote, "Covid-19 has given me more time to focus on things that I love outside of work and school to do things like share music, and DJ." He rarely had time to explore his passion before the quarantine because he worked two part-time jobs while attending the university full time. At the start of the pandemic when classes went online, Xavier had to quit his jobs and move back home with his parents, providing him with more free time.

> Since the pandemic started in early March, my social media changed from a way to unwind and de-stress to a tool for self-promotion. This has allowed me to mobilize and get my first DJ gig performing in front of people and has enabled me to get another gig doing a wedding. I hope this gives me momentum to build clients and keep getting gigs after the pandemic ends.

For Xavier, the pandemic provided him with time and space to explore the possibility of turning his passion into a business, something he would not normally have been able to squeeze into his busy life.

A few students wrote about friends who had begun promoting their OnlyFans profile through Instagram stories during the quarantine. OnlyFans, known for its sexual content, is a subscription website that allows users to lock their content behind paywalls and charge a fee for accessing it. A *New York Times* article dubbed OnlyFans "the paywall of Porn," describing it as a site "where subscribers—mostly male; straight, gay and beyond—pay models and social media influencers a fee, generally $5 to $20 a month, to view a feed of imagery too racy for Instagram."[9] A quick Google search uncovered many pages of popular media articles highlighting the rise in popularity of this site during the pandemic. OnlyFans reported a 75 percent increase in content creators in early April of 2020, coinciding with mass global layoffs due to the pandemic.[10] By the end of 2020, OnlyFans had 90 million users and over a million content creators, up from 219,000 in 2019.[11]

One woman commented on the drastic shift in social media posting norms with the rise of OnlyFans:

> On social media, there are unwritten rules that people collectively have come to terms with over time. Usually, you are not supposed to post certain images, like nudes of yourself, but people have now started to do this more on OnlyFans.

Autumn noted that she has three friends who started promoting their OnlyFans profiles on Instagram and Twitter after losing their jobs during the quarantine. She wrote that seeing her friends resort to such desperate measures for income saddened her.

Autumn explained that people use the site to "sell nude content, sexual content, you name it, it's on there." She wrote, "Many college students lost their jobs due to the quarantine. I wonder how many more young women joined the sex industry, even temporarily, due to unemployment from Covid-19." Autumn's final comment is important in light of how popular OnlyFans became in just a few months during the pandemic. Future ethnographic research exploring sex work among college students would illuminate the extent to which college student participation on such sites has been a temporary financial stop-gap measure during the pandemic or if it endures. For students who participated in these sites, self-objectification, concern about the body, and posting to attract maximum attention remained prominent aspects of online sociality.

Increased Surveillance on Social Media

In their narratives, it was clear that surveillance of others and awareness that others were closely monitoring their own behavior were important topics of concern. Many student essays described extreme backlash on social media when people posted themselves disregarding social distancing or mask guidelines. Several students described how others had commented on their posts, jumping to conclusions about how they had behaved "carelessly" in terms of mask wearing. As a result, some students expressed concern about how to post appropriately during the pandemic without attracting negative attention and comments. Grace, for example, said that she remained cautious about what she posted after she faced "a lot of backlash for being careless" in July 2020. She insisted, however, that she had been careful about wearing a mask, and had just removed it before taking the photo. At the time, she was visiting her best friend at the beach and they both wore masks every time they left the house; after returning home, she quarantined for two weeks. Nonetheless, others had criticized her unmasked posts at the beach. Her narrative speaks to the ease of misinterpretation in a time of heightened surveillance.

Allison described a similar experience, despite her attempts to mitigate the possibility of receiving negative comments on her posts. Aware of how others might respond, Allison expressed concern about her posting on social media during the summer of 2020 when she was on a road trip through national parks with her roommate. Even though she followed social distancing guidelines while outside, she was aware of how she was "second guessing every post," even when hiking.

> I did not want to be controversial for posting without a mask on, even though I was at least a mile from humanity in the middle of a canyon hiking trail. I know many people have been shamed for certain posts or

have talked about others behind their backs for choosing to post questionable group photos.

Although Allison was adhering to Covid-appropriate behavior, she remained unsure of how others would respond. Based on student narratives, it appeared that the social norms of posting had shifted, although there was uncertainty about what the new norms were during the pandemic. One thing was clear—posting on social media in relation to mask wearing had become a fraught, anxiety provoking experience.

Partially due to concerns of intense surveillance, many emerging adults chose to post outdoor activities, such as camping or hiking. Brooke offered a comparison between one friend who posted herself camping and another friend who posted at a club, showing a bottle of vodka in a bucket of ice.

> There were no people shown in the photo, but there were seven cups in the background and a half empty bottle of vodka, so it's easy to assume there are quite a few people with him at the club. The posts of my friend responsibly hanging out (camping with friends) got twice as many likes as the photo of the vodka bottle.

Brooke's explanation for this was that people did not want to see others going out and breaking social distancing rules on their social media. Photos that would have been very cool before the pandemic had become a source of contention almost overnight. Even if friends understood and supported drinking with others, there may have been a reluctance to comment positively on such behavior. Social norms of acceptable behavior were undergoing continual, rapid change across the months of the pandemic, and it was difficult to ascertain where your followers were on this continuum. In a time of social isolation, it could be a risk to established friendships if you appeared to be crossing a line.

Bianca explained that she "tried to watch for markers" in order to ascertain if people were still going out; what measures they were taking to reduce the spread of the virus, such as wearing a mask or maintaining distance from others; and generally what types of activities her friends were engaging in on social media. From time spent on Instagram, Bianca assessed that about half of the people she followed "went about their usual lives, while others were still in a mode of safety and precaution." One of her friends, Alicia, had recently posted a video of herself and her boyfriend unmasked at a bar, with other unmasked bar-goers in the background. Alicia held up proof of her negative Covid-19 test results, perhaps as justification for being out with friends in places where social distancing was difficult to accomplish. The example highlights Alicia's misinterpretation of what it means to behave safely during the pandemic and a lack of understanding about transmission of the virus.

Alicia appears to be re-embracing and taking back "living her best life." Because posting photos of yourself at a bar during the pandemic might be considered inappropriate and unsafe during Covid-19, Alicia attempts to "mask" this behavior by instead highlighting her test results. Nonetheless, in posting at the crowded bar, Alicia shows that she is not afraid to take a risk; she appears to throw caution to the wind in her expression of personal agency. Alicia is not alone in her behavior; her photo displays many other unmasked people in the bar. Her behavior indexes a new norm among some emerging adults that supersedes health concerns.

Shifts in Social Relations during the Pandemic

Although many students were critical of posts that involved physical risk to one's health during the height of the pandemic, others were careful to reserve judgment of their friends. In her research on smoking among college students, Mimi Nichter found that many felt sensitive to seemingly dogmatic impositions from others.[12] As a result, non-smoker friends were hesitant to say anything about quitting to friends for fear of offending them. To some extent, we observed a similar attitude among college students with regard to Covid-19-related behavior, with some expressing reluctance to make critical comments about their friend's unmasked posts on social media. Elizabeth, for example, explained:

> I try not to judge too hard about, like, if they have a mask on in a post or not, because I don't know the circumstance, you know? I've posted pictures of myself outside without a mask, but I was working out alone. I did post a picture of myself when I went out with friends wearing a mask. So it depends, but if I do know the person and where they were or what they were doing, and if they did not wear a mask, I just think how careless they are.

Still, Elizabeth was reluctant in such contexts to post a negative comment because she recognized that although there was physical risk involved in her friend's behavior, there was also the social risk to their friendship that could result if she commented in a truthful manner, revealing her disappointment and annoyance.

Similarly, Paula, an outgoing anthropology major who wrote at length about her struggles with pandemic-related social isolation, also felt reluctant to risk a friendship over unmasked behavior. She was quick to give others the benefit of the doubt when a friend posted on Instagram without their mask; she needed to understand the context before she would pass judgment on another's behavior.

I assume they took their mask off for the picture or maybe they're practicing social distancing. . . I mean, it could be that they are not being
compliant with the mask rule, in which I would have to be disappointed.
The posts that I see about a house party or bars are very different. . .no
one in the picture—not even the people in the background—are wearing
masks. So I am not sure why the person would post such an event, let
alone participate in it, seeing as how "controversial" the entire pandemic
seems to be.

Paula went on to explain that she would never put herself or someone else at
risk just "for the gram." She had her limits in relation to the behavior she found
acceptable from her friends though she was careful not to post this online.

Other students, however, felt that seeing their friends engage in what they
deemed to be careless behavior resulted in a changed opinion of their friend.
David had continued working as a server in a restaurant throughout the quarantine and contracted Covid-19 during the summer of 2020. He described this
experience as "worse than the flu." David observed high school friends posting
online without masks or wearing them ineffectively, like under their chin or
dangling from an ear. When asked how he felt about these posts, he said that
it made him feel at odds with people he had felt close to previously. One of
his friends, Mallory, who he described as "very liberal," posted a picture at a
house party without a mask. When he messaged her out of fear for her health,
she claimed not wearing a mask was okay because "She knew everybody at
the party and her new boyfriend had chastised her for wearing a mask since he
believed the Covid-19 virus was a myth."

David was sure that Mallory had the common sense to understand the seriousness of the pandemic but expressed disappointment in her for succumbing
to her boyfriend's pressure. He said this made him want to stop thinking about
his friend entirely.

I didn't shut her out completely, but it just made me wary of how much
I could actually trust her. . . if she was willing to put her health at risk
for the sake of being on someone's good side, it made me question everything else about our friendship.

While it was unclear whether he discussed his concerns with Mallory beyond
his initial response, this is a good example of how a friend's posts on Instagram
during the pandemic can alter one's perception of them and, by extension, social relations between them.

Isla's narrative mirrored that of David as she often saw friends on Snapchat
posting in public with masks nowhere in sight. She wrote:

I won't delete somebody because they make dumb decisions, but I think
it says a lot about a person's priorities. If someone isn't willing to protect

themselves, then they for sure don't care to protect others, including myself, and that doesn't sit well with me.

Isla believed that masks were "as important as a phone nowadays when going out in public." Taking a broader perspective, the pandemic provided Isla with insight into how her generation reacted in the face of danger given that it was the first global issue that affected all of them directly. Overall, she was not impressed with what she saw.

Claire observed that viewing friends' posts during the pandemic "had made it very easy to see people's true colors." This, in turn, changed her opinions and relationships with people offline.

> Seeing that people I know and were once close friends with absolutely refuse to wear a mask or social distance has made me feel a sort of anger towards them. It makes me feel like they're selfish, that they would not do anything to help others. They are refusing to do something that could save people's lives and help keep those around them healthy because it's slightly uncomfortable to them or because they believe it's against their rights . . . It just seems so inconsiderate and pointless. If they can't do something as simple as wearing a mask to help someone besides themselves, then it makes me reconsider if is someone who I want to be close with.

Claire went on to write, "Subconsciously, there is some anger and jealousy towards people who are out doing things, whether they are following the rules or not, as we see them doing things we wish we could be doing." She felt, however, that not following the masking and social distancing rules made people "look selfish or uneducated, as they are posting about doing things that we have been warned not to do in a global pandemic." Claire referenced a recent post of a friend eating out with a large group at a new taco restaurant in Austin, and although she realized they might have been wearing masks and taking precautions before eating, she still felt angry. She understood her friends' desire for a return to normalcy, but also recognized that "they are part of the problem, preventing the return to normal."

Amelia wrote that she felt both hurt and infuriated when she saw Instagram posts of "young stupid college students" and her co-workers—women in their 30s and 40s—at bars having drinks with no masks. She wrote, "These are people I've liked and respected at work who I thought were better than this, but this pandemic has shown a lot about people . . . in regard to how selfish or intelligent they are." Because Amelia was staying in and had little to post, she spent less time on Instagram. When she did post,

> It's to rage about the Covid rates in a shamefully passive aggressive jab at the people who think it's time to start partying again. I don't like to burn

bridges or hold grudges, but I recently unfollowed a bunch of people I worked with and was friendly with because the content they were posting was too irritating for me to handle.

As a result, her feed had become more impersonal, filled with ads and influencers, rather than with friends.

For Stephanie, annoyance with her friends' behavior led her to stop viewing their posts altogether "due to the carelessness and lack of empathy for others during the pandemic." Stephanie was a caretaker for her grandfather, which made it even more unsettling for her. She explained:

> . . . to see such recklessness, which in turn created a cloud of anxiety anytime I left my home. Students weren't wearing masks, carried on in large groups, and many of them I knew personally. I wouldn't say I was jealous of their activity, but disappointed that they would risk their families and friends' lives.

She believed that not wearing a mask was having a ripple effect, leading others to believe this behavior was acceptable, describing a mentality of, "If that person can do it, then I can too." Stephanie noticed that many people she knew stopped posting to avoid the scrutiny and judgment of being out without a mask, while they "continued to act as if they were living in a normal world." Her main concern was that she could get Covid-19 from other students and bring it home to her household, especially her aged grandfather.

Shifting the Performance

When asked how social media had changed during the pandemic, Amy, an avid social media user, wrote, "It's the same as it always was. . . . I still use it to check in on people, and people are still performative. Just . . . what they're performing about has shifted a little bit." She explained that the "preening" that one typically does on social media has remained the same.

> It's the same principle as in, like, Twitter activism. People want to pretend like they're political activists and preen over re-tweeting a petition. They'll guilt others for not doing the same, when really, they're not doing their part either. They just want the image, the persona. It's all about what others think of you, instead of what you think.

She wrote about how, even in the pandemic, people pretended as if they care deeply about the unspoken, social distancing rules if only to "virtue signal" to others.

Amy went on to discuss her roommate, Annette, who was a prime example of virtue signaling to demonstrate her moral character:

> Annette often preaches about safety, and what one should and shouldn't be doing in order to be the most responsible Samaritan they possibly can. She's the first person to make posts about how bars and restaurants shouldn't be re-opening but is also the first person in line up at their doors when they do. She often makes posts about how heinous and irresponsible people are being, while immediately going out and acting on the behavior she outwardly condemns. It's difficult to tell whether she's aware of her hypocrisy or whether she completely believes herself.

Amy observed that this was not new behavior for Annette, who in pre-pandemic times had envisioned herself as a "very righteous political activist, despite doing nothing but making posts on Twitter." Amy concluded by noting:

> It's this general performative attitude. . . . You want people to see you as sage, wise and responsible. So you get on the internet and lie about being sage, wise and responsible. . . . Whether it's about the pandemic or about whatever else.

In her opinion, social media was rooted in false presentations of self, which had continued and amplified over the past year.

Virtue signaling was not just a behavior among college students. Marina, who was living at home with her parents during the quarantine, voiced a similar sentiment about her family's behavior; they continued to go to restaurants during the pandemic, but also wanted others to see them as good, moral people. Her parents navigated this dilemma by not posting any public pictures. This irked Marina, who felt that her parents were lying about how they were living their day-to-day lives. For Annette and for Marina's family, concern of others' judgment influenced what they were willing to post, while having little impact on their actual behavior.

Both Marina and Amy recognized that social media affected their friendships and familial relationships, both before and during the Covid-19 pandemic. "Again, it's all about performing. The subject just changed a bit, in the past few months," wrote Amy.

> The problem is dishonesty and disingenuousness. That never changed. It's just a matter of what specifically you're being dishonest about. Right now, it's the pandemic and a willingness to take basic precautions to protect yourself and others. In general, it's infuriating when you have to knowingly watch people pretending to be something they're not.

Marina also felt like her relationships had changed during the pandemic, but she noted:

> I feel bad talking about it. Like, we're all adults. . . . I can't tell my friends and family what to do. But it's just so appalling, you know? Like, is it so hard to stay home? Or even just to wear a mask? It upsets me in my heart that people don't want to make even small sacrifices for the safety of people around them. . . . And it makes me mad! But I don't know where to put it all. I'm not a perfect person in any way, so I don't want to pass judgement on others. But it's frustrating.

Similar to over-editing in pre-pandemic online sociality, appearing inauthentic elicited derision from others who mostly gossiped behind the person's back. The heightened sense of frustration expressed by students in this chapter has to do with what is at stake. Inauthentic self-presentation before the pandemic signaled a desperate plea for attention and compliments; however, inauthentic self-presentation during the pandemic signaled indifference about others' health and well-being, even further, a willingness to risk harming others in pursuit of a good time.

Clearly, not all students on campus would share this level of frustration about Covid-related behaviors. The narratives these students presented reflect insights at a point of transition during the pandemic, as emerging adults moved from the height of fear to experimenting with a return to normalcy.

Social Comparisons during the Pandemic

Social comparison has been a prominent theme throughout the book. We have discussed the pressure students felt to edit their photos so they appeared as flawless as everyone else, the importance of appearing to have an exciting life, the need for a respectable amount of attention online in the form of likes and comments, and of course, the endless iterations of body comparisons. Here we highlight two drastic shifts in online social comparison. One has to do with a new focus on comparing productivity and quarantine routines, and the other is a shift away from social comparison toward greater self-acceptance.

Brooke estimated that she was spending upward of 5 hours a day on Instagram when the quarantine began. After a few weeks, Brooke deleted her accounts because she realized that she was becoming increasingly self-critical as she compared herself to others who seemed so much more productive at the site of the body. She wrote:

> Seeing fitness instructors post selfies of their bodies and workout/dieting routines while I was gaining quarantine weight made me feel guilty that I wasn't exercising or taking care of myself in already difficult and stressful

circumstances. Or even seeing people post an "outfit of the day" photo while I had been wearing the same leggings for three days straight made me feel like I wasn't doing enough "self-care." Deleting my Instagram didn't make me stop comparing myself to others altogether, but at least now I'm seeing more realistic responses to the stresses of the pandemic, rather than just a curated response for the internet.

Brooke's comments underscore the continued impact of various forms of everyday self-measurement during the pandemic that appears to have carried over from pre-pandemic days. Her comparisons left her dissatisfied as she failed to meet the benchmarks set by other women. She describes a sense of feeling left behind and out of control because she has not lived up to online expectations that demonstrate a certain level of productivity, measured by weight loss and regular workouts. Deleting her Instagram account was an attempt at self-empowerment.

Claire noticed during quarantine that many of her friends were posting about weight loss, healthy eating, and exercising, making it all look effortless.

Seeing a post from a friend who started working out during quarantine posting about how she found it so easy to work out every day or that she was eating only healthy food and anyone could live like this was incredibly discouraging. It made me feel like what I was doing was not enough. I find that if I stay on social media for too long, I can begin to question if I am too boring or uninteresting or if I have a right to be happy when I'm not being as productive as other people are.

Like Brooke in the example above, Claire became increasingly self-critical and responded by deleting her social media accounts. The resulting transformation she described was profound:

I found that getting off social media was a great motivator to be a more confident and healthier person because I was doing it for myself, not to impress other people. I got to the point where I was excited to work out because when I was no longer worried about keeping up with other people and their posts, I realized I enjoyed exercising and the way it made me feel. Being able to grow and work on myself without the influence of others has been a very liberating experience; it has allowed me to make changes that I wanted to make, not ones I felt I had to make to fit in.

Claire's self-reflection offers insight into the value of seeking affirmation from within instead of relying on others for validation. She gained confidence and a greater sense of pleasure from working out when she began doing it for herself rather than for the approval of social media followers. The pandemic allowed

Brooke and Claire a modicum of freedom they had not experienced before the pandemic when they felt compelled to post their best lives. These two women described the act of deleting all of their social media apps as freeing—for them, opting out altogether was the only way they could release the constant worry about never living up to an unrealistic online standard.

Unlike the experience of Brooke and Claire, who reduced their comparisons to others by deleting their social media accounts, several students reported feeling jealous of others' outings during the pandemic. Some who responded to the pandemic with extreme caution and heeded public health warnings about socializing in person envied their less risk-aversive friends. Rachel wrote that seeing posts of friends going out in groups during the quarantine made her wonder if she was being overly cautious.

> Even though I knew there was a pandemic and that I was doing the right thing by staying home, seeing my friends go out made me feel like I was taking the pandemic a little too seriously. Looking back, I don't regret staying home, but at the time it was hard for me to see the positives of those decisions when I was constantly seeing all the things people were doing on Instagram.

Reflecting on the emotional impact of social media during Covid-19, Rachel explained:

> Social media has never been a healthy outlet for me, and Covid only made it worse by allowing me to compare my reactions to the pandemic to every other person on social media. The world was already full of stress and uncertainty. I didn't need an app to add to that!

Amelia, another student who strictly quarantined, found herself feeling jealous of friends who were going out, "whether it was partying or just running errands."

> I can't help when I see other people going out and about with their lives but wonder if I'm the crazy one, or if I need to move out (of my parents' house) right away, or if I'm letting the pandemic inhibit me too much.

Considering how much more time some students were spending on social media, it is no wonder social comparison intensified. It is one thing to spend hours scrolling through your sites amidst the noise of a busy life that includes going to classes, working, and socializing offline with friends. However, when the normal pace of life stops abruptly, as it did with Covid-19, and the focus of one's day becomes staring at social media for 6–10 hours, as was the case with most of these students, context disappears. Before the pandemic when students were out in the world, they had a strong sense of the fake, constructed nature of social media posts. However, without the ability to compare online images with offline context, it is easy to lose perspective.

Other students described a shift away from social comparison toward greater self-acceptance. Some students reflected that feeling less pressure to post exciting content resulted in an internal shift away from comparison to others. Some felt more relaxed. Allison reflected:

> Having more time with myself and being less busy has meant less comparison to others through social media because I have limited access to things I can post. Less travel is occurring, as well as fewer social gatherings. I can still feel jealous of someone's fashion on social media, but I have become more comfortable with myself.

The drastic shift in everyday life provided space to slow down and consider the influence of social media on their sense of self; the result was greater self-acceptance as they abandoned the practice of posting and scrolling through social media.

Summary

This chapter highlights the contiguous relationship between online and offline worlds. As daily life offline changed drastically with Covid-19, so too did daily life online. At the onset of the pandemic, students' social media feeds shifted focus from a display of adventure, positivity, and highly curated selves to constant news about the pandemic that pervaded all of their sites. Stuck at home with nothing to do, most stopped posting altogether for a while, even as their screen time spiked. Students felt distressed and anxious at the nonstop news coverage of death, illness, and social unrest, but they were unable to look away.

Even in the brief span of a year, online social norms shifted from an abstention of posting to gradually posting a broader range of content than before the pandemic. Students had to rethink and redefine their digital multiples overnight. When you can no longer post about your busy and exciting life, what defines your online presence, and what do you post? Some shared glimpses of their mundane, unfiltered quarantine life, while others dabbled in upbeat aspirational posts despite the daily tragedy unfolding offline. Some students found online communities with shared interests as they diverted their boredom into developing a hobby or passion project. Others used the downtime quarantine provided to try out business ventures, like selling arts and crafts online or pursuing music endeavors, which they otherwise would not have time to squeeze into their busy schedules.

The convergence of anxiety and boredom during the long quarantine led to a hypervigilance of social media posts among students, initially focused on news and later focused on how friends were navigating social distancing and masking rules. Many students expressed disappointment at seeing posts of their friends gathering in public without masks, seemingly unconcerned with the potential consequences of their actions. These reactions partially stemmed from fear that their parents or other elderly family members, who were most at risk for Covid-19 complications, might contract the virus from the careless actions of others. Their friends' cavalier behavior referenced something much deeper, a contentious divide between those who believed the science behind Covid-19 and those who thought it was a hoax or did not care how their behavior might affect the health of others. Importantly, online posting behavior influenced offline relationships. Students' reactions to seeing their friends' posts ranged from tuning out their posts for a while to deleting them from their sites. Many wondered if they could handle being friends with someone who appeared not to care about the welfare of others.

The stress of being stuck at home—many once again under the same roof as their parents—scrolling through their sites all day long only to see a combination of distressing news, boring quarantine life photos, and anger-inducing photos of friends flouting pandemic-related safety guidelines quickly became overwhelming. Most turned to TikTok for entertainment and escape. Viral TikTok videos of dances that students could practice at home or funny skits about college pandemic life that they found relatable served as welcome distractions. These fun videos also provided a sense of connection with others, a reminder that people all over the world are sharing an experience.

Social comparison remained a prominent theme online during the pandemic. The content of online comparison shifted in tandem with offline daily life. During the pandemic, students compared their quarantine routines, level of productivity, and adherence to pandemic safety guidelines with others' posts; this represented a dramatic shift away from the pre-pandemic focus on body image, attractiveness, accomplishments, and adventure.

Students scrolled through posts highlighting exercise and diet routines and felt inadequate as they sat on the couch; they watched others post about their hobbies and entrepreneurial ventures and felt boring in comparison; they watched friends move boldly out of quarantine to resume a "normal" life of socializing and worried that they were being overly cautious or paranoid in comparison. Paradoxically, some students found the absence of glamorous, exciting posts to be liberating. Instead, they found posts of friends engaged in mundane everyday activities, such as hanging out with their pets and cooking, to be comforting and relatable during the pandemic. It lessened the pressure to outdo others online and opened a space to experience a degree of contentment.

Notes

1 *New York Times* 2021a, 2021b.
2 Browning et al. 2021; Son et al. 2020; Wang et al. 2020.

3 Fruehwirth, Biswas, and Perreira 2021.
4 Browning et al. 2021; Sreenivasan 2021.
5 Healthy Minds Network 2020.
6 Browning et al. 2021.
7 Healthy Minds Network 2020.
8 Ibid.
9 Bernstein 2019.
10 López 2020.
11 Friedman 2021.
12 Nichter 2015.

References

Bernstein, Jacob. 2019. "How OnlyFans Changed Sex Work Forever: OnlyFans Has Put X-rated Entertainment in the Hands of its Entertainers. Call it Paywall Porn." *NYTimes.com,* February 9, 2019. https://www.nytimes.com/2019/02/09/style/onlyfans-porn-stars.html.

Browning, Matthew H. E. M., Lincoln R. Larson, Iryna Sharaievska, Alessandro Rigolon, Olivia McAnirlin, Lauren Mullenbach, Scott Cloutier, Tue M. Vu, Jennifer Thomsen, Nathan Reigner, Elizabeth Covelli Metcalf, Ashley D'Antonio, Marco Helbich, Gregory N. Bratman and Hector Olvera Alvarez. 2021. "Psychological Impacts from COVID-19 among University Students: Risk Factors across Seven States in the United States." *PLoS One* 16 (1): e0245327.

Friedman, Gillian. 2021. "Jobless, Selling Nudes Online and Still Struggling." *The New York Times,* January 13, 2021. https://www.nytimes.com/2021/01/13/business/onlyfans-pandemic-users.html?auth=login-google.

Fruehwirth, Jane Cooley, Siddhartha Biswas, and Krista M. Perreira. 2021. The Covid-19 "Pandemic and Mental Health of First Year College Students: Examining the Effect of Covid-19 Stressors Using Longitudinal Data." *PLoS One* 16 (3): e024799.

Healthy Minds Network. 2020. *The Impact of Covid-19 on College Student Well-Being.* American College Health Association. https://healthymindsnetwork.org/wp-content/uploads/2020/07/Healthy_Minds_NCHA_COVID_Survey_Report_FINAL.pdf.

López, Canela. 2020. "People are Turning to OnlyFans to Earn Money After Losing their Jobs During the Pandemic." *Insider.com,* June 17, 2020. https://www.insider.com/people-are-creating-onlyfans-accounts-after-losing-jobs-during-pandemic-2020-6.

New York Times. 2021a. "Coronavirus in the U.S.: Latest Map and Case Count." https://www.nytimes.com/interactive/2021/us/covid-cases.html.

New York Times. 2021b. "Coronavirus World Map: Tracking the Global Outbreak." https://www.nytimes.com/interactive/2020/world/coronavirus-maps.html.

Nichter, Mimi. 2015. *Lighting Up: The Rise of Social Smoking on College Campuses.* New York: New York University Press.

Son, Changwon, Sudeep Hegde, Alec Smith, Xiaomei Wang, and Farzan Sasangohar. 2020. "Effects of COVID-19 on College Students' Mental Health in the United States: Interview Survey Study." *Journal of Medical Internet Research* 22 (9): e21279.

Sreenivasan, Hari. 2021. "Rethinking College: How the Pandemic is Impacting College Students' Mental Health." *PBS News Hour,* January 19, 2021. https://www.pbs.org/newshour/show/how-the-pandemic-is-impacting-college-students-mental-health#:~:text=College%20students%20have%20long%20been, series%2C%20"Rethinking%20College.

Wang, Xiaomei, Sudeep Hegde, Changwon Son, Bruce Keller, Alec Smith, and Farzan Sasangohar. 2020. "Investigating Mental Health of U.S. College Students during the COVID-19 Pandemic: Cross-Sectional Survey Study." *Journal of Medical Internet Research* 22 (9): e22817.

CONCLUSION

Throughout this book, we have shown how students navigate their online lives, attending to the exigencies of various social media platforms. College students whom we spoke with unveiled a busy online life, which they described as exhausting and anxiety producing at times, but also satisfying and fun. Their digital multiples required intensive labor as they competed for likes amidst an attention economy where the half-life of a single post was short.

We have explored how social norms, most of which are tacit rather than explicitly stated, guide participation in social media. Like many societal rules for appropriate behavior, there is no playbook; one learns through a process of trial and error. On social media, the number of likes you receive and the tenor of comments, which can range from positive to ambiguous to brutally frank, can quickly help you ascertain the success or failure of your post. All too often, a person who violates social media norms (e.g., a woman whose online and offline appearance does not match) becomes the target of gossiping and joking behind her back. The blurry boundary between these contiguous worlds can be difficult to navigate and, for many, serves to heighten anxieties about posting.

At the macro level, a key social norm among emerging adults was an imperative to maintain a continual and vibrant online presence. Those who went offline for even two or three days worried that they might lose followers; those who had long-standing streaks with friends expressed anxiety about the mere thought of missing a day, which would sever their online relationship. Those who did not maintain active social media accounts were outliers. As Hailey explained, "Their social lives are a lot different because they don't know what people are doing on a daily basis. . . . I can't imagine not knowing my friend's milestones and not being able to comment on their lives."

DOI: 10.4324/9781003182047-7

In effect, those who opt out of social media are excluded from others' lives and must actively reach out to their friends (usually by text) if they want to stay in touch. Hailey's observation raises several important points. First, given the instantaneous speed of communication on social media, frequently checking your sites is a requirement to ensure that you stay on top of what is happening in the lives of your friends and acquaintances. Second, the norms of friendship dictate that you must respond with a like or a comment. Not to do so violates the rules of online friendships. Thus, opting out of social media removes you from the normative means of connection for your generation.

Given the lure of continuously checking social media, college students struggled to determine appropriate rules for social etiquette when spending time with friends. With many students on social media for upward of 5–7 hours a day, staying offline while with friends was difficult. Though some tolerated quick phone checks when hanging out with friends, others did not. Rules for behavior were largely unspoken until a person crossed a line of privileging their online friends over a friend in their immediate social space.

Students described this violation of social etiquette as rude and annoying; it signaled that your friend was bored with you or whatever conversation you were having with them. The response to this offensive behavior was sometimes non-verbal: grabbing the phone from a friend's hands or waving at them to remind them of your physical presence. Some groups of friends, particularly women, created guidelines for appropriate behavior, such as putting their phones away while at a restaurant together. However, if one person transgressed this rule by checking their phone when it pinged, others were left feeling that online friendships were more important than in-person connections. It was clear that these were negotiated interactions subject to frequent change.

Social norms for posting about one's emotions online appeared to be among the most established and readily known, perhaps because they overlapped to some degree with offline rules for behavior. Students understood the requirement to post how they were "living their best life," which meant conveying a sense of adventure and excitement. To post ordinary life was to risk being seen as a person who had little going on, and by extension, a person who was leading a boring life.

Going to parties, even if you did not participate fully, provided an opportunity (sometimes specious) to take photos to create an image of popularity, fun, and being fully engaged in life. In contrast, students recognized that it was inappropriate and against social convention to post about your sadness, depression, anxiety, and frustrations. As one woman unabashedly explained, "When people I follow start posting about sad things in their life . . . and this sounds bad . . . I just unfollow them. I'm like, 'I followed you to be distracted, and now you're doing this?'" Showing need and vulnerability was not what social media followers signed on for, and most people had internalized this rule of appropriate behavior, particularly on Instagram.

Among other key themes that emerged in our research was the proliferation of digital multiples in the online presence of college students. Given social norms for self-presentation, posting on multiple sites was an all-encompassing endeavor made ever more complicated by the requirement of frequent life updates. The creation and maintenance of digital multiples was a time-consuming process, requiring hours of planning, editing, and posting. This was particularly true for women. Digital multiples necessitated fluid identities; that is, being flexible in one's presentation of self in relation to specific contexts and social spaces.

The mandate to remain consistent with online and offline presentations of self further complicated the creation of digital multiples. Our interviews were peppered with discussions of "real" and "fake," indexing the invisible line that one can inadvertently cross in contiguous online and offline worlds, at times when one's presentations of self fail to match. While discussions of digital multiples gone awry mostly referred to appearance, it could also relate to one's affect (e.g., an introverted person who appeared excited and upbeat online but painfully shy in person). As participant observers to college students' lives on social media, we became attuned to the complexities and tensions inherent in the maintenance of digital multiples.

Based on our analysis of student narratives, we unpacked key contradictions, including presenting a self that appears both authentic and highly edited; appearing excited and upbeat even during emotionally difficult times; and exuding body positivity even when frustrated with how you look. While the name of the game was to get attention, it was equally important not to appear needy. Students struggled with what we came to understand as a series of impossibilities.

For students who experimented with their look and failed to get sufficient positive feedback, they could delete their posts and try again. Social media provided an infinite number of "do-overs." Similar to how college offers an opportunity to reinvent yourself, so too does social media. Yet, social media provides the added benefit of flexibility with its access to sophisticated editing tools. Online appearance enhancement features allowed students to try on new selves and experiment with degrees of "fakeness." Students were aware that if they over-edited or failed to impress their audience, they could become a source of gossip. The only indication that they got it wrong might be fewer likes than usual on a particular post, which is why they closely monitored feedback.

On the surface, a social media post that fails to get the right kind of attention can be deleted, which seems simple enough. However, at a deeper level, students talked about feeling disappointed and self-conscious when their posts received too few likes—one woman said she wonders if she did something wrong. When Morgan experimented with posts that revealed her "authentic" self she received fewer likes than when she showed off her body in revealing clothes. Thus, even after students deleted an unpopular post, the residue of disappointent remained; they had internalized the audience response and carried forward a deep sense of inadequacy.

While social media use was ubiquitous among women and men, our research found that the effects of being online were far more pernicious for women, particularly at the site of the body. Some women considered Instagram to be a toxic platform as it perpetuated unrealistic expectations of the physical body. Among our participants, social media heightened comparisons to other women's bodies and resulted in increased dissatisfaction and self-consciousness with one's appearance. Women in our study felt scrutinized and evaluated by others, which led them to close inspection of their own bodies so they could airbrush and erase their imagined flaws before posting.

The gendered work of beauty and maintaining a recognizable brand image required college students to perform invisible labor that necessitated time, skill, and strategy. Most women recognized that a sure-fire method to obtaining maximum likes and positive feedback was to post photos in revealing clothes; however, this required a level of self-confidence that eluded many. "It isn't even real," one woman complained, "and you feel hopeless like you can't do anything about it because you can never get to that fake standard." Many students longed to present a more authentic self, but they understood this to be a risky venture that could result in the loss of followers.

The Upsides of Social Media

Beyond the difficulties and frustrations of being on social media, many students offered a balanced perspective of being online, often articulating both benefits and challenges of immersing themselves in these online worlds. They saw social media as a space for exploring different sides of themselves and experimenting with ways of being that might otherwise feel too risky. On the one hand, site affordances, social norms, and perceived audience expectations constrained their self-presentation; on the other hand, engaging across multiple sites, each with its own unique set of cultural mandates, provided an opportunity to cultivate digital multiples.

For some students, social media felt like a safe space for intensive identity work. Chelsea, the hula hoop enthusiast, presented herself online as sexy, confident, and artistic, in stark contrast to her shy, self-conscious offline demeanor. Diego, the aspiring rapper, saw social media as a safe space to experiment with bold clothing choices. And Natalie, who described herself as socially awkward and appeared so as she fidgeted throughout her interview, felt upbeat about her self-portrayal on Instagram as a provocative and edgy woman.

Despite the labor-intensive process entailed, and the consequent disappointment if a post did not turn out as expected, some students enjoyed the process of constructing the self as an artistic endeavor. For them, social media was a medium for developing their creative skills through editing tools. One participant explained that he had few artistic abilities and considered himself a mediocre photographer. He told us that his art and passion is editing average quality photos into something eye-catching: "Social media is my art because I feel like it's a reference to something creative I did. Anytime I get a photo, I'm in my zone. It's a time-consuming process, but I love it. It's worth it to me." As one student explained, "You really are like your own little artist on your phone screen."

Another positive aspect of social media was that it facilitated social connection for students, especially those who were shy and introverted. One man explained that offline he is painfully shy, but in Snapchat he is funny and outgoing. Receiving positive feedback for his Snapchat stories gave him the self-confidence to try out his jokes and share his sense of humor among friends offline. For this student and others who were introverted, joining social media student groups allowed them to get to know others from the safety of their screen before meeting them in person. Communicating online gave them time to think up an appropriate response, rather than feeling nervous and unable to speak, which was how they felt in offline conversations.

Experimenting on social media was like a dress rehearsal for "real life," which could be difficult to navigate, as it could throw a "curve ball" (i.e., something unexpected). Several shy students said they would have struggled to make friends in a large public university setting without the help of online student groups. For example, Daniel explained:

> I really wouldn't have friends if it weren't for social media. It's a good way to stay in touch with people you don't see every day, and it's a good way to get to know people before meeting them in person.

Daniel's university notified him about his assigned dorm roommate several weeks before they moved in together. They immediately connected through social media and corresponded online regularly. Daniel said, "On move-in day it felt like we already knew each other even though we had never actually met before."

Many students said that social media allowed them to maintain strong connections with their childhood friends as well. They were able to retain old friendships while developing new ones; social media provided a means for managing a larger number of relationships than would otherwise be possible. The various feedback mechanisms, all of which required differing degrees of effort, from a quick click to a personal message, provided a range of options for communication. Students could simply like someone's post while scrolling through their feed, which functioned as a quick nod of acknowledgment and approval; they could respond to the post with a comment for a slightly more personal touch; or they could take the time to send someone a more intimate, detailed note through the direct message feature. For those who had streaks, there was the option of quickly sending a generic group message or taking the time to construct individualized messages in order to maintain these contacts. During the pandemic, social media became one of the only ways for students to socialize safely with friends—it gave them a sense of community during a prolonged period of social isolation.

Is Social Media "Good" or "Bad"?

As to the question of whether social media is "good" or "bad," which appears to be at the heart of every discussion about youth and technology, our findings reveal that the answer is complex. Certainly, much of the research on this topic has focused on negative aspects, playing on our worst fears about youth losing their ability (and desire) to socialize offline, develop meaningful friendships, and even empathize with others.[1]

As a counterpoint to the overwhelming negative press on youth and social media, a recent study found that teens who are online almost constantly are just as likely to socialize regularly offline as their less-connected peers.[2] This study suggests we have a lot more to learn about how screen time affects teens and emerging adults. We cannot assume time online is replacing in-person sociality—the reality is much more complicated. Conflicting research findings and popular narratives about the effects of social media on youth underscore the importance of ethnography as a way to understand these issues from the perspectives of young people.

Social media scholar danah boyd argues that characterizing social media as "good" or "bad" obscures the complexities of how youth experience online sociality.[3] She highlights the contiguous nature of offline and online worlds:

> The internet mirrors, magnifies, and makes more visible the good, bad, and ugly of everyday life. As teens embrace these tools and incorporate them into their daily practices, they show us how our broader social and cultural systems are affecting their lives.[4]

Online worlds offer complimentary environments for attaining a deeper understanding of identity and sociality among youth.

Our findings align with boyd's concept of social media as a mirror that reflects and magnifies everyday life. Students' body image concerns and their struggles with social comparison and authentic emotional expression that emerged online were an outgrowth of issues they confronted offline. The maintenance of digital multiples across online spaces—each with their own set of rules, editorial mandates, and audience expectations—intensified identity work.

Some imperatives seemed impossible to navigate—how could students possibly present a flawless, glamorous online self while maintaining a commitment to authenticity? Everyone knew that images they saw online were fake, yet many students worked hard to perfect the ability to mask their editorial efforts in an image that appeared natural and effortless. While this editorial tight rope was stressful to navigate, students took pride in cultivating their skills and enjoyed the positive feedback from others when they got it right.

On the one hand, students expressed cynicism and frustration with social media—they struggled with the seeming inauthenticity of editing and self-presentation imperatives, and they sometimes wondered if online friendships were merely transactional. On the other hand, students enjoyed the creative freedom to play with their identities, from the more superficial elements of fashion and physical appearance to deeper aspects of emotional expression and authentic self-presentation. Students said that social media helped them stay in touch with old friends and meet new friends; yet, some felt frustrated with the obligation of maintaining the continual online presence required to sustain relationships.

Even as students lamented the time- and work-intensive process required for creating an Insta-worthy post, they described the adrenaline rush they felt when they clicked "post" and their sense of pride at watching likes accumulate. Others embraced editing practices as an immersive artistic endeavor from which they derived pleasure. Students certainly struggled with social comparison and feelings of inadequacy and jealousy at seeing their friends' adventures and accomplishments; yet, they enjoyed sharing their own successes and milestones online, especially when they received many likes. During emerging adulthood, when identity exploration and sociality is often a focal point, social media provided multiple spaces and tools for experimentation.

Are College Students Addicted to Social Media?

In interviews, students struggled to estimate how much time they spent online mostly because they checked their social media sites throughout the day and late into the night. While the focus of our study was not on social media addiction or dependency, the topic did emerge spontaneously in some interviews and in student essays. It is certainly a topic that appears regularly in the popular media and is of increasing concern to parents, to colleges, and to students themselves. As this is a relatively new field of research, a plethora of terms have been used to describe problems related to social media use, including social media addiction (or smartphone addiction), excessive social media use, social media dependence, and social media disorder.[5] There appears to be little consensus on the definition of these terms.

Results of a recent large-scale study among over 1,000 university students in the U.K. found that almost 40 percent self-reported having a smartphone addiction. Sixty-nine percent of participants with smartphone addiction reported having poor sleep quality.[6] In other studies, those who report social media addiction describe decreased interest in face-to-face interactions, preoccupation with checking their sites, problems with concentration, and a sense of anxiety when they cannot use their phones.[7]

Some studies report that smartphone addiction is associated with reduced productivity and lower academic attainment.[8] Higher levels of media multitasking (being on social media while doing schoolwork or hanging out with friends) is related to the ability to properly sustain attention.[9] In fact, those who become accustomed to constantly switching between activities eventually lose their ability to focus on a single subject or activity.[10]

Of late, researchers have created a number of scales to measure this emergent phenomenon.[11] One widely used scale is the Social Media Disorder Scale, which measures frequency of daily social media use, self-reported addiction, preoccupation, withdrawal, use of social media as an escape, and feeling restless or irritated when you cannot be online, to name a few.[12] Some of these questions are similar to measures of addiction in other domains, such as smoking, where addiction is measured by variables such as how long after waking up one smokes, withdrawal, preoccupation, and number of cigarettes smoked each day. As in the field of smoking, it is important to examine markers of dependency and addiction as understood by youth themselves.[13]

Medical anthropologists Gilbert Quintero and Mark Nichter have discussed the importance of studying the semantics of addiction, pointing out that in everyday speech, several terms are associated with addiction, including habit, dependence, obsession, and abuse, among others.[14] They raise questions about the meaning of these concepts to laypersons and highlight the importance of studying how people interpret and use such terms in their everyday conversations.

As a case in point, anthropologist Jeffrey Snodgrass and colleagues found that researchers who study online gamers "are unable to consistently distinguish 'problem' online play from healthy 'engagement' and interest in gaming as a hobby."[15] Their analysis, which draws on interviews with emerging adult gamers, suggests that the "addiction" frame used by hardcore gamers can indicate their passion for online play but can also be a way for them to signal distress, such as depression and loneliness. The authors suggest that the clinical category, Internet Gaming Disorder, be used sparingly as "the medical and gamer understanding of 'addictive play' differ so markedly."[16] In this example, we see how the point of view of cultural insiders is critical to an understanding of user's perspective on an issue.

What Do Students Say about Social Media and Addiction?

Returning to social media use, how do emerging adults distinguish between normative use of social media and addiction? As we have discussed throughout, college students need to maintain a continuous online presence, a sign that they are popular and living their life well. What, then, is addiction? Are there signs or markers that youth have crossed the line with social media to unhealthy use or addiction?

One of our participants, Brody, a recent college graduate who was teaching yoga, explained that being a "heavy user" did not necessarily mean that the person was addicted to social media. Brody believed that addiction was more about how a person used social media, particularly if they did so "in a meticulous and premeditated way." Brody analogized this to a drug user who plans how they will obtain drugs and use them. He explained:

> This (addiction) can include maintaining a precise following to follower ratio, having apps that track who unfollows them, apps that demonstrate a mock-Instagram page to plan what picture to post next, how it will look on the actual Instagram page among existing photos, or even editing apps with personal schedules that will post your pictures for you. Addicts will regularly shop for new filters, keep updated on the best editing apps and spend hours picking out, then perfecting a single photo.

In Brody's example, the person who is fully engaged in time-consuming, premeditated behaviors can be considered a social media addict. This person is obsessed with cultivating the perfect online self, making it a priority in their life.

Other students talked about friends who prioritized checking their phones even when they were in social situations. This inability to disentangle themselves from their online worlds was considered a sign of addiction; someone who devoted so much time to social media that it impaired their offline social relationships. Some students considered themselves addicted when it became increasingly difficult to complete class assignments in a timely manner because they felt compelled to continually check their social media sites.

Others looked at the phenomenon of craving as a marker of addiction. They talked about needing the thrill of "that dopamine rush" they got when they posted a new photo and anxiously waited for positive feedback. Many felt enthralled by this immediate gratification, which, in the short term at least, could improve their mood. Amber enjoyed the mood shift she got from likes and positive feedback. In her interview, she sheepishly admitted that her addiction to social media was "totally connected" to the feedback she received. While Amber recognized that her sense of self relied on this feedback, she also felt powerless to change. This was frustrating to her even though she knew she was not alone; several of her women friends seemed caught in the same feedback loop.

Others talked about experiencing withdrawal when they misplaced their phones for even a short time or when they were unable to go online because they were at work or in class. One woman described feeling overcome with anxiety when she could not check her phone for 4 hours while she was at her busy workplace.

Did Students Want to Spend Less Time Online?

Even if an emerging adult wants to reduce their time on social media, it is not easy to do so. Smartphones are engineered to provide constant cues that draw our attention. As we have seen, many young people have invested significant time in building their online brand, so opting out of social media means letting go of your hard work. Given the strong expectation that you will like and comment on your friends' posts in a timely manner, what happens when you do not respond? Failure to respond is a social risk as providing feedback is necessary for maintaining connections. Indeed, keeping up with your social media feed is a requirement for social relations in the digital age. Given the connectivity imperative, is there a time when youth want to step away from social media, and if so, how do they accomplish this?

As an antidote to their smartphone addiction, several women explained that it was important to have a "social media cleanse" occasionally, particularly around final exams. This was thought of as a periodic fast, which allowed their sleep cycle to improve and their brain fog to lift. Typically, cleanses were short-lived and announced in advance, as students feared that if they went "cold turkey" without notification, their friends might worry about them. You had to let others know you were taking a break. Some students worried their friends might forget them if they were no longer visible online. They also spoke about how being offline for even a short period of time could result in feeling excluded from conversations with friends, as they would not know what had been going on.

Staying off social media was challenging, but those who were determined to do so experienced positive results. Without continuously scrolling through their feed, students described feeling more connected to the "real world," less anxious as they stopped comparing themselves to others, and more in touch with themselves. As Brittany explained, "It's difficult to define yourself as an individual when having direct access to others' lives and comparing them to your own life." This realization was often short-lived given the stakes of going offline for longer periods. So, even after a cleanse, chances were high that before too long you might be pulled back into the same cycle of social media use.

Shifts in Social Media Use after College Graduation

During interviews with college seniors who were nearing graduation, we wondered about whether they would "age out" of the social media practices they had become accustomed to during college. Would they still spend as much time online? Would the same apps remain popular? Before addressing what students had to say about these questions, it is worth examining what is known more broadly about the lives of recent college graduates in the U.S. At some point after college, at least as the script was once written, post-college life was conceptualized as a movement toward adulthood: finding a job, having a stable living environment, and eventually settling down with a partner. Today, this script seems outdated and is far from the reality of many recent college graduates.

Research conducted prior to the pandemic found that 54 percent of about-to-be graduates planned to move back home.[17] During Covid-19, many young adults (52 percent) returned to their parents' house. These trends, especially pronounced among 18–24-year-olds, are occurring across gender, racial, and ethnic groups. Fifty-eight percent of Hispanic youth, 55 percent of Black youth, 51 percent of Asian youth, and 49 percent of white youth have been living at home with their parents during the pandemic.[18]

Clearly, college students have had good reasons for moving back home during the pandemic and after graduation. Since February 2020, emerging adults have been more likely than other age groups to either lose their jobs or get a pay cut, making it difficult (if not impossible) to maintain living on their own. Among those who have continued working during the pandemic, many now contribute a portion of their earnings to support their family households. For college seniors, shortly after graduation they will need to begin repayment of student loans. Approximately 43 million young adults have student loan debt; the average amount owed is over $39,000.[19] Given the disruptive nature of Covid-19, it is unclear how long students plan to stay in their parents' home or if this living arrangement is stigmatized. One survey found that living with one's parents becomes an embarrassment only at age 28.[20]

Overall, many of the post-college milestones for emerging adults appear to be delayed. More than 50 percent of recent college graduates are unemployed or underemployed; it is common to have two or three part-time jobs simultaneously. In relation to social media, as students near graduation they become increasingly cautious about what they post online for fear of self-sabotaging any potential job opportunity.[21] Their online presentation of self shifts from highlighting their best life to a focus on their professional accomplishments. And for good reason: Nowadays, 70 percent of employers and recruiters check social media during the hiring process, and more than one-half report that they have chosen not to hire someone because of content on their social media.[22]

Envisioning the Future

In an essay assignment, we asked students to reflect on how they thought their social media might change after graduation. Many believed that the amount of time they spent on social media would diminish as they entered the "adult world" where they would have greater responsibilities and less time to spend online. Some thought they would prioritize their own experiences and their own lives after graduation rather than compulsively checking and comparing themselves to what other people were doing. One woman observed that friends who were recent graduates had already made their social media accounts private, and they refrained from posting or sharing about politics, religion, and personal opinions, which their employers or co-workers might find offensive.

Some students provided a different outlook on their future with social media. Rachel, for example, believed that the amount of time she spent on social media after graduation would vary depending on what kind of job she found. If she worked in her major (psychology), she did not see herself needing to do a lot of self-promotion. However, if she worked as a small business owner or in an artistic field, social media would be necessary to promote her services and products. Several women had friends who had started an online business from Instagram, and they believed that "social media is a place that makes anything possible." For these digital natives, it was hard to imagine not being on social media in some form. Abigail expanded on this idea:

> I don't think college students will age out of using social media but rather may change platforms to reflect where they are in life. The purpose for the apps may be geared more toward gathering knowledge and social networking as we transition from college to the business world. Apps like LinkedIn that allow you to search, create a resume, and apply for jobs will be very popular because having a job lined up right after you graduate isn't always in the cards, especially if you are still unsure what it is you want to do with your degree. And once you find yourself working, it may be with people from an older generation who frequently use Facebook. You might then consider signing up to keep in touch and fit in. . . . The idea that college students will age out and abandon most social media platforms (like Instagram) and end up like our parents, solely using Facebook, is bogus. Social media for my generation is something we grew up with and is an integral element that has shaped the way we connect and view the world.

Another participant, Bianca, shared Abigail's idea that after graduation she and her friends would continue to post on their favorite platforms—Instagram and Snapchat—although "they would probably talk about different things and post different kinds of pictures" when they were on those sites. She added, "If we continue to label Facebook as the platform for old people, I think it's safe to say that eventually Instagram will become the Facebook of my generation." It is interesting to note that a recent study contradicts what these young women envision as their future on social media. Researchers found that as youth move into their late 20s, Facebook and YouTube become increasingly popular, while Instagram and Snapchat decrease in popularity.[23]

Some students wrote that after they graduated, if they were still obsessively looking at what others were doing and were experiencing fear of missing out (FOMO), it would be a sign that they had not matured adequately during their 20s, that their emotional and cognitive growth had been stunted somehow.

Rachel, who considered herself dependent on social media, wished that she would age out of her compulsion to check all of her platforms repeatedly throughout the day, a practice she used to distract herself from dull or uncomfortable situations. She wrote, "I appreciate that social media is an extension of myself and can be used as a means of self-expression, but I hope to find more meaningful ways to present myself in the future." Students like Rachel were hopeful that their futures would include less reliance on social media.

One college senior said that he was growing "fonder of privacy every day" and resented the sense of vulnerability he experienced on social media. As he got older, he envisioned himself "craving more and more human connection," which meant spending time with friends in person rather than online. Several students said that once they had a career and a family, they would focus more on living their lives fully rather than documenting their activities for others.

In these narratives, we see divergent opinions of how social media use may shift as emerging adults move further along the continuum into adulthood. Given the fluctuations in living situations that occur after graduation, the difficulties in finding appropriate employment, and the separation from one's friends that occurs after college, it is easy to imagine that social media use will persist, albeit in new forms. As students noted throughout interviews and essays, staying connected with others online was integral to their sense of well-being. Social media was a way to accomplish this goal. After graduation, students will have fewer spontaneous everyday connections with friends than they had on campus. Thus, social media will remain a beacon for maintaining friendships and a sense of community. In addition, as the average age of marriage has become progressively older (33 for men; 31 for women), it is reasonable to assume that emerging adults will continue to use the ever popular social media dating apps. Future research should explore how social media continues to play a role in the development and maintenance of friendship and romantic/sexual relationships.

Social media use among emerging adults can change quickly, as we learned from students' reflections during Covid-19. Their social media feeds shifted overnight from posts highlighting excitement and adventure to a singular focus on the pandemic and social unrest. Suddenly isolated, lonely, and anxious about events unfolding offline, students began spending increasing amounts of time online to feel connected and informed. Social norms related to posting and interacting online shifted from adventure to everyday life at home; TikTok emerged as a favorite site for escape, entertainment, and a sense of community; and the nature of online surveillance and social comparison changed and intensified because of Covid-19. Rather than observing how attractive or "cool" a person looked, followers focused their gaze on whether a person was wearing a mask or whether they were engaged in inappropriate pandemic behavior, like going to a bar. This led us to recognize how quickly social media norms could change among college students and how apps could rise and fall in popularity in just a short period.

We noticed another major shift in social media use among some participants who had graduated. In preparation for our book, we followed up with students online as part of an ongoing collaborative consent process. Given how popular Instagram had been among our participants, we figured this would be the best way to reach them. We were surprised to find that some were no longer as active on that site as they once had been. Many of our direct messages went unread, and we noticed that some students had not posted in several months. Others had wiped their accounts clean and started over, posting only a handful of photos featuring nature, art, or some other relatively neutral scene. Most had made their Instagram accounts private, and a few had deleted their accounts altogether. Several students who had been Instagram enthusiasts during the study remained so; they continued to post "living their best life" images that exuded enthusiasm, happiness, and adventure. For many of the students whose social media sites we checked—about one-quarter of our sample—their accounts seemed abandoned and neglected, like a ghost town, when compared to what we had seen just six months earlier.

Surprisingly, we found Facebook to be the best site for reconnecting with students. Most of their accounts were active with recent and regular posts, and we could see that they were frequently on the site. Our direct messages generally received instantaneous responses on Facebook. In accordance with social norms on that site, their posts were family friendly and entirely appropriate for a potential employer who might browse their social media. Images appeared candid (truly!), unedited, and featured the more mundane aspects of life, like smiling with a pet, having dinner with a friend, or gathering with family. Most of these students were either approaching graduation or had recently graduated. Some were graduate school bound, while others were beginning their careers as educators, real estate agents, and various entry-level office positions. Some did not list employment information, and their trajectory was unclear. This shift in social media use was striking, but it aligns with research findings that these digital natives are extremely perceptive about posting once they enter the professional job market.[24]

As we look toward the future, it will be important for research to explore questions that emerged from our study: How does the production of a filtered self change after graduation? As students enter their next phase of life, to what extent do they maintain their online personas and digital multiples? Does the intense desire for online attention and feedback abate? Do the imperatives and contradictions identified throughout the book continue to affect their sense of self and shape their online behavior? Answers to questions such as these will help us understand the trajectories of social media use among emerging adults as they move into their late 20s and beyond. Future studies of online interaction and identity production will need to be attentive to gender, sexuality, and ethnic differences.

More than 90 percent of college students are on social media daily. It remains to be seen whether emerging adults continue to embrace time-intensive online identity and sociality practices, and if their level of engagement changes after graduation. Arguably, the evolution of online communication, and specifically social media use, is among the most important topics to explore in the foreseeable future. New apps will no doubt appear on the horizon and will find their place in an already crowded online marketplace. Ethnographic studies will be needed to track these changes as they unfold in contiguous online and offline worlds.

Notes

1 Turkle 2015, 2017; Twenge 2017, 2018.
2 Jiang 2018.
3 boyd 2014.
4 Ibid., 24.
5 Paschke, Austermann, and Thomasius 2021.
6 Sohn et al. 2021.
7 De-Sola Gutierrez, de Fonseca, and Rubio 2016.
8 Duke and Montag 2017; Grant, Lust, and Chamberlain 2019.
9 Van der Schuur et al. 2015.
10 Ibid.; Wallis 2010.
11 Marin, Nunez, and Martins de Almeida 2021.
12 van den Ejinden, Lemmens, and Valkenburg 2016.
13 Nichter 2015.
14 Quintero and Nichter 1996; Nichter 2015.
15 Snodgrass et al. 2019, 750.
16 Ibid., 748.
17 Friedman 2019.
18 Fry, Passel, and Cohn 2020.
19 Hanson 2021.
20 Friedman 2019.
21 Quraishi 2019.
22 Ibid.
23 Perrin and Anderson 2019.
24 Quraishi 2019.

References

boyd, danah. 2018. *It's Complicated*. New Haven, CT: Yale University Press.
De-Sola Gutiérrez, José, Fernando Rodríguez de Fonseca, and Gabriel Rubio. 2016. "Cell-Phone Addiction: A Review." *Frontiers in Psychiatry* 7 (2016): 175.
Duke, Éilish, and Christian Montag. 2017. "Smartphone Addiction, Daily Interruptions and Self-Reported Productivity." *Addictive Behaviors Reports* 6: 90–95.
Friedman, Zach. 2019. "50% of Millennials are Moving Back Home with Their Parents after College." June 6, 2019. https://www.forbes.com/sites/zackfriedman/2019/06/06/millennials-move-back-home-college/?sh=1e07db3638ad.

Fry, Richard, Jeffrey S. Passel, and D'Vera Cohn. 2020. "A Majority of Young Adults in the U.S. Live with their Parents for the First Time Since the Great Depression." *Pew Research Center,* September 4, 2020https://www.pewresearch.org/?p=374511.

Grant, Jon, E., Katherine Lust, and Samuel R. Chamberlain. 2019. "Problematic Smartphone Use Associated with Greater Alcohol Consumption, Mental Health Issues, Poorer Academic Performance, and Impulsivity." *Journal of Behavioral Addictions* 8 (2): 335–342.

Hanson, Melanie. 2021. "Student Loan Debt Statistics." *EducationData.* February 28, 2021. https://educationdata.org/student-loan-debt-statistics.

Jiang, Jingjing. 2018. "Teens Who are Constantly Online are Just as Likely to Socialize with their Friends Offline." *Pew Research,* November 28, 2018. https://www.pewresearch.org/fact-tank/2018/11/28/teens-who-are-constantly-online-are-just-as-likely-to-socialize-with-their-friends-offline/.

Marin, Maísa Gelain, Xiomara Nuñez, and Rosa Maria Martins de Almeida. 2021. "Internet Addiction and Attention in Adolescents: A Systematic Review." *Cyberpsychology, Behavior, and Social Networking* 24 (4): 237–249.

Nichter, Mimi. 2015. *Lighting Up: The Rise of Social Smoking on College Campuses.* New York: New York University Press.

Paschke, Kerstin, Maria Isabella Austermann, and Rainer Thomasius. 2021. "ICD-11-Based Assessment of Social Media Use Disorder in Adolescents: Development and Validation of the Social Media Use Disorder Scale for Adolescents." *Frontiers in Psychiatry* 12 (April): 661483.

Perrin, Andrew, and Monica Anderson. 2019. "Share of U.S. Adults Using Social Media, Including Facebook, is Mostly Unchanged since 2018. FactTank, Social Media Usage in the U.S. in 2019." *Pew Research Center,* April 10, 2019. https://www.pewresearch.org/fact-tank/2019/04/10/share-of-u-s-adults-using-social-media-including-facebook-is-mostly-unchanged-since-2018/.

Quraishi, Hafsa. 2019. "Under Employers' Gaze, Gen Z is Biting its Tongue on Social Media." April 13, 2019. https://www.npr.org/2019/04/13/702555175/under-employers-gaze-gen-z-is-biting-its-tongue-on-social-media.

Quintero, Gilbert, and Mark Nichter. 1996. "The Semantics of Addiction: Moving Beyond Expert Models to Lay Understanding." *Journal of Psychoactive Drugs* 28 (3): 219–228.

Snodgrass, Jeffey G., H. J. Francois Dengah, II, Evan Polzer, and Robert Else. 2019. "Intensive Online Videogame Involvement: A New Global Idiom of Wellness and Distress." *Transcultural Psychiatry* 56 (4): 748–774.

Sohn, Sei Yon, Lauren Krasnoff, Phillipa Rees, Nicola Kalk, and Ben Carter. 2021. "The Association between Smartphone Addiction and Sleep: A UK Cross-Sectional Study of Young Adults." *Frontiers in Psychiatry* 12 (March): 629407.

Turkle, Sherry. 2015. *Reclaiming Conversation: The Power of Talk in a Digital Age.* London: Penguin Books.

Turkle, Sherry. 2017. *Alone Together: Why We Expect More from Technology and Less from Each Other.* 3rd ed. New York: Basic Books.

Twenge, Jean. 2017. "Have Smartphones Destroyed a Generation?" *The Atlantic,* September 2017. https://www.theatlantic.com/magazine/archive/2017/09/has-the-smartphone-destroyed-a-generation/534198/.

Twenge, Jean. 2018. *iGen: Why Today's Super-Connected Kids are Growing Up Less Rebellious, More Tolerant, Less Happy—And Completely Unprepared for Adulthood—And What that Means for the Rest of Us.* New York: Atria Books.

Van den Eijnden, Regina J., Jeroen S. Lemmens, and Patti M. Valkenburg. 2016. "The Social Media Disorder Scale." *Computers in Human Behavior* 61: 478–487.

Van Der Schuur, Winneke A., Susanne E. Baumgartner, Sindy R. Sumter, and Patti M. Valkenburg. 2015. "The Consequences of Media Multitasking for Youth: A Review." *Computers in Human Behavior* 53: 204–215.

Wallis, Claudia. 2010. *The Impacts of Media Multitasking on Children's Learning and Development: Report from a Research Seminar.* New York, NY: The Joan Ganz Cooney Center and Stanford University. https://www.renevanmaarsseveen.nl/wp-content/uploads/overig2/MediaMultitaksen%20-%20effect%20on%20children_030510.pdf.

INDEX

Note: *Italic* page numbers refer to figures.